# Through the Bible Devotions

# Through the Bible Devotions

From Genesis to Revelation in 365 days

Mark Littleton

Standard PUBLISHING
CINCINNATI, OHIO

 Project editor: Greg Holder. Cover and interior design: Tobias' Outerwear for Books.

ISBN 0-7847-1474-6

10 09 08 07 06 05 04          9 8 7 6 5 4 3 2 1

For Gardner Littleton (born Sept. 29, 1997), my first and only son. May he one day find these pages an encouragement and a source of illumination.

Week 1: Monday

# God Had You in Mind from the Beginning

**In the beginning God created the heavens and the earth.** Genesis 1:1

**Main Reading:** Genesis 1 • **Optional Reading:** Genesis 10, 11

How would you like to have been there when God threw that first spangle of light out into the blackness of the universe? Pretty cool, huh? Like the best fireworks show ever.

Have you ever wondered why God took the trouble to create the world? After all, he knew what would happen in it—sin, hatred, murder, and even the death of Jesus.

Why do you think he still did it?

He wasn't lonely. He had Jesus and the Spirit as best friends.

He wasn't bored. God can never be bored.

He didn't just want to do something different. Every moment is perfect to God.

So why did he do it?

For one reason: he looked down through time and he saw you. He loved you so much that he decided to create a whole universe, full of people like you that he could love forever.

Do you ever feel unloved? Then remember what God did: he created you to be his friend and worshiper. That makes you pretty important, don't you think?

**Prayer:** Lord, thank you for creating me. Help me never to forget you love me. Amen.

# Something for Everyone!

**The Lord God placed the man in the Garden of Eden to tend and care for it.** Genesis 2:15

**MAIN READING:** Genesis 2 • **OPTIONAL READING:** Genesis 20, 21

Sally sat in her Sunday school listening intently. The teacher said that morning that God had a job for everyone. Everyone mattered to God. And he would use all who asked him in the work of his kingdom.

It seemed incredible to Sally. What could she possibly do?

The teacher referred to Adam, how God created him to work and tend the Garden of Eden. Suddenly, the teacher said, "God has work for all of us to do, work that we will enjoy. Work that will make us feel important, and loved."

Sally raised her hand. "What am I supposed to do?"

The teacher smiled. "There are many things, Sally. You can help around your house. You can encourage your mom. You could be an assistant here in Sunday school to lead the kids in learning."

Sally loved drawing. "Could I teach kids to draw?"

"You bet," the teacher said, and went to the cabinet for supplies.

God has work for you to do. Not boring work. Not stupid work. But the work of his kingdom. Where do you think you could fit in this week? What is your talent?

**PRAYER:** Father, show me my talents, so I can use them for you. Amen.

# The Big Lie

**"You won't die!" the serpent hissed. "God knows that your eyes will be opened when you eat it. You will become just like God, knowing everything, both good and evil."** Genesis 3:4, 5

**Main Reading:** Genesis 3 • **Optional Reading:** Genesis 26

Have you ever been walking along and a thought suddenly beams into your mind. "Turn over Mrs. Chambers's trash cans." Or, "Throw a rock through that window." Or, "You've had a tough day. Go ahead and cuss."

It's a temptation. It's the Devil trying to get you to do something wrong.

What usually happens? You might say to him, "That's wrong. I shouldn't do that!"

And the Devil comes back at you with, "Hey, it'll be fun. There's nothing in the Bible that says you can't do that. And anyway, why should you have to listen to the stupid Bible? It's not your king!"

Satan has the power to plant thoughts in our minds, just like he did with Eve in Genesis 3. At the same time, he deceives us, tempts us, goads us, pushes us to do bad things.

Eve should have realized the Devil was lying to her. But she was deceived. Watch out! Satan will deceive you too. How do you stop him? By knowing the Bible and obeying it. By learning what God says. That way you'll send the Devil running.

**Prayer:** Jesus, don't let me give in to temptation. Help me obey your truth. Amen.

Week 1: Thursday

# The Awful Power of Anger

**"Why are you so angry?" the Lord asked him. "Why do you look so dejected?"** Genesis 4:6

**MAIN READING:** Genesis 4 • **OPTIONAL READING:** Genesis 5

Everyone gets angry sooner or later.

Your sister steals one of your favorite posters. You're ready to punch her lights out.

Your little brother messes up your room. You want to smack him in the face.

Anger can strike in an instant. One second we're laughing, and the next we're ready to kill.

In this story about Cain in the Bible, we see a man who was angry. Why? Because God rejected the offering he brought. God accepted his brother Abel's offering, and that only made it worse.

Cain's anger would lead him to kill his brother.

All through the world you'll find angry people. Some, like terrorists, murderers, and abusers, commit horrendous acts. Anger can be controlled, though, and overcome. How? With the help of God, a desire to obey him, and a commitment to his leadership. Ask God for his power, and God promises to give it.

**PRAYER:** Father, teach me to control my anger. Let me never hurt others. Amen.

Week 1: Friday

# Sometimes God Hurts

**So the Lord was sorry he had ever made them. It broke his heart.**
Genesis 6:6

**MAIN READING:** Genesis 6 • **OPTIONAL READING:** Genesis 7—9

Can people hurt God? Can God feel pain?

According to this verse of the Bible, he can. Here, the world had turned into a murderous, lying, cheating, stealing mess. People destroyed others for their own gain. Sin happened everywhere.

When God looked down and saw it, Genesis 6:6 says he was grieved. That means he mourned, he felt deep pain in his heart over the things people did. He couldn't simply ignore it. He couldn't go away for a rest and forget about it. He couldn't start beating up on them as they sinned.

No, God hurt and he had to do something. In this case, he would send a flood that would destroy the world.

But what about you? What does God do when you sin? God probably won't flood you out. But he will discipline you. He will convict you and tell you gently what you're doing is wrong. He'll try to get you to change and become a better person.

Are you disobeying God? Have you hurt others? Stop! Today! Refuse to live an evil, hateful life, and go to God, asking him to help you live rightly.

**PRAYER:** Lord, keep me from sinning. I want to please you. Amen.

Week 1: Saturday

# What We Do When We Have Faith

**Then the Lord told Abram, "Leave your country, your relatives, and your father's house, and go to the land that I will show you."**
Genesis 6:6

**Main Reading:** Genesis 12 • **Optional Reading:** Genesis 13—15

Imagine this. One day God says to you, "Go up to your class in school. Stand on your desk and tell the kids the gospel. Don't be afraid. I will be with you."

Wouldn't that be incredible? "Well," you say, "I'd probably be scared out of my wits. And everyone would think I'm totally weird."

But what if God himself told you to do this?

It has happened before in history. One of the first great examples comes from Abram (whose name had not yet been changed to Abraham). One day God told him to leave his country and go to a land God promised to show him. The Bible shows us that Abram obeyed, and he became the father of the Jews.

There will always be times in our lives when God asks us to do things that make us fearful. "I want you to be a missionary." Or, "Go to the school bully and tell him about me." Or, "Invite your weird neighbor over for lunch."

It could happen to you today. Be listening. God is there, and he wants to use you to change his world.

**Prayer:** Jesus, help me to listen for your voice. I want to follow you. Amen.

Week 1: Sunday

# The God Who Sees

**Thereafter, Hagar referred to the Lord, who had spoken to her, as "the God who sees me," for she said, "I have seen the One who sees me!"**
Genesis 16:13

**MAIN READING:** Genesis 16 • **OPTIONAL READING:** Genesis 17—19

Have you ever felt like no one cares about you? Like you don't matter to anyone?

Everyone has those feelings now and then. For Hagar in this story in the Bible, the feelings were intense. A slave, her owner Sarah, wife of Abraham, had allowed her to bear a special child for Abraham. This was an old practice. When a woman couldn't have children, she often allowed a slave or servant to bear children that she'd adopt. In Hagar's case, Sarah's jealousy when Hagar became pregnant upset the whole house. Hagar ran away. She felt alone, rejected, and hated.

But Hagar lived in a special house: Abraham's. God had chosen to bless Abraham in many ways, and those in his house would be blessed as well. God saw Hagar in her misery and visited her. He told her to go back to Sarah, and things would improve. Hagar reacted with the words, "You are the God who sees me." God knew about her trouble, and helped her.

Do you ever think that God sees you? He knows all about your problems, your hurts, your worries. Like Hagar, if you turn to him for help, he will answer. God never turns anyone away who seeks his love and friendship.

**PRAYER:** Jesus, I know you see me. Let me never forget that you care. Amen.

Week 2: Monday

# God Provided the Sacrifice

**"God will provide a lamb, my son," Abraham answered. And they both went on together.** Genesis 22:8

**MAIN READING:** Genesis 22 • **OPTIONAL READING:** Genesis 23—25

Imagine this situation. One day your dad comes into your room. "Come with me," he says. "God has asked me to do something important."

He takes you down to the living room. There, he ignites a fire and soon flames shoot up from the wood. Then he asks for your hands. You stick them out. He ties them up, and then ties up your feet. "What are you doing?" you ask.

"God wants me to sacrifice you on the fire to prove I really love him," your dad says.

You are terrified. Your dad picks you up. He's about to throw you in, when God stops him. "Here," God says, "here's a loaf of bread you can put into the fire. But now I know you really believe."

Crazy—right? But it actually happened. God told Abraham to sacrifice his son to prove his faith. At the last minute, God provided a sheep to use instead.

God has also provided the perfect sacrifice for everyone. No one ever need fear that God will ask this again. Jesus was the sacrifice, and when we believe in him we prove our faith. Have you proven yours by believing in Jesus? If not, do so today!

**PRAYER:** Father, thank you that Jesus died for me. I do believe. Amen.

Week 2: Tuesday

# Tricking Dad

**Go out to the flocks and bring me two fine young goats. I'll prepare your father's favorite dish from them.** Genesis 27:9

**MAIN READING:** Genesis 27 • **OPTIONAL READING:** Genesis 28—30

Dad stepped in the front door and yelled for Jesse. "Get down here," he called.

Jesse hurried down the stairs and stood in front of his dad. "You lied to me," he cried." You paid your friend Billy to clean up the garage. But I asked you to do it. You lied to me."

Jesse hung his head. "I didn't want to do it. I'm sorry."

"Trickery! Lying! It's a bad way to live," his dad said. "Now go apologize to Billy for using him."

Jesse clomped off, feeling guilty and miserable.

Trickery! Lying! Some of us do it all the time. You even find such things in the Bible. In this story, Jacob and his mother tricked his father into giving him the blessing that his father intended to give to his brother, Esau. It cost Jacob dearly, for he soon had to run away to the north and live with relatives because Esau threatened to kill him.

Do you ever lie to your parents (or anyone else)? Do you use trickery and deception to get what you want? Stop! Confess it to God and start being honest. It's a trap of the Devil which he will use to destroy you, if he can.

**PRAYER:** Lord, let me not use trickery and lying to get my way. Ever. Amen.

Week 2: Wednesday

# The Wrestling Match

**A man came and wrestled with him until dawn.** Genesis 32:24

**Main Reading:** Genesis 32 • **Optional Reading:** Genesis 31, 33, 34

Karin lay in bed thinking. From somewhere deep in her mind, she heard the words, "Go ahead, give the test to your friend, Stacey. No one will know, and you will help her."

A second voice spoke: "You know that's cheating, Karin. You know that displeases God."

"But Stacey is having a hard time in math. Shouldn't I help her?" the first voice said.

And the second: "You can help Stacey by spending some time showing her how to do those formulas. That's a better way."

And so it went. Sometimes we "wrestle" in our minds with God about things we want to do but which we know are wrong. Jacob experienced a similar wrestling in this story in the Bible. He was afraid of his brother, and he worried that he would die. God came to him and wrestled with him about the right thing to do. In the end, God changed Jacob's name from "cheater" (which is what Jacob means) to Israel, which means "one who struggles with God."

Do you ever see your Christian life as a struggle? Well, the truth is, it often is a struggle. Forces all around us fight for our loyalty and love. Whom will you love most—God, the Devil, or yourself? That's the struggle!

**Prayer:** Jesus, let me make the right decision to follow you today. Amen.

# The Dreamer

**One night Joseph had a dream and promptly reported the details to his brothers, causing them to hate him even more.** Genesis 37:5

**Main Reading:** Genesis 37 • **Optional Reading:** Genesis 35, 36, 38

Kyle woke up in a sweat. "Wow, what a weird dream!" he muttered.

In his dream, he had stood in a stadium and told a Super Bowl crowd about his faith in Jesus. And everyone started laughing at him. It was horrible. He woke up feeling as if he would scream.

Dreams can be strange, comforting, weird, or wild. You just never know. In ancient times, though, God sometimes communicated to people by dreams. He did so with Mary and Joseph, the parents of Jesus. He also gave dreams to Daniel, the wise men, and others. Joseph, in this story today, dreamed many strange but prophetic dreams. His dreams actually told what would happen in the future.

Few if any of our dreams will do that. Joseph's mistake was to tell his family the dreams, which made him look important and powerful and made them look inferior and like slaves. It would all lead to bad things for Joseph. When pride strikes and we begin to think we're really something important, we are on dangerous ground.

Do you ever think of yourself as better, or more important, than others? Watch out. You might be in for a terrible surprise!

**Prayer:** Father, help me to think rightly of myself and not be proud. Amen.

Week 2: Friday

# Who Is WITH You?

**The Lord was with Joseph and blessed him greatly as he served in the home of his Egyptian master.** Genesis 39:2

**MAIN READING:** Genesis 39 • **OPTIONAL READING:** Genesis 40—42

Joseph made some big mistakes as a boy. Number one, his father loved him more than his other brothers, and Joseph let everyone know about it. He even wore a special coat, showing how important he was. Joseph also dreamed great dreams that madehim look like a god and his brothers like slaves. That just made everyone angry. Eventually, Joseph's brothers came up with a plot and sold Joseph into slavery.

As you read the rest of the story of Joseph, you'll be amazed. Every time someone threw a curve to Joseph and got him into trouble, Joseph seemed to make the most of it. He ended up on top even though it seemed everyone was trying to put him down.

Why did this happen? The Bible reveals one basic reason: God was with him.

Do you sense that God is with you? How can you tell? Several ways. One, you'll defeat temptation more than you'll give in to it. Two, you'll experience joy and peace in your heart. Three, you'll see some success in life, and you'll know it's not just because of you. It's because God opened the door and led you through.

If you're a Christian, God is with you. He will lead, help, and encourage you every step of the way. So trust him.

**PRAYER:** Father, I praise you that you're with me. Keep me thinking about you. Amen.

Week 2: Saturday

# When You Love Someone

**"I am Joseph!" he said to his brothers. "Is my father still alive?"**
Genesis 45:3

**Main Reading:** Genesis 45 • **Optional Reading:** Genesis 43, 44, 46

"Can I see that knife?" Jason asked from the group of four boys who stood in Gabriel's dad's garage.

The knife thudded onto the ground and Gabriel stared in horror. That knife had once belonged to Jason, but Gabriel's father kept it in the garage now. Gabriel had stolen it from Jason a couple of years before.

Jason picked up the knife and gazed at it. Gabriel's mind whizzed through several strategies, but suddenly he knew only one was right: tell the truth.

He said, "Do you recognize that knife?"

Jason nodded. "I think."

"I stole it from you," Gabriel said. "I'm sorry. Will you forgive me?"

Jason looked up. "Uh, sure," he said. "But . . ."

"You can have it back," Gabriel said. "I shouldn't have done that. But I'm a Christian now."

Jason shook his head. "You amaze me, Gabe."

Gabriel smiled. "I'm just trying to do what's right."

When you sin against a friend, how do you make it up? By admitting your wrong and offering to make it right. It's that simple. In the above passage, that's what Joseph did with his brothers. It's a great example to follow.

**Prayer:** Jesus, help me to be forgiving, always. Amen.

Week 2: Sunday

# God Meant It for Good

**As far as I am concerned, God turned into good what you meant for evil. He brought me to the high position I have today so I could save the lives of many people.** Genesis 50:20

**MAIN READING:** Genesis 50 • **OPTIONAL READING:** Genesis 47—49

Ally waited in line at the theater with her friends. Her heart was troubled. That afternoon, she learned her grandfather had suffered a stroke. In the hospital in the West, miles from where Ally lived, the doctors were saying it was touch and go. Ally's parents told her to go to the movie tonight to take her mind off the disaster, but she couldn't. She found herself praying according to a verse she'd learned that week in Wednesday night youth group. "Jesus, please make Granddad well, and make this work for good in his life."

Ally's grandfather wasn't a Christian. A hard-driving man, he cussed and drank and lived a rough life. But she loved him.

A week later, Ally's parents flew her out West to see her Granddad. As she sat by his bedside, he took her hand. "You been prayin', haven't ya?" he whispered.

Ally nodded.

"Well, it's workin'," he said. "I'm feelin' ready to get right with God."

Ally told him about her prayers and the verse and he smiled. "Sounds like God's been answerin'."

Before he died, Granddad did accept the Lord, and Ally realized God had worked the stroke for good, just like he had with Joseph and his brothers.

**PRAYER:** Lord, show me how you're working good in my life. I need to see it. Amen.

# "Who Am I?"

**"But who am I to appear before Pharaoh?" Moses asked God. " How can you expect me to lead the Israelites out of Egypt?"** Exodus 3:11

**MAIN READING:** Exodus 3 • **OPTIONAL READING:** Exodus 1, 2, 4

Carey stared at the assignment: "Write and then speak without notes a story you have made up. It can be any story." He gulped. Talking in front of the class was the one thing that made his legs weak and his stomach about to vomit. How could he do it?

Carey explained to his dad what he had to do, and his dad smiled. "You know, Moses had the same problem."

"Moses?" Carey replied. He had heard plenty about Moses in church over the years, but nothing about a speaking problem.

"Oh, yeah," his dad said. "The Bible tells us that Moses was clumsy with words. He was very reluctant to speak to Pharaoh."

"What happened?" Carey asked. He knew Moses had turned into one of the great leaders of history, guiding the Jews as they left Egypt to their own country.

"God told him he would be with him," Carey's dad explained. "He also gave Moses a sidekick, his brother Aaron. But we know Moses was the leader."

As his father went into more details about Moses, Carey gained confidence. Finally, he told his story in class and got a solid B+.

Are you ever afraid you won't be able to do something—in school, church, or home? Remember: God is with you. Turn to him, and he will lead.

**PRAYER:** Lord, help me to remember that you are always with me when I'm afraid.

Week 3: Tuesday

# Trouble!

**So Moses went back to the Lord and protested, "Why have you mistreated your own people like this? Why did you send me?"**
Exodus 5:22

**MAIN READING:** Exodus 5 • **OPTIONAL READING:** Exodus 6—8

Trouble happens to everyone. Sooner or later, trouble will invade your life. School, church, your family, your friends. Trouble finds us all.

In Moses' day, God had commanded the leader to barter with Pharaoh (the king of Egypt) and lead the Jews out of slavery. Moses, after trying to get out of the whole thing, finally went along with God. When Moses appeared before Pharaoh, things got worse. Pharaoh told Moses to get out of his palace, and then he ordered that the Jews make bricks without straw. This was a dire problem, because without straw the bricks were much harder to make.

When Moses got back to the Jewish leaders, they screamed at him. How could he do this to them? What was he thinking?

Moses ran into his tent and complained to God. "How could you do this to ME?" he cried.

In the end, though, God showed Moses he was completely in charge. He made it possible for the Jews to escape from Egypt, but only after more trouble occurred.

Having troubles is not always a bad thing. God sometimes sends them for one reason: so we'll run to God and ask for his help. Do you have trouble today? Maybe you need to go to God and get some divine help!

**PRAYER:** Father, let me never forget that you are there to help me. Amen.

Week 3: Wednesday

# The Plagues on Egypt

**So they gathered soot from a furnace and went to see Pharaoh. . . . Moses tossed the soot into the air, and terrible boils broke out on the people and animals throughout Egypt.** Exodus 9:10

**MAIN READING:** Exodus 9 • **OPTIONAL READING:** Exodus 10, 11

Imagine one morning that you awake and your bed is covered with frogs!

You run to the shower to wash yourself off, and blood comes out of the faucet.

A few days later, flies infest your home, so many you can hardly breathe without sucking a couple down your throat.

Days later, your animals all die. And one day, a darkness that you can feel comes on the land. You can't see a thing, even your hand in front of you. It's terrifying.

Finally, a few days later, your father, who is the first son of your grandparents, and your older brother are stricken with a horrid disease. That night, they both die.

Pretty miserable situation, wouldn't you think? Yet, that's exactly what God did to the Egyptians when they wouldn't let the Jewish people go free. God sent 10 plagues in all. The last one involved the death of every firstborn son and animal.

God did this to Egypt to show his power. He wanted the world to know that he ruled in heaven and earth and no one could resist him.

Do you see God as a great God of power? He is. He can do more than we'd ever ask or think. So why not ask today?

**PRAYER:** Father, I praise you that you're all-powerful. I trust you to strengthen me. Amen.

Week 3: Thursday

# The Lamb of God

**Then Moses called for the leaders of Israel and said, "Tell each of your families to slaughter the lamb they have set apart for the Passover."**
Exodus 12:21

**MAIN READING:** Exodus 12 • **OPTIONAL READING:** Exodus 13—17

Imagine that one day your dad comes home with a new pet. It's a little lamb. He says, "We're keeping the pet in the house for a few days."

The lamb is cute and you have fun with it. You teach it a trick or two. At night, it sleeps on your bed. During the day, you run around with the lamb and it bleats and gambols and rolls over. It's the greatest fun you've ever had.

But on the last day of the week, something terrible happens. Dad takes that lamb away. Later, he returns with a dead lamb and its blood in a bowl. He splashes the blood on each side of your front door.

Would you weep? Would you be angry?

God gave the Jews this very situation in the Passover. Jews kept the lamb and then put it to death so none of their own children would have to die.

The lamb represents Jesus. He is the one who died in our place. Have you put your trust in the lamb? Is he your Savior? Why not settle the issue today?

**PRAYER:** Lord, it hurts to see innocent animals die. But I know it was your way of showing us how we should feel about Jesus. Thank you for sending him for me. Amen.

# Don't Misuse God's Name

**Do not misuse the name of the Lord your God. The Lord will not let you go unpunished if you misuse his name.** Exodus 20:7

**Main Reading:** Exodus 20 • **Optional Reading:** Exodus 18, 19, 21—23

God gave us the Ten Commandments. You find them in Exodus 20 and also Deuteronomy 5. God wrote them on tablets of stone and ordered that they be put into the ark of the covenant, the special box that symbolized God's presence in the temple. God didn't want his people to forget what was important.

Do you know the Ten Commandments? Why not read them right now, just to refresh your memory.

Are there any that you're violating? Are there any you find difficult?

Probably the most difficult commandment for people of all ages is the one that tells us not to misuse God's name. Sometimes people use God's name wrongly when they cuss and swear and add bad words to the name of God. But there are many ways to misuse God's name. When we just mutter, "God," when something goes wrong, that's misusing it. When we say, "Jesus," and are not talking to him directly, we're also misusing his name.

Watch what you say. God is listening. He wants you to have a pure mouth, one that speaks truth and good things. How are you doing today?

**Prayer:** Teach me not to misuse your name, Lord, so I can please you. Amen.

Week 3: Saturday

# God's Glory

**The Israelites at the foot of the mountain saw an awesome sight. The awesome glory of the Lord on the mountaintop looked like a devouring fire.** Exodus 24:17

**Main Reading:** Exodus 24 • **Optional Reading:** Exodus 25—27

What would it look like if God suddenly appeared on the street, or in your classroom, or at the front of the church? What do you think you would see?

A ball of fire?

A thick cloud or fog?

A giant face?

A bolt of lightning?

A planet?

God did appear to people long ago. Not himself, but his glory. What is his glory? It's the aspect of God that makes him most impressive, most powerful, most beautiful in our eyes. In Israel's day, his glory was like the verse above describes—a consuming fire on top of the mountain. That's a fire that burns up everything in its path. It's totally awesome and inspiring. No one can stand before it.

One day, the book of Revelation says, we will see God's face (22:4). No one has any idea what that will look like. But it will be an awesome moment, don't you think?

Something to look forward to in heaven!

**Prayer:** Lord, I'd like to see you, but let others see you in my life. Amen.

Week 3: Sunday

# Worshiping an Idol

**Then Aaron took the gold, melted it down, and molded and tooled it into the shape of a calf. The people exclaimed, "O Israel, these are the gods who brought you out of Egypt!"** Exodus 32:4

**MAIN READING:** Exodus 32 • **OPTIONAL READING:** Exodus 28—31

Carly's room had more posters than any of her friends' rooms. All the posters were of one person too. A movie star that she thought was the greatest. There was one of the movie star standing by a car. Another of his face, huge and smiling, right in the middle. Over on another wall, one of the movie star strumming a guitar. And another of him surrounded by a bunch of fans.

She had a poster of this movie star for just about every occasion. When she stepped into her room each afternoon after school, she felt close and loved by this movie star, even though she'd never met him.

What was Carly's problem? Some people like Carly very nearly worship the idols they find in the music world, movie world, TV world, and so on.

And idol can be anything. In Hebrew times it was an actual sculpture or image. In our day, it could be money, popularity, pleasure, a movie star, or something else that catches our attention. How do you know if something in your life has become an idol? By how much you think about that thing or person. By how much you spend on buying stuff related to them.

Have you fallen prey to an idol? Turn back to God and tell him you want to give him first place in your life.

**PRAYER:** Father, remove the idols from my life and let me worship only you. Amen.

Week 4: Monday

# Who God Really Is

**He passed in front of Moses and said, "I am the Lord, I am the Lord, the merciful and gracious God. I am slow to anger and rich in unfailing love and faithfulness."** Exodus 34:6

**Main Reading:** Exodus 34 • **Optional Reading:** Exodus 33, 35, 36

Who is God really? The big guy in charge of the world? Someone who demands that we worship and love him, or he'll send us to hell? An all-powerful person who supposedly can do anything, but mostly doesn't?

We all have many ideas about who God is and what he is like. One of the best pictures is found here in Exodus 34. Here, God told Moses exactly what he was like. What was that?

Compassionate. God understands where we hurt and he feels that hurt with us. He wants only to help us and make us feel safe in the world.

Gracious. God has many gifts. He owns the whole world. And his grace means he wants to give those gifts to all of us. He wants to make eternity in heaven one huge Christmas celebration.

Slow to anger. You may think God gets angry easily, but he really doesn't. If he ever got truly angry with us, where would we be? But God is slow to anger. He is constantly patient, giving us the time and opportunity to change.

Abounding in loving-kindness. God is full of love. First John 4:16 says he is love itself. "God is love." He wants to pour out his love on each of us.

Does that give you a better picture of who God is?

**Prayer:** Lord, I praise you that you are the greatest of all, and I trust you. Amen.

# God Is Near

**The cloud of the Lord rested on the Tabernacle during the day, and at night there was fire in the cloud so all the people of Israel could see it.** Exodus 40:38

**MAIN READING:** Exodus 40 • **OPTIONAL READING:** Exodus 37—39

Moses often talked with God in the Tent of Meeting. He wasn't just praying the way you and I do—Moses was in the physical presence of God!

When Moses came out of the Tent of Meeting, his face actually glowed. In fact, his face was so bright that everyone else had to look away.

Why did this happen? Because spending time in the presence of God is a wonderful thing. In some ways, it's like sitting near a hot fire that warms you and makes you feel secure and protected. It cleanses you, so that you become clean in his eyes. It comforts you during cold and lonely nights, so that you know you're not alone. You come away joyful and filled with the Spirit. You might even have a bit of a "glow" about you.

Spending time with God is what helped Moses become such a powerful leader of Israel. It made him realize that because of God, he could be strong and never alone.

One day we will all bask in the physical presence of God and see him face to face. His love, comfort, and care will keep us warm and happy through all eternity.

**PRAYER:** Lord, let me draw near to you to live in your presence and warmth. Amen.

Week 4: Wednesday

# A Sacrifice Without Blemish

**If your sacrifice for a whole burnt offering is from the herd, bring a bull with no physical defects to the entrance of the Tabernacle so it will be accepted by the Lord.** Leviticus 1:3

**Main Reading:** Leviticus 1 • **Optional Reading:** Leviticus 2—4

Ever buy a CD or a toy or something else that was broken, didn't work, or was otherwise messed up? It's a pain, isn't it? You expect to get a working item and it turns out it doesn't work at all. You have to take it back, stand in line, go through all kinds of questions, all to get back what should have been right in the first place.

When God first instructed Israel about sacrifices, he required the people to sacrifice only the very best animals—ones with "no physical defects."

Why did God require this? Because a sacrifice represented something that would take the punishment in place of you, the sacrificer. You had committed a sin, or said something out of line. Now you had to pay for it. God made up a system where animals paid for the sins of the people.

What God wanted the Israelites to understand was that Jesus would one day take on the sins of the world. He had to be perfect—meaning without sin.

The point was that, in order to pay for the sins of the world, Jesus needed to be perfect. Otherwise, he would have to pay for his own sins first.

It was an amazing system. Through it, God shows us how he thinks and works. Jesus was the perfect sacrifice. We never need to fear God's anger again.

**Prayer:** Jesus, thank you for paying for my sins. I'll never forget it. Amen.

Week 4: Thursday

# Guilty!

**If any of the people sin by unintentionally defiling the Lord's sacred property, they must bring to the Lord a ram from the flock as their guilt offering.** Leviticus 5:15

**MAIN READING:** Leviticus 5 • **OPTIONAL READING:** Leviticus 6—8

Lisa turned around to say something to her friend Jenna in class. Immediately, the teacher, Mrs. Simpson, clapped her hands. "I said no talking, girls. You are guilty! Now who will pay for what you've done?"

Lisa stared in astonishment at her teacher. Pay for talking? With what? Money? A time out? What?

When we do something wrong, we're guilty. That guilt means someone has to pay for what was done. Sometimes, the victim of your wrongdoing might offer forgiveness. But in God's eyes, someone still must pay. Why? Because that's the way justice works. You do wrong, you pay. You take drugs and get caught, you pay. You lie about a situation and the teacher finds out, you pay. It's the way the whole world works.

What was God trying to teach the Israelites when he showed them the system of sacrifices and payments? That guilt must be punished.

The joy for us is that Jesus took the punishment. When he died on the cross, he paid for the sins of everyone in the world. In other words, God demands payment, and then he paid it through his Son. That's how much he loves us.

**PRAYER:** May I always remember that you paid that I might be free, Lord. Amen.

Week 4: Friday

# Cleansed by Blood

**His sons brought him the blood, and he dipped his finger into it and put it on the horns of the altar. He poured out the rest of the blood at the base of the altar.** Leviticus 9:9

**MAIN READING:** Leviticus 9 • **OPTIONAL READING:** Leviticus 10—12

Blood. It's red. It's wet. It's a liquid. And it runs through our bodies. Without blood flowing in our veins, we would die.

That's why Jesus' dying on the cross is so important. As he hung there, he spilled his blood. That blood was a sacrifice to God to pay for sin, for guilt. When Jesus gave his blood for us, he was giving his very life. God accepted it as the just payment for the sins of the world.

Next time you get a cut or lose some blood, look at it. Notice how rich and red it is. Notice how it hurts when your skin breaks. Blood is precious. If we lose too much of it, we will die, like Jesus did.

God requires that someone pay for our sins with blood. Jesus did that for you. Have you accepted what he did? Do you believe it? Then you belong to God forever, and he forgives you for everything.

**PRAYER:** Lord, praise you that Jesus died for me. Amen.

Week 4: Saturday

# The Most Holy Place

**The Lord said to Moses, "Warn your brother Aaron not to enter the Most Holy Place behind the inner curtain whenever he chooses; the penalty for intrusion is death."** Leviticus 16:2

**MAIN READING:** Leviticus 16 • **OPTIONAL READING:** Leviticus 13—15

Do you have a secret place? Do you keep special things there? Is this the place you go to think and work out problems and read your best books?

Not all of us have a special place, but perhaps you can imagine one. In the Bible, God had a special place. No one could go into it except once a year when a high priest entered and put some blood on the ark of the covenant. This represented the payment for the sins of Israel. God forgave them for everything each year when this happened.

This special place of God's is called the holy of holies or the most holy place. The word holy means that it was utterly different and separate from everything else. It was God's alone, and no one could even look inside without God's permission.

The most holy place represents the most intimate and personal place we can meet with God. When Jesus died on the cross, the Bible tells us that the veil, which stood in front of the most holy place, was torn in half. From that point on, it showed that anyone could enter the secret place of God and talk to him.

Are you spending time with God? Then you have entered his most holy place.

**PRAYER:** Father, let me come into your holy place often, so I can talk to you. Amen.

Week 4: Sunday

# Witchcraft

**Men and women among you who act as mediums or psychics must be put to death by stoning. They are guilty of a capital offense.**
Leviticus 20:27

**MAIN READING:** Leviticus 20 • **OPTIONAL READING:** Leviticus 17—19

Patricia invited several of her friends to a sleep-over. There, she pulled out a Ouija® board game. Patricia explained that as they all sat around it, closed their eyes and concentrated, the board would talk to them. It would answer questions. It would tell secrets.

Everyone wanted to try it except Abby. She had been a Christian for several years. In church she heard about such occult objects, and she knew they were forbidden by God. Her friends called her a scaredy-cat and a goody-goody, but Abby just called her mom and went home that night.

Several months later, one of the other friends from that night told Abby, "I play with the board all the time. I've learned all kinds of secrets. It's fun." But Abby noticed her friend had changed. She cussed a lot now, and lied, and had even tried drugs.

Talking boards and similar things are related to witchcraft. In the above Scripture, God even commanded that people who used such things be put to death. We wouldn't do that today, but we should know that such things get us talking to demons, fallen angels who want to trick us. Don't be deceived. They're dangerous.

**PRAYER:** Lord, keep me from ever getting involved in witchcraft. Amen.

Week 5: Monday

# Passover

**First comes the Lord's Passover, which begins at twilight on its appointed day in early spring.** Leviticus 23:5

**Main Reading:** Leviticus 23 • **Optional Reading:** Leviticus 21, 22, 24

Do you like Christmas? Is it a special holiday to you?

How about Easter? Do you get candy in a basket and maybe some chocolate Easter bunnies?

We all have holidays during that year that help us remember great events of the past. Christmas reminds us of Jesus' coming into the world. Easter makes us think about Jesus' dying on the cross and then rising from the dead.

The Jews also had holidays. Through them, they learned about important events of history, and even of the future. The Passover was probably their most important holiday. In it, they remembered when the Lord "passed over" them as he went through Egypt and slew all the firstborn sons of the Egyptians.

Passover represented many important things. It reminded the people of their slavery in Egypt and of their escape from Egypt. Especially, it told them about the lamb God would provide to give them new life. The Passover lamb, which was killed and eaten at Passover, had its blood painted on the sides and top of their front doors. When the Lord saw the blood, he "passed over" that house and killed no one.

Jesus is your passover. When we trust him, God passes over us when he judges the world.

**Prayer:** Lord, thank you for passing over me. I trust you forever. Amen.

Week 5: Tuesday

# Obedience Brings Blessing

**If you keep my laws and are careful to obey my commands, I will send the seasonal rains. The land will then yield its crops, and the trees will produce their fruit.** Leviticus 26:3, 4

**Main Reading:** Leviticus 26 • **Optional Reading:** Leviticus 25, 27

God blesses obedience," the youth pastor said. "He doesn't bless disobedience or rebellion."

Aaron thought about the past week. He'd almost had a fight with his sister. But at the last minute, he stopped himself, and asked her not to sneak into his room when he wasn't there. So far, she had complied and even been nice to him.

At school, he spent much time studying for a test. And he'd done well.

He invited one of his friends to a church concert with the band from the kids' group. Jeffrey had come and enjoyed it.

That night, he knelt by his bed and prayed, "God, haven't I been obedient? But where's the blessing?"

The next week he asked the youth pastor about it. The young man said, "Well, you have a better relationship with your sister, right? That's a blessing. A good grade on the test is a blessing. Your friend came to church. Couldn't that have been the blessing?"

Aaron thought about it. Maybe God's blessings weren't gifts and rewards and other things like that all the time, but blessings that were linked to the obedience. It made sense to him, and he decided to look for his blessings in that way.

**Prayer:** Jesus, your blessings are all very good. Thank you. Amen.

# The Meeting Place

**The Tabernacle will be located at the center of these tribal compounds.** Numbers 2:2

**Main Reading:** Numbers 2 • **Optional Reading:** Numbers 1, 3, 4

God wants to meet with you.

Did you know that? The awesome, creator God wants to be your friend, talk with you, and hear what's on your mind. Anytime you're ready!

Yes, God desires to meet with you at different times during your week. Perhaps you plan to spend some time reading the Bible. God in turn will meet with you then. He'll put thoughts into your mind about the Bible. He'll speak to you if you're listening. He'll be there, ready when you read.

God wants to meet with you in church and in your youth group. Maybe he will reinforce something in your heart that your leader says. Maybe you'll feel a special warmth about a song or something from the church service. God meets with us in many ways. We can never be sure how, just that he will.

Have you been meeting with God regularly? God wants a relationship with you, a friendship. If you take the time, he will take the time too. It could be the best moment of your week.

Prayer: Lord, let me remember always to meet you each week. Amen.

Week 5: Thursday

# The Leading of God

**When the cloud lifted from over the sacred tent, the people of Israel followed it. And wherever the cloud settled, the people of Israel camped.** Numbers 9:17

**MAIN READING:** Numbers 9 • **OPTIONAL READING:** Numbers 5—8

Many young Christians struggle with God's leading.

What does God want me to do now? What about school—should I run for president of my class, or not? And my family—would God tell me how to get along better with my little brother?

God longs to show you the way in this world. The Israelites in the passage above had a perfect guide from God. When he appeared in the cloud by day and the pillar of fire by night, they knew exactly when he wanted them to move on. All you had to do was look up and you knew what God's will was.

For us it's not so simple. But here are some guidelines.

1. God will lead you through the words of the Bible. Study it, and you'll know what to do in many situations.

2. God leads through prayer. Talk to God, and he will help you.

3. God will lead you through others. Listen to your Christian friends and leaders.

Use these methods, and you will not fail.

**PRAYER:** Lord, I will look for your leading. Help me to see it. Amen.

Week 5: Friday

# Criticism

**While they were at Hazeroth, Miriam and Aaron criticized Moses because he had married a Cushite woman.** Numbers 12:1

**Main Reading:** Numbers 12 • **Optional Reading:** Numbers 10, 11

"You're just an idiot, Maddie," Erin said. "You always do things wrong!"

"What did I do wrong?" Erin cried. "I did everything we said."

"No, you didn't. You didn't do the picture right, and you didn't write it up properly."

Erin and Maddie worked on the school newspaper together. Erin acted as managing editor. Maddie worked as a reporter. She didn't like what she was hearing from her friend at the moment.

Everyone gets criticized for something. Your clothing. Your looks. Your way of talking. Acting out of line. Making a mistake. It can be anything. Some people will jump on you and yell and scream no matter how careful you are.

Moses received criticism from his brother and sister in the story we're looking at today. They criticized him about his marriage to Zipporah, but the real problem was that they were jealous of him because God used him so much. Sometimes criticism is like that. The critic is jealous, or angry about something else, or in a bad mood.

Don't let criticism stop you. If you believe you're doing the right thing, have prayed about it and asked God for his guidance, then trust that he will give it. We all get criticized, but it's the one who keeps the course who succeeds.

**Prayer:** Father, help me not to worry about criticism. Let me worry about pleasing you. Amen.

Week 5: Saturday

# A Lone Voice

**But Caleb tried to encourage the people as they stood before Moses. "Let's go at once to take the land," he said. "We can certainly conquer it!"** Numbers 13:30

**Main Reading:** Numbers 13 • **Optional Reading:** Numbers 14—16

Sometimes you will have to stand alone.

In the story of the 12 spies in the book of Numbers, we see 10 scared men who gave a bad report about the land they'd seen. The people were powerful. Their cities were fortresses. Some of them, the sons of Anak, were virtual giants. The Israelites couldn't take the land.

One man stood out, and then another joined him. Caleb assured everyone they could take the land with God's help. Joshua agreed. But in the end, the people didn't listen to them. Why? Because they didn't have the kind of faith that these two men had.

There will be times when you have to stand alone. Maybe in school, or church, or even your family. You might be the only Christian in your group of friends. That will bring many times when you have to speak up for the truth. No one else may agree with you.

All through history, Christians have often stood alone. Two examples are Martin Luther King, Jr.—and the person he was named after, Martin Luther, who started the Reformation of the church and changed history too. Many Christians have been persecuted. But they stood firm. Why? Because they had faith. Faith always gives you courage because God is with you.

**Prayer:** Lord, help me not to be afraid to stand up for what is right. Amen.

Week 5: Sunday

# Big Mistake

**Then Moses raised his hand and struck the rock twice with the staff, and water gushed out. So the people and their livestock drank their fill.** Numbers 20:11

**MAIN READING:** Numbers 20 • **OPTIONAL READING:** Numbers 17—19

Could you do something so terrible that you would lose God's blessing and love?

In the story from the Bible today, we see Moses committing a grave sin. God told him to speak to the rock to bring forth water. But Moses, in anger at the people's complaining, struck it twice with his staff. God's anger was immediate. He told Moses because of this sin he would never enter the land of milk and honey, the land of Israel. He would only see it from the top of a mountain.

All of us will sin many times in this life. Some sins are minor. We confess them and receive forgiveness. But every now and then we may do something that brings God's anger. We won't lose his love or the right to go to heaven. God won't turn against us. But he will discipline us. He will make us face the consequences of our sin.

You can't lose God's love through sin, but you can lose his blessing. You can lose the right to succeed in some special way. God hates sin and he will discipline us when we sin. Be careful. Sin is lurking. It wants to destroy you. But if you live by faith, you will win over it.

**PRAYER:** Jesus, keep me from sin. I want your blessing on my life. Amen.

Week 6: Monday

# God Provides

**From there the Israelites traveled to Beer, which is the well where the Lord said to Moses, "Assemble the people, and I will give them water."**
Numbers 21:16

**MAIN READING:** Numbers 21 • **OPTIONAL READING:** Numbers 22, 23

Montel sat at the table as his dad folded his hands to pray. "We've got a serious need," his father said.

Montel's family listened in silence as his dad told them he was being laid off from his job and it would be hard to find a new one. It scared Montel deeply. Where would they live? What about their house? How long would his dad be unemployed?

Nothing much changed in Montel's life over the next few weeks, except his father stayed home all the time. Montel decided to pray about the situation every day.

Then one night, Montel's father had another announcement before dinner. "I'm starting my own business as a consultant," he said. "It'll be tough, but I think that's what God's leading me to do. Pray now that God would give me some clients."

Again, Montel prayed. His dad found four solid clients over the next month, and more were coming. In Sunday school one morning, Montel talked about how God had answered his prayer. "I guess God really does provide," he said. The joy in him felt like a little shooting star.

God does provide. He meets needs. Keep trusting, and God will answer.

**PRAYER:** Lord, help me to always put my trust in you during times of trouble. Amen.

Week 6: Tuesday

# The Star

**I see him, but not in the present time. I perceive him, but far in the distant future. A star will rise from Jacob; a scepter will emerge from Israel.** Numbers 24:17

**Main Reading:** Numbers 24 • **Optional Reading:** Numbers 25—27

When the wise men were looking for the place where Jesus was born, what brought them there? A star, right?

How had the wise men learned about this special star? Possibly from Daniel, a Jew who served in Babylon as the king's highest adviser. Daniel would have been very familiar with the prophecies in the Old Testament, and he might have told the wise men about a star that would one day announce the birth of the new king of the Jews.

Where could Daniel have gotten this idea of a star? Possibly from Numbers 24:17. There, the non-Jewish prophet Balaam tells about a star that would appear when the king arrived.

Some scholars believe that this information was passed down through the centuries from one generation to the next. However it actually happened, God made sure that the right people knew the right information at the right time. The wise men saw the star, traveled to Bethlehem, and brought Jesus gifts of gold, frankincense, and myrrh.

Isn't it amazing how God works? He never leaves anyone who wants to know about him without the truth. Trust him to bring that truth to your family, your friends, and all the people of the great wide world. For he will.

**Prayer:** Jesus, you are the king, and you are my king. I worship you. Amen.

# Gathered to Your People

**Take vengeance on the Midianites for leading the Israelites into idolatry. After that, you will die and join your ancestors.**
Numbers 31:2

**Main Reading:** Numbers 31 • **Optional Reading:** Numbers 28—30

How did people in the Old Testament know about the resurrection?

Only a few Scriptures give us an inkling about a resurrection of the dead. Some are found in Daniel, others in Job, one in Psalm 16. But there is an old Hebrew expression that all Hebrews used that indicates their confidence in heaven. It's found in Numbers 31:2, as well as many other places. "Join your ancestors."

What does that mean?

The Hebrews believed that when you died, you were brought back together with your ancestors. You were drawn in like a fish on a hook to your people. They were all those who had died before you in the faith. You came back to them in heaven, and were with them forever.

Think about it: one day you will die and, if you're a Christian, you will be gathered to your people. You'll see all those who have gone before who believed in Jesus. Your grandparents and great-grandparents, all the way back to Abraham and Abel and Adam. There, you will experience happiness and joy.

**Prayer:** Lord, praise you for making a way for all of us to live forever. Thanks. Amen.

Week 6: Thursday

# God Cares About the Details

**They said, "Sir, the Lord instructed you to divide the land by sacred lot among the people of Israel. You were told by the Lord to give the inheritance of our brother Zelophehad to his daughters."** Numbers 36:2

**Main Reading:** Numbers 36 • **Optional Reading:** Numbers 32—35

Many families pass on land, or homes, or businesses from one generation to the next. The children in a family inherit what their fathers bought or started.

Is it like that in your family?

In my family, one of the things I inherited was a diamond ring from my grandmother. It had been passed down from her mother, and maybe even before that. In my family, that diamond ring was special. I gave it to my wife when we got engaged.

In the land of Israel, one thing was most sacred of all: land. Strict rules governed how land was passed down from one generation to another. In the above situation, a man did not have any sons, only daughters. If they married outside men who were not in the same ancestral line, that land would pass out of the family's hands.

These people were so concerned about this that they came to Moses. They asked him to find out from God what to do. God answered and solved the problem easily.

You might think that something like this was really a minor problem. But God cares about all problems we face, big and little ones. What problem, small or big, can you bring to God today?

**Prayer:** Father, remind me always that you want to help with everything. Amen.

Week 6: Friday

# Don't Go It Alone

**At that time I told you, "You are too great a burden for me to carry all by myself."** Deuteronomy 1:9

**Main Reading:** Deuteronomy 1 • **Optional Reading:** Deuteronomy 2—4

Have you ever been elected to a position of leadership? In school? In your Sunday-school class? On a sports team?

Such a job can be daunting. How are we to lead effectively? How can I be in charge of so many people?

Leaders all through history have felt that tension. In Deuteronomy 1:9, Moses tells the Jews about his feelings when he decided to lead Israel out of Egypt. How could he care for so many people? How could he possibly make right judgments? How could he lead his friends and family in way that succeeded?

When you get a chance to lead, here's one word of wisdom: don't try to do it alone! We all need help. God wants to give us help wherever we need it.

God will help you find people who can lead with you. He will guide you about decisions you might need to make. He will give you wisdom greater than any you could ever dredge up on your own. Trust him. He'll get you where you want to go.

**Prayer:** Lord, guide me so that I lead with you beside me. Amen.

Week 6: Saturday

# Walk in the Way

**Stay on the path that the Lord your God has commanded you to follow. Then you will live long and prosperous lives in the land you are about to enter and occupy.** Deuteronomy 5:33

**Main Reading:** Deuteronomy 5 • **Optional Reading:** Deuteronomy 6, 8, 9

Have you ever wondered why the spiritual life is so often compared to walking along a path? What does it mean to walk spiritually?

Walking is slow and steady. You can walk without getting tired for a lot longer than you can run. Remember Aesop's fable of "The Tortoise and the Hare"? The slow and steady tortoise completed the race ahead of the hare because he was not distracted from the goal.

God wants you to be steady, not hurried in growing up spiritually. When you walk, you plod along, but you're not racing. You get where you need to go, one step at a time.

When you walk in the Spirit, you will never get bored or tired of your spiritual life. It will seem like an adventure.

Walk in the path of Christ, and like others before you, you will please God.

**Prayer:** Jesus, please help me stay on the path you want me to follow. Amen.

Week 6: Sunday

# Fear

**Perhaps you will think to yourselves, "How can we ever conquer these nations that are so much more powerful than we are?"**
Deuteronomy 7:17

**MAIN READING:** Deuteronomy 7 • **OPTIONAL READING:** Deuteronomy 10—12

The three boys slumped by the wall of the store and stared at Kelsey. She stopped and looked away. Was she really going to walk by them? Would they try anything?

Kelsey hesitated, then thought to pray. "God, let me not be afraid. Keep me safe. I'm going to walk by them. Tell me not to if that's what you want."

She walked to the mailbox near the corner. In her mind, a thought registered, "Turn around and go in the opposite direction.
Go behind the store and the street there."

Kelsey swallowed. Was this the Spirit of God talking? She decided to heed the voice and soon walked toward home without mishap.

Kelsey was in a situation that could easily provoke great fear. God wants each of us to know we're in his hands. He protects us. If we listen for his voice, he will help us make wise and good decisions. He doesn't want us to go through life afraid. We belong to him and he will lead the way, if we seek him.

**PRAYER:** Father, let me always come to you when I'm afraid. Amen.

Week 7: Monday

# The Tenth

**You must set aside a tithe of your crops—one-tenth of all the crops you harvest each year.** Deuteronomy 14:22

**Main Reading:** Deuteronomy 14

**Optional Reading:** Deuteronomy 13, 15, 16

Ally opened the birthday card. As she expected, a check had been tucked into it. She quickly scanned the check. Her grandmother had sent her $150. "Be careful how you spend it," Gram had written. "And remember to give some to the Lord."

Ally grinned. Gram always wanted her to do the right thing when it came to God. And she knew her grandmother was serious. She took the check to her dad.

"I'd like you to give me $15 from it so I can give it in church this Sunday," she told him. "I'd like to put $15 in savings, and then . . ."

Her father nodded. "And then . . ."

"I spend the rest."

Her father chuckled. "Good thinking, honey. I'm glad you're willing to tithe. That's an important step."

"What does tithe mean anyway, Dad?" Ally asked.

"It means a tenth. It all goes back to Abraham who gave to a great priest a tenth of some winnings he'd gotten in a battle. Since then, Christians have followed that pattern."

Tithing is an important practice. It's not for God so much as for us. When we learn to give from the heart, we give the way God wants.

**Prayer:** Jesus, may I never hold back what I should give to your work. Amen.

Week 7: Tuesday

# The Prophet Like Moses

**I will raise up a prophet like you from among their fellow Israelites. I will tell that prophet what to say, and he will tell the people everything I command him.** Deuteronomy 18:18

**MAIN READING:** Deuteronomy 18

**OPTIONAL READING:** Deuteronomy 17, 19, 20

Prophecies of what will happen in the future are an important feature of the Bible. We find prophecies in many books of the Old Testament, and in some of the New. The Book of Revelation is almost all prophecy.

One of the most ancient prophecies we have is this one from the words of Moses. Here, God told the Jews to look for a prophet to arise who would be like Moses. What characteristics should they look for?

He would be a great leader.

He would set free people who were enslaved.

He would provide a way for people to be forgiven of their sins.

He would speak mighty words that live on after him.

He would do miracles.

Can anyone guess who this prophet might be? You probably nailed it. The person Moses spoke of was Jesus. Jesus alone fulfills all these requirements.

God inspired prophets to foretell the coming of Jesus. There are over 300 prophecies concerning Jesus in the Bible. God didn't want anyone to be misled.

**PRAYER:** Lord, thank you that you have given us many ways to know about Jesus. Amen.

Week 7: Wednesday

# Obedience to Your Parents

**They must declare, "This son of ours is stubborn and rebellious and refuses to obey. He is a worthless drunkard."** Deuteronomy 21:20

**Main Reading:** Deuteronomy 21

**Optional Reading:** Deuteronomy 22—24

Disobedience is serious in the eyes of God. Many times the Bible talks of ways parents can keep their children in line. Parents are never to abuse their little ones, but they are to discipline them when they do things wrong.

Sometimes young people start doing far worse things than coming home late or telling a little lie. Sometimes they get into drugs, drinking, sex, and many other things that can lead to their destruction. When parents today must give up on a son or daughter because of their sin, they usually let them go off on their own and suffer the consequences of their bad behavior.

In the Old Testament, though, disobedience invited a much worse fate than that. A young man or woman could be stoned (executed) because of his or her sin. It was that serious.

We don't resort to such measures today. God tells us to show mercy and compassion, even to very bad people.

Disobedience is a serious matter in the eyes of God. Take a look at your life. Are you disobeying your parents about some situation or problem? Are you sinning against them and others? Stop! Confess it to God and make it right with your parents. Then your life will be blessed and preserved.

**Prayer:** Father, help me to learn to obey even when I don't feel like it. Amen.

# Honesty

**Yes, use honest weights and measures, so that you will enjoy a long life in the land the Lord your God is giving you.** Deuteronomy 25:15

**MAIN READING:** Deuteronomy 25

**OPTIONAL READING:** Deuteronomy 26—28

"Give me your money and I'll buy the CD for you," Dean said to his friend, Roberto. "I can get it tomorrow."

Roberto gave him $15.

Roberto had recently moved to the U.S. from Brazil. He didn't know much English, and he wasn't used to American stores. But Dean planned to cheat him. He would purchase the CD from a discount store instead of the music store, and keep the change that was left over from the purchase.

Do you think that's fair, or right, or even Christian?

Certainly not. Roberto obviously trusted his new friend, but Dean wasn't much of a friend. He wanted to cheat Roberto.

There are a million ways kids can cheat each other today. But in the old days of Israel, one way to cheat people was common. We see it in Deuteronomy 25:15. Some people kept two sets of weights used to parcel out grain, bread, milk, and other things. Merchants used the lighter weights when they intended to give the buyer less than he really paid for.

God hates such practices. Cheating others is a very bad thing in God's eyes. It hurts the people who pay good money for your help, and it angers God.

**PRAYER:** Lord, help me beware of ever cheating anyone, in school or anywhere else. Amen.

Week 7: Friday

# Secret Things

**There are secret things that belong to the Lord our God, but the revealed things belong to us and our descendants forever, so that we may obey these words of the law.** Deuteronomy 29:29:

**MAIN READING:** Deuteronomy 29

**OPTIONAL READING:** Deuteronomy 30, 31

Have you ever wondered about some of these things:

Why one person is good at music, and someone else isn't—

Why some kids get better grades than others, even though the others may study just as hard—

How you came to be born where you did, in the family you did, while other people are born to a king in a palace—

Why some people like Tiger Woods have great talent, and others who wish they had it just don't—

What does God call the answers to these questions? The secret things. Such secrets belong to God and God alone. He knows why he created Tiger Woods the way he did and why he made you the way you are. The important thing is to trust that God knows all about you, why he made you the way you are, and what he intends to do with you. That's a secret thing he will reveal to you, if you ask.

**PRAYER:** Jesus, show me what I can do in your world today. Amen.

Week 7: Saturday

# God's Oath

**Then the Lord said to Moses, "This is the land I promised on oath to Abraham, Isaac and Jacob, and I told them I would give it to their descendants. I have now allowed you to see it, but you will not enter the land."** Deuteronomy 34:4

**Main Reading:** Deuteronomy 34

**Optional Reading:** Deuteronomy 32, 33

When people testify in court, they swear on a Bible to tell "the truth, the whole truth, and nothing but the truth, so help me God!"

When someone wants to make a point and show how strongly he feels about it, he may swear: "I swear that's the truth."

What happens when God swears?

In Deuteronomy 34:4, we see one of the times God swore about a situation. Long before, in the book of Genesis, God had sworn to give the land of Canaan (later, Israel) to Abraham, then Isaac, and finally Jacob. God made it clear that nothing would stop him from keeping that promise.

Do you know what happened?

Over the centuries, Israel lived in the land. Sometimes they labored under the power of Babylon or Greece or Rome or other nations. But for much of the time, they were free. Today, the land of Israel is occupied mostly by Jews.

God keeps his promises. You can trust him with your life. What promises from Scripture do you know that you'd like God to fulfill?

**Prayer:** Father, let me trust your promises and live by them every day. Amen.

Week 7: Sunday

# God Will Be with You

**I command you—be strong and courageous! Do not be afraid or discouraged. For the Lord your God is with you wherever you go.** Joshua 1:9

**MAIN READING:** Joshua 1 • **OPTIONAL READING:** Joshua 2—4

When I was 14 years old, I went on a trip to Philmont Scout Ranch in New Mexico. It's the greatest experience for any Boy Scout, and I was excited. All the way out there, though, I kept hearing about the bears. "Don't put any food in your tent," our leaders warned us, "or a bear will come in, take the food, and possibly eat you too."

Scared? You bet. Until I met Buzzy Woodward. Buzzy was our guide the first few days on the trail. He carried a giant hunting knife, could walk silently through the woods like a Native American, and wanted to be a Green Beret. Buzzy had one special ability, though: he could hiss and roar like a mountain lion. He told us, "Bears are only scared of one thing: mountain lions."

One night, we put him in a tent with all the food. He wanted to show us what happened when a bear heard a mountain lion. The bear would go into the tent, Buzzy would do his roar, and that bear would run.

Unfortunately, the bear never showed up. But can you imagine how I felt around Buzzy? Like I could face anything.

Being a Christian is a little like having a divine Buzzy Woodward on your side. God is with you. God goes before you. God protects you. God is always there. That's what he told Joshua in Joshua 1:9, and that's what he tells you too. "I am with you!"

**PRAYER:** Jesus, help me always to feel you at my side. Amen.

Week 8: Monday

# God Saves the Faithful

**The young men went in and brought out Rahab, her father, mother, brothers, and all the other relatives who were with her. They moved her whole family to a safe place near the camp of Israel.** Joshua 6:23

**Main Reading:** Joshua 6 • **Optional Reading:** Joshua 5, 7, 8

Remember Rahab?

When the two Jewish spies scouted out Jericho, Rahab helped them. When the police of Jericho searched her home, she hid the spies. Then she asked the two to remember her when the whole nation of Israel came up against Jericho.

Why did Rahab do this?

Undoubtedly, Rahab had heard the stories of how God destroyed Egypt with the 10 plagues when he set the people of Israel free. Maybe she knew about the parting of the Red Sea. Perhaps she'd heard how the God of the Hebrews was powerful and could do anything. Maybe she knew something of the prophecies of Balaam (see Numbers 22—24) that said God would bless Israel forever.

Whatever Rahab knew, it was enough to stoke her faith in the living God. She knew Jericho's idols would not protect them. So she decided to go with the Jews.

As a result, she helped the two spies, and when Jericho fell, she was saved.

God loves faithful people. And he helps and preserves them.

**Prayer:** Lord, I want to be a faithful person. Help me to be that way, always. Amen.

Week 8: Tuesday

# No One Can Withstand You

**"Do not be afraid of them," the Lord said to Joshua, "for I will give you victory over them. Not a single one of them will be able to stand up to you."** Joshua 10:8

**MAIN READING:** Joshua 10 • **OPTIONAL READING:** Joshua 9, 11, 12

The army stood on the hill overlooking the field of battle. Against them, iron chariots lined up in an array of power. The generals conferred, and they almost decided that they should hightail it and run for cover. No one could withstand an assault by men and horses with iron chariots.

Then God spoke. General Joshua listened. He looked at his men, standing with swords slack in their hands, their spears dipping slightly from exhaustion and worry.

Yes, he said to God, yes, he believed God. But how?

"My power!" God told Joshua.

And it was so. The Jews defeated everyone they came against in the land of Israel. No one could withstand their power. Why? For one reason: because God's power was with them.

Do you have opponents, maybe even enemies? Are you afraid? Does it look impossible for you to face those people?

Be like Joshua. Listen to God. God will guide you and be with you and grant you success. It may not happen the obvious way. But God will show you his way. And his way always finds the victory.

**PRAYER:** Father, sometimes I'm afraid, but I ask you, fill me with your Spirit. Amen.

# Convictions

**I was forty years old when Moses, the servant of the Lord, sent me from Kadesh-barnea to explore the land of Canaan. I returned and gave from my heart a good report.** Joshua 14:7

**MAIN READING:** Joshua 14 • **OPTIONAL READING:** Joshua 13, 15, 16

Conviction!

It's written on the face of General George Washington as he encourages his men during the Revolutionary War while they camp at Valley Forge.

It's in the eyes of Abraham Lincoln as he signs the bill that will set the slaves free.

It's in the voice of Martin Luther King, Jr., as he tells a crowd of thousands that he has a dream.

And you hear it in the words of a young man as he tries to interest a friend in Jesus.

You can be a person like these, a man or woman of conviction. What does that mean? It means to be convinced so completely that nothing will change you from that belief. What beliefs should you be convinced of? That Jesus is God. That Jesus died for the sins of the world. That he rose again. That he will come again to the earth and take all those who believe in him home to heaven.

Convictions are what life is all about. Are you a person of conviction?

**PRAYER:** Lord, teach me to have firm and unwavering convictions. Amen.

Week 8: Thursday

# Encouragement

**They said, "The hill country is not enough for us, and the Canaanites in the lowlands around Beth-shan and the valley of Jezreel have iron chariots—they are too strong for us."** Joshua 17:16

**MAIN READING:** Joshua 17 • **OPTIONAL READING:** Joshua 18—20

Israel stood up against tough odds. Iron chariots. Towering cities. The sons of Anak, who were giants. Goliath was probably descended from these giants, and he was over nine feet tall.

What does a leader do when his people face big problems?

He encourages them.

"We can do it!"

"They won't win!"

"We have the brains and the brawn, so let's go."

"God is with us. God is on our side."

"God won't let us fail."

Leaders say many different things, but it all comes down to one principle: all of us need encouragement. In school. In church. In our families. We can't survive without people around us who can encourage.

What if you decide today to be an encourager? What might you say to your friends, your family, the guys on the basketball team, and the girls on the cheerleading squad?

**PRAYER:** Jesus, make me an encourager. Amen.

# Whom Will You Serve?

**But if you are unwilling to serve the Lord, then choose today whom you will serve. Would you prefer the gods your ancestors served beyond the Euphrates? Or will it be the gods of the Amorites in whose land you now live? But as for me and my family, we will serve the Lord.**
Joshua 24:15

**MAIN READING:** Joshua 24 • **OPTIONAL READING:** Joshua 21—23

Everyone serves someone or something.

For you, it might be sports. You think about sports all the time. You imagine yourself in a winning game. You see yourself stepping up to the plate, or hurling the football. Sports are always on your mind. You're probably serving a god named sports, if you're not careful.

For some young people getting good grades is what it's all about. When you see your dad or mom smile at a great report card, you're happy. You live for such smiles.

Perhaps it's rock music. Or videos. Or video games. You pour all your money and extra time into those activities. It's easy to become a slave to things like that.

Are you serving someone or something other than Jesus? Take a hard look at your life. Where do you spend your time and money? How much do you put into those things, compared to how much you put into serving the Lord?

You don't have to think about Jesus every minute to put him first. It's a matter of mind-set, of attitude. Who's first in your life?

**PRAYER:** Father, let me learn to put you first in everything. Amen.

Week 8: Saturday

# The Promise-Keeper

**The angel of the Lord went up from Gilgal to Bokim with a message for the Israelites. He told them, "I brought you out of Egypt into this land that I swore to give your ancestors, and I said I would never break my covenant with you."** Judges 2:1

**MAIN READING:** Judges 2 • **OPTIONAL READING:** Judges 1, 3, 4

God is the great promise-keeper. He makes promises about many things. For instance . . .

He will never leave you or forsake you (Hebrews 13:5). He will stick with you no matter what.

He will lead you to full maturity in Christ (Philippians 1:6). He wants you to grow into a great man or woman of God, and he will help you every step of the way.

He will get you to heaven safely and blamelessly (Jude 24). God won't leave you behind. He makes sure all his children get home at the right time. We may have troubles on Earth, but God promises to get us to his trouble-free heaven without question.

He will reward you for doing good (Galatians 6:9, 10). No good you do will ever be forgotten or cast aside. God plans to reward you for every good deed, small or great.

Those are just a few of God's promises. You can count on these truths. God never lies, nor does he ever forget anything he's ever said to you.

**PRAYER:** God, let me rely on your promises and claim them every day. Amen.

Week 8: Sunday

# Make Music

**Listen, you kings! Pay attention, you mighty rulers! For I will sing to the Lord. I will lift up my song to the Lord, the God of Israel.** Judges 5:3

**MAIN READING:** Judges 5 • **OPTIONAL READING:** Judges 6—8

God loves music. Church music. Contemporary music. Rock music. Rap. Classical.

You name it, God loves it—as long as it shows strong values and moral truth. God doesn't like music with cuss words, music that glorifies violence or hatred, or music that tells us to do evil things. But he does like any music that promotes goodness and love and truth, especially when it's his goodness and love and truth that's being sung about.

Do you ever sing to the Lord? Do you ever simply let it rip in the woods, or in the shower, or alone in your room? Do you sing out strong and clear in church?

God loves people to sing to him. He enjoys the voices, and he hears the hearts.

Make a joyful noise to the Lord. Today. Tomorrow. Every day.

God will be pleased.

---

**PRAYER:** Lord, fill my heart with your music, so that I'm always singing for you. Amen.

Week 9: Monday

# God's Anger

**Again the Israelites did evil in the Lord's sight. They worshiped images of Baal and Ashtoreth, and the gods of Aram, Sidon, Moab, Ammon, and Philistia. Not only this, but they abandoned the Lord and no longer served him at all. So the Lord burned with anger against Israel, and he handed them over to the Philistines and the Ammonites.** Judges 10:6, 7

**MAIN READING:** Judges 10 • **OPTIONAL READING:** Judges 9, 11, 12

God gets angry. About sin. About hatred. About the bad things people do to each other. About lying and stealing. About people who break the Ten Commandments. About cussing and swearing and saying nasty things.

Does God like these things? No. Does he forgive us for these things? Yes, when we confess them and stop doing them.

In the book of Judges, we see Israel doing all kinds of evil things. They stole from each other. They cheated each other. They gossiped about each other. They put down and hated good people for being good. Sometimes they even murdered innocent people, worshiped idols, and sacrificed their children to those gods.

God warned Israel again and again that if they didn't change their ways, terrible things would happen to them. In spite of God's warnings, they turned their backs on him and resisted everything God stands for.

God controlled his anger against Israel until it was clear they had rejected him and would not change. He punished them because he is holy and just and he always does what he says.

**PRAYER:** Father, let me be one person who follows your rules. Amen.

Week 9: Tuesday

# One Last Prayer Request

**Then Samson prayed to the Lord, "Sovereign Lord, remember me again. O God, please strengthen me one more time so that I may pay back the Philistines for the loss of my eyes."** Judges 16:28

**MAIN READING:** Judges 16 • **OPTIONAL READING:** Judges 13—15

Samson messed up big time.

Always reckless, he didn't regard his special relationship with God as special. He treated it like an inconvenience. He ran after bad women. He made enemies of nearly everyone in his life. In the end, he suffered harsh consequences as a result of his foolish and rebellious behavior.

But Samson had faith. God departed from Samson when the big guy sold out to a loose woman named Delilah. He told her the secret of his strength was his hair. It had never been cut because Samson was a Nazirite. A Nazirite was a man utterly dedicated to God. He never cut his hair. He didn't drink wine. He drew close to God his whole life. Samuel was a Nazirite, and some scholars believe John the Baptist was too.

Samson broke his vow, though, when he told Delilah about cutting his hair. When she cut it off, Samson lost his power and God's presence.

But Samson had faith. At the end, with his eyes gouged out and the Philistines openly mocking him, he prayed a prayer for God's power. God gave it because he always honors faith. And Samson had his revenge on the Philistines.

God answers the prayer of faith. Do you pray like that? Do you believe God is listening and will answer? If you have faith like that, you can be sure God will answer.

**PRAYER:** Lord, help me to be a kid of faith, always. Amen.

Week 9: Wednesday

# Everyone Did As He Saw Fit

**In those days Israel had no king, so the people did whatever seemed right in their own eyes.** Judges 17:6

**MAIN READING:** Judges 17 • **OPTIONAL READING:** Judges 18—21

"No one tells me what to do," Brad informed his friends.

"I do what I like," Tomie answered. "I go my own way."

"Do your thing is what I always say," Allin added. "Do what makes you happy."

Ever hear kids talk like that? Probably all of us have said such things at one time. Millions of people throughout history have lived according to those statements too. You know what happens in a world like that?

It goes crazy. People hurt each other because they're doing what they want to do. People slam each other around because everyone's doing his own thing. That was what happened in the land of Israel in the time of the judges. Everyone "did whatever seemed right in their own eyes." No laws. No rules. Every person out for himself.

When Israel lived like that, plenty of problems arose. Sin happened everywhere. God disciplined them by sending enemies into their country to make them slaves and take their food. God can't let people live by their own rules. Why? Because the stronger people always take over the poorer and weaker people. If you're poor or weak, you get trampled on. God cares enough about the poor and weak not to let that continue.

Are you living by your own rules? Are you making it up as you go along?

Watch out. God may send you a wake-up call soon.

**PRAYER:** Jesus, help me always to live the way you want me to live. Amen.

Week 9: Thursday

# True Loyalty

**But Ruth replied, "Don't ask me to leave you and turn back. I will go wherever you go and live wherever you live. Your people will be my people, and your God will be my God."** Ruth 1:16

**Main Reading:** Ruth 1 • **Optional Reading:** Ruth 2—4

The three girls stood in the hallway, talking. "I can't believe she said that to Mrs. Urichi. Urichi is the hardest teacher of all," Joni said.

"She's gonna flunk, I bet," Joni's best friend Ally answered.

Joni came back with the words, "She's just an idiot, that's all. I don't like her."

Kelly, the third member of the troop said, "She's not really an idiot. She just doesn't know how to control her mouth."

"You're always defending her, Kelly," Ally said. "What's she to you?"

"Nothing much," Kelly answered. "We were friends in first and second grade. We're still friends."

"Well, she's gonna mess it up for everybody," Joni added.

"I'll talk to her," Kelly finally said.

Although you may not know what these girls are talking about, you probably recognize something about Kelly that stands out. What is it? She's loyal. She doesn't diss her friend, even though her friend has made a big mistake. And she's willing to talk to her friend to help her out.

Loyalty is hard to find in the world today. Ruth had it toward Naomi. Do you have it toward your friends?

**Prayer:** Father, help me to be a loyal friend even when it hurts. Amen.

Week 9: Friday

# The Prayer That Gives It All Up

**And she made this vow: "O Lord Almighty, if you will look down upon my sorrow and answer my prayer and give me a son, then I will give him back to you. He will be yours for his entire lifetime, and as a sign that he has been dedicated to the Lord, his hair will never be cut."**
1 Samuel 1:11

**MAIN READING:** 1 Samuel 1 • **OPTIONAL READING:** 1 Samuel 2—4

What would you give up to get what you wanted? Your video game console and the games? Your baseball mitt? Your favorite stuffed bear?

It probably depends on how much you want it. For some things in life, many of us would be willing to sacrifice.

In this story in the Bible, we see Hannah willing to give up her son to God if only God would give her a son. She had been unable to have children for years. It wore her down. But in the end, she prayed a prayer of relinquishment. What is that? It's when you bow your head before God and say something like, "Lord, I cannot make this happen. But you can. I'm willing to humble myself before you and I offer to tithe for the rest of my life if you'll give it to me."

People offer God different things: to pray every day. Go to church every week. Hannah was willing to give God her firstborn son.

She wasn't making a deal with God as much as humbling herself. It must have been a hard decision. But the next year God answered: she gave birth to a son. And when the time came, she gave him back to God.

**PRAYER:** Jesus, let me always be willing to give up to you what you desire. Amen.

# How to Get What You Want from God

**Then Samuel said to all the people of Israel, "If you are really serious about wanting to return to the Lord, get rid of your foreign gods and your images of Ashtoreth. Determine to obey only the Lord; then he will rescue you from the Philistines."** 1 Samuel 7:3

**MAIN READING:** 1 Samuel 7 • **OPTIONAL READING:** 1 Samuel 5, 6, 8

What impresses God?

Your giving $15 in the offering plate one Sunday, after receiving a fat check from your grandpa for your birthday?

Your telling your friends about Jesus, even though some of them laugh at you?

Your reading the Bible every day?

Your going to church and singing your head off in the service?

All these things are good things. But the Bible passage above gives us an indication of what God really wants from us: to turn from sin and live holy lives before him.

See what the prophet told the people of Israel. They had to "return" to the Lord. And they were required to destroy their idols.

God wants a holy, pure, open relationship with each of his children. He longs to bless us when we live before him like that. When we obey God about sin—turn from it—and come close to him in prayer, that's when we get his attention.

**PRAYER:** Lord, help me to grow in grace so that I have a holy relationship with you. Amen.

# When God's Spirit Takes Over

**Then the Spirit of God came mightily upon Saul.** 1 Samuel 11:6

**MAIN READING:** 1 Samuel 11 • **OPTIONAL READING:** 1 Samuel 9, 10, 12

Jeff felt terribly afraid. Tonight he had to give a testimony in church for more than 200 people, and he would be baptized afterwards. He had tried to think of what he might say. Just because he was a believer didn't mean he was a public speaker. Telling a crowd about his life scared him to death.

As Jeff and his parents talked about it, they showed him a passage in Matthew 10 that tells about God's Spirit. "Don't worry about what to say in your defense, because you will be given the right words at the right time. For it won't be you doing the talking—it will be the Spirit of your Father speaking through you"(vv. 19, 20).

"Don't worry or be afraid," Jeff's dad said. "God will give you the words and the power."

When Jeff finally stood up to speak, he shook at first. But then the nervousness left him. He talked like a pro for the next five minutes.

The Spirit also worked on a young man named Saul many centuries ago. God gave him spiritual power to lead the people of Israel.

In your life, God will give you many tasks. Often you will find yourself in situations where you feel afraid. But don't worry. God will give you the power you need right when you need it. Trust him, and all will be well.

**PRAYER:** Father, I know your power is great. Help me to trust you. Amen.

Week 10: Monday

# What God Delights In

**What is more pleasing to the Lord: your burnt offerings and sacrifices or your obedience to his voice? Obedience is far better than sacrifice. Listening to him is much better than offering the fat of rams.**
1 Samuel 15:22

**Main Reading:** 1 Samuel 15 • **Optional Reading:** 1 Samuel 13, 14, 16

One fifth grader refuses to dance at a school dance. Another one offers to help her mother do the dishes after a fine dinner.

A sixth grader tells his friends he won't play cards with them. It's against his religion. Another helps out in church to get ready for a large meeting.

A fourth grader decides he won't watch movies. Another gives his teacher a Bible for her birthday.

What is happening here? The first young person in each paragraph is keeping man-made rules. Nothing in the Bible says you can't dance, play cards, or go to movies. Many Christians keep such rules. But doing so doesn't impress God.

The other young people mentioned do positive things. They help their parents, work at church, and give a gift.

Which is better—keeping rules, or obeying the voice of God?

In the Bible story about Saul today, King Saul failed to obey God's commands. He thought that, by giving special sacrifices of various animals, God would overlook the fact that he didn't obey him in more important matters.

God honors obedience. God is pleased when we listen to his voice. Keeping rules is OK. But obeying God's Word is better.

**Prayer:** Lord, may I always keep your Word in my life. Amen.

Week 10: Tuesday

# Spiritual Weapons

**David put it on, strapped the sword over it, and took a step or two to see what it was like, for he had never worn such things before.**
1 Samuel 17:39

**MAIN READING:** 1 Samuel 17 • **OPTIONAL READING:** 1 Samuel 18—20

Joseph picked up his father's baseball glove. It was great in helping his dad catch a softball on the softball team. But it was too big for Joseph.

"It's too big, Dad," Joseph said. "I'm not used to catching with it." He grabbed his own glove, worn and used, but also something he knew well. "I'd rather use this one if it's OK with you."

Using equipment and "weapons" we're used to ensures victory. When we pick up tools we've never tried before, we're in danger.

In the Bible story above, David wanted to fight Goliath. King Saul gave David his armor and sword. But when David put it on, he found it was far too big. David picked up his slingshot and told everyone he was used to that, and that was what he'd fight Goliath with.

In your spiritual life, employ "tools" that you know how to use. Learn what the Bible says, and how to use a concordance, Bible dictionary, and Bible encyclopedia. Ask your parents and teachers to help you understand the Bible. Grow in knowledge and faith as you practice using God's Word.

**PRAYER:** Jesus, help me to work with the tools you've given me. Amen.

# Knowing God's Will

**David asked the Lord, "Should I go and attack them?" "Yes, go and save Keilah," the Lord told him.** 1 Samuel 23:2

**MAIN READING:** 1 Samuel 23 • **OPTIONAL READING:** 1 Samuel 21, 22, 24

Well, are you gonna run for president of the class or not?" Julie asked her best friend, Marcie. "You're the most popular girl in the class. You'll win."

"I'm not sure."

"What's to be sure about?"

Marcie took a long breath. She had become a Christian about a year before. In church she learned about doing God's will. She wanted to please the Lord. Did he want her to run?

"Is this one of those God things you have?" Julie finally asked.

"It's important to me," Marcie answered. "God is important to me. I have to do what he wants."

"Fine, then pray about it, and see what happens."

"OK." Marcie went home that night and prayed. God soon answered in a matter of days, giving her what she thought was a go ahead.

Is God concerned about things like a class election? God wants to be involved in every aspect of your life. It's not so he can control you. It's so he can lead you to fulfillment.

Do you want to know what God wants today? Start with prayer. Talk to God. He'll tell you.

**PRAYER:** Father, I want to do your will, not mine. Lead me. Amen.

# Don't Mess with God's Chosen One

**But the Lord forbid that I should kill the one he has anointed! But I'll tell you what—we'll take his spear and his jug of water and then get out of here!** 1 Samuel 26:11

**Main Reading:** 1 Samuel 26 • **Optional Reading:** 1 Samuel 25, 27, 28

"Our teacher is such a jerk," Josh commented to his friend Giles as they left the Sunday-school room.

"He's just trying to give us good lessons," Giles answered.

"But they're all so stupid. I wish I didn't have to go to this stupid Sunday-school class."

"Maybe if we support him, it'll go better," Giles said.

"Oh, so you're on his side now?" Josh replied.

Criticism. Have you ever spent some time criticizing your pastor, your leaders, your teachers? Of course you have. It's a normal thing to do.

But that doesn't make it right. In the Bible story we're looking at today, we see David in a difficult situation with King Saul. Saul wanted to kill David. Meanwhile, David fled here and there, managing always to escape. But in this situation, David had a chance to eliminate King Saul once and for all. Strangely, David refused. Why? Because he knew God had made Saul king. To hurt Saul, much as he deserved it, would invite God's anger.

Criticizing and putting down the people God has put into positions of leadership in your life is wrong. God wants you to respect and value those people, even if they do flub up now and then. What will you do next time someone criticizes your leaders?

**Prayer:** Jesus, help me to support my leaders, even when I think they're wrong. Amen.

Week 10: Friday

# Talking to Demons

**Saul then said to his advisers, "Find a woman who is a medium, so I can go and ask her what to do."** 1 Samuel 28:7

**Main Reading:** 1 Samuel 28 • **Optional Reading:** 1 Samuel 25—27

Mrs. Gibbs was one strange woman, Jesse thought. He didn't know how to respond to her.

Mrs. Gibbs, Jesse's neighbor, believed she had a spirit guide named Yunga. She talked about Yunga all the time, the things he had told her, the ideas he passed on about life, friendship, death, and other things. She said that she was "channeling" Yunga now. That meant he could take control of her at times and speak through her.

Jesse didn't know what to make of it. Was the lady nuts?

New Age ideas have filtered into our culture. Many people believe in such things as spirit guides, channeling, and other practices. What these really are, though, are demonic influences. Yunga may say he's from the planet Zorg, but he's really a demon bent on getting a foothold in the lives of open people.

When King Saul consulted a medium in the Bible story for today, great danger lurked. God had mercy on Saul and sent Samuel from the dead to speak to him. But Saul's act was blatant disobedience.

Trying to speak with demons, whatever way you try it, is filled with danger. Run as fast as you can from people who do that. They will often try to snare you too.

**Prayer:** Lord, keep me from the power of demons. Amen.

# Suicide

**Saul groaned to his armor bearer, "Take your sword and kill me before these pagan Philistines run me through and humiliate me." But the armor bearer was afraid and would not do it. So Saul took his own sword and fell on it.** 1 Samuel 31:4

**MAIN READING:** 1 Samuel 31 • **OPTIONAL READING:** 1 Samuel 29, 30

Suicide is a serious problem today for young people. It's one of the leading causes of death among elementary school children. Why do people commit suicide? Usually, it's because their lives have gone terribly wrong. Some sin or problem—bad grades in school, a bully situation, a parent's death or divorce—has struck, and the young person feels depressed and angry inside. He or she may try to end it all to relieve the pain.

In the story we're looking at today, King Saul had lost an important battle. His fighting sons were killed, including Jonathan, David's best friend. Saul saw no way out. In the darkness of the hour, he saw only one course of action: to die.

So Saul fell on his sword and killed himself.

Thoughts of suicide are nothing to be played with. If you feel depressed and suicidal, get help. Talk to your counselor and your parents. Such people will know how to encourage you. Don't keep it to yourself, and remember that God is with you. He will help you through this. He knows his plans for you and assures you that better days are coming, no matter how bad it looks now. Don't let this time of pain and darkness destroy you.

**PRAYER:** Father, let me turn to you for help when I'm feeling down. Amen.

# Loss of a Loved One

**How I weep for you, my brother Jonathan! Oh, how much I loved you! And your love for me was deep, deeper than the love of women!**
2 Samuel 1:26

**Main Reading:** 2 Samuel 1 • **Optional Reading:** 2 Samuel 2—4

All of us will face it sooner or later.

A close friend is killed in an auto accident.

Or a beloved uncle or grandfather dies of a heart attack.

Or an innocent teacher is struck down when a holdup occurs at a store she's visiting.

It can happen anywhere, anytime. God does not keep us from facing such losses. They happen to all of us.

When David learned of the death of his best friend, Jonathan, he grieved. The process of grief—when you work through your feelings over loss of a loved one—can be long and painful. Feelings of anger, depression, and other pain strike us. We may slip into deep despair if we're not careful.

When you lose a loved one, talk about the situation with your parents, your friends, your church leaders. God does not tell us to act as if nothing has happened, or even to pretend we're fine when we aren't. He wants to go with us through the grief and show us the way beyond it. He will not simply zap us to eliminate all our bad feelings.

When you grieve, it's OK to cry, OK to feel anger, even at God. Tell the truth about how you feel. That is the way through it.

**Prayer:** Lord, help me to look to you when grief strikes. I know you understand. Amen.

# Your Throne Forever

**Your dynasty and your kingdom will continue for all time before me, and your throne will be secure forever.** 2 Samuel 7:16

**Main Reading:** 2 Samuel 7 • **Optional Reading:** 2 Samuel 5, 6, 8

God made a tremendous promise to King David. He told him that his kingdom would never end, it would be the final and great kingdom of the world.

When you read the Bible, though, you find that King David's line did end. When Israel was taken into slavery by Babylon, no king would ever sit on David's throne again. Other nations would rule over Israel for centuries.

Was God's promise wrong? Did God make a mistake?

Actually, God saw things from a different perspective. He knows the end from the beginning, and a few centuries without a king was no problem. Why? Because the kingdom God had spoken about was Jesus' kingdom. Jesus, a descendant of David through both Joseph and Mary, will one day reign on King David's throne. His kingdom will never have an end.

Many times in the Bible, things do not look quite right if we study them from a human perspective. But when we see the meaning and truth as God sees it, we discover that God was right all along.

When you think you've found a contradiction or problem in the Bible, don't despair. Sometimes the answer isn't right on the surface. You have to dig deep to see what God really meant.

**Prayer:** Jesus, may I always trust your Word as the truth. Amen.

# God Honors Kindness

**But David said, "Don't be afraid! I've asked you to come so that I can be kind to you because of my vow to your father, Jonathan."**
2 Samuel 9:7

**MAIN READING:** 2 Samuel 9 • **OPTIONAL READING:** 2 Samuel 10—12

The new kid rolled into class in a wheelchair. Several kids simply avoided him. But Cal walked over and introduced himself. "I'm Cal Thurston," he said. "What's your name?"

The disabled boy held out a bony, gnarled hand. "I'm Steve."

Soon they were good friends. Cal wheeled Steve wherever he needed to go, and Steve felt like a king.

A similar thing happened long ago in Israel. David could have killed Mephibosheth. After all, he was an enemy. King Saul fought against David every step of his life after David became famous. But David had sworn to his best friend, Jonathan, that he would take care of his children.

Mephibosheth was disabled. He certainly couldn't lead a troop against David's army. He might try to rally the people behind him in the name of Jonathan and King Saul. But he had no interest in that. He simply wanted to survive.

David showed kindness to Mephibosheth. He gave the young man a place at his table. He honored the youth with friendship and grace. God ultimately rewarded David for his kindness too.

God loves kindness. Who can you be kind to today?

**PRAYER:** Father, teach me to be a kind person to everyone. Amen.

Week 11: Wednesday

# Sin Leads to Disaster

**David's son Absalom had a beautiful sister named Tamar. And Amnon, her half brother, fell desperately in love with her.** 2 Samuel 13:1

**MAIN READING:** 2 Samuel 13 • **OPTIONAL READING:** 2 Samuel 14—16

Have you ever wanted something that was forbidden?

Maybe it was a special knife your dad kept in his desk. You liked it, wanted to throw it, wanted to carve with it. But Dad made it clear that knife was off limits.

Perhaps it was a beautiful figurine your mom kept in a special cabinet. You wanted to play with it. But Mom told you no, it was valuable.

Forbidden things can take many forms. In David's kingdom, he had a son Amnon who wanted to marry a half-sister, Tamar. Normally, marrying someone in your own family was forbidden. But Amnon figured out a way to get what he wanted by force. It was a horrible sin.

King David did nothing about it. But another son, Absalom, who was Tamar's brother, conspired to kill Amnon. It seemed like disaster after disaster happened to David's family during that time.

Why did such bad things happen? Because David himself had sinned with Bathsheba. God judged David and warned him that there would be consequences for his disobedience.

Sin always has consequences. When we sin, God responds by disciplining us with problems and trouble. Are you about to sin? Think! It could lead to disaster!

**PRAYER:** Jesus, keep me from sin. I don't want to go through what David did. Amen.

# True Leadership

**Now go out there and congratulate the troops, for I swear by the Lord that if you don't, not a single one of them will remain here tonight. Then you will be worse off than you have ever been.** 2 Samuel 19:7

**MAIN READING:** 2 Samuel 19 • **OPTIONAL READING:** 2 Samuel 17, 18, 20

Say something, Harry," Luke whispered. "You're captain of the team."

Harry stammered and hemmed and hawed. What could he say? They were losing the game. There was no way they could come back.

"What are we gonna do?" another member of the team asked.

Harry prayed in his mind. "Please, God, help me. I don't know what to do to encourage these guys."

No sooner had he prayed than a thought came to him. "Remember that movie about the kids' football team that was way behind and they came back?" he asked.

Someone named the movie.

"That's right. That's what we're going to do. We're not gonna let this team steamroll us. We're going down fighting. Let's hit it, guys. We're on a roll!"

The team went back to the field and played their hearts out.

Leaders need to step into tough situations and lead. Are you a leader? Sometimes, like David in the Bible story for today, you will need to jump into a situation and offer words of encouragement. Don't duck out. Young people need leaders as much as adults. So give it your best, and leave the rest in the hands of God.

**PRAYER:** Lord, show me how to lead in school, church, and on my team. Amen.

Week 11: Friday

# God Is a Rock

**The Lord is my rock, my fortress, and my savior; my God is my rock, in whom I find protection. He is my shield, the strength of my salvation, and my stronghold, my high tower, my savior, the one who saves me from violence.** 2 Samuel 22:2, 3

**Main Reading:** 2 Samuel 22 • **Optional Reading:** 2 Samuel 21, 23, 24

Have you ever come upon a huge rock—in the forest, by a lake, or in your backyard? How do you feel when you stand on that rock? Doesn't it give you a feeling of solidity—like no one could knock you off?

The Bible calls God our rock because we feel strong when we stand on him. A rock seems powerful, centered, unmovable. No matter how much blasting and hitting someone might do, that rock won't budge.

God is our rock. When we stand on him, we find stability, security, strength. He won't move. He's powerful, and like a rock, he cannot be overcome.

God is your rock in three ways:

1. He provides stability and strength. You won't be defeated or overwhelmed when you're standing on him.

2. He shelters you in the storm. Ever sit under a ledge of rock in a rainstorm? It's comfortable, dry, safe. God is like that. He gives us safety in the storm.

3. He cannot be moved by others. Real rocks can be dislodged or broken up. But not God. He's a rock the size of the universe.

Stand on the rock today. Feel his power. Feel his safety. You can be sure no one will be able to knock you off this rock!

**Prayer:** Father, you are my rock and I will stand on you forever. Amen.

Week 11: Saturday

# An Amazing Offer

**That night the Lord appeared to Solomon in a dream, and God said, "What do you want? Ask, and I will give it to you!"** 1 Kings 3:5

**MAIN READING:** 1 Kings 3 • **OPTIONAL READING:** 1 Kings 1, 2, 4

What if God appeared in your bedroom and said, "Ask whatever you want. I will do it for you. Anything."

What would you ask for? A new video game? A special friend? Straight As in school? Money?

Unfortunately, God made such an offer only once in history. He came to King Solomon, the new king of Israel, and offered to give him anything. Solomon, perhaps in a stroke of genius, asked for just the right thing: wisdom to lead his people. God liked that request and gave him wisdom. But he also threw in wealth, grandeur, power, fame, and plenty of friends, too, just because Solomon had answered so wisely.

Would you ask for wisdom, if God gave you that choice? Through wisdom you can live a successful, happy life. Through wisdom, you can solve your problems with speed and skill. With wisdom in your heart, you might become an adviser to a president, or you might even become a president. Wisdom is the key to many things.

You know what? God offers you the same thing right now. He will give you wisdom, if you ask him, the same kind he gave Solomon.

Why not ask God to start giving you wisdom today? You'll be surprised at what happens if you do.

**PRAYER:** Lord, give me wisdom that I might be great at what I do. Amen.

# God Deserves the Best

**As the priests came out of the inner sanctuary, a cloud filled the Temple of the Lord.** 1 Kings 8:10

**MAIN READING:** 1 Kings 8 • **OPTIONAL READING:** 1 Kings 5—7

Does God deserve the best from us? Our best praises? Our best service? Our best love?

King Solomon thought so. He wanted to build God a place to live on Earth. It would be the most magnificent temple ever built. He called for the most skilled workmen. He paid for the best gold, silver, and wood. He commanded the whole nation of Israel to work on the temple with all their hearts.

It took years. But one day it was done. The greatest temple the world has ever seen was finished. It was truly a wonder to behold. Many people journeyed long distances to see the temple in person. Solomon outdid himself.

Was God pleased? You bet. God came down and dwelt in the holy of holies deep inside the temple. There, a cloud filled the temple, shining and glorious. This was to be God's home on Earth.

Solomon's Temple has long been destroyed. But God has other temples to live in. Do you know what they are? The hearts of his people. God makes our heart his home while we are on Earth. Have you given your heart to God for him to dwell in?

Why not tell God right now that you want him to make a temple of your heart and live inside you?

**PRAYER:** Jesus, come live in my heart and make it your home. Amen.

Week 12: Monday

# Hang With the Right People

**He had seven hundred wives and three hundred concubines. And sure enough, they led his heart away from the Lord.** 1 Kings 11:3

**MAIN READING:** 1 Kings 11 • **OPTIONAL READING:** 1 Kings 9, 10, 12

Hanging around with the wrong people can lead to disaster.

King Solomon is a perfect example. He liked having beautiful women around him. He enjoyed making them his wives. In those days, some kings of Israel practiced polygamy. That means marrying more than one woman at a time. Solomon went to such an extreme that he married 700 women during his reign.

God had warned the kings of Israel not to marry foreign women. He also warned them not to have multiple wives. Solomon disobeyed both laws.

Those wives from other countries worshiped idols. This was also forbidden. But apparently, Solomon didn't care. He was the wisest man who ever lived, yet he acted stupidly in this matter.

Those wives liked worshiping idols. They told Solomon about it. They pestered him. They nagged. "Come, worship Baal." Or, "It's not hard. Try my goddess Ashtoreth."

Solomon was sucked in. He began to worship idols. God was very angry. He punished Solomon by taking half his kingdom from his son, Rehoboam.

Who you hang with matters. Bad people want to do bad things. They will drag you into sin, if you're not careful. Choose your friends wisely. It's a matter of life and death.

**PRAYER:** Father, help me always to choose good friends to hang with. Amen.

Week 12: Tuesday

# He Did Right

**Asa did what was pleasing in the Lord's sight, as his ancestor David had done.** 1 Kings 15:11

**MAIN READING:** 1 Kings 15 • **OPTIONAL READING:** 1 Kings 13, 14, 16

If you had someone write a line or two about you in the Bible, what would you like them to say?

"He sinned constantly."

"She was a decent person, but she didn't follow God."

"He made some mistakes, but he always turned back to God."

"She did right in the sight of God!"

When you read about the history of Israel, you will find this expression "he did what was pleasing in the Lord's sight" frequently. The authors of 1 and 2 Kings, and 1 and 2 Chronicles, often referred to a king's reign that way. Such kings weren't necessarily powerful, like King Saul. Or famous, like King David. Or fabulously rich, like King Solomon. But they did one thing right: they did right in the sight of God.

How would you like that as the one sentence about you? It's a good one, isn't it? "He did right." It means the person obeyed God's commandments. He worshiped God. He took God seriously. And God blessed him mightily.

What can you do to "do right in the sight of God" today?

**PRAYER:** Jesus, may I do right all my days. Amen.

# Proven Once and for All

**And when the people saw it, they fell on their faces and cried out, "The Lord is God! The Lord is God!"** 1 Kings 18:39

**MAIN READING:** 1 Kings 18 • **OPTIONAL READING:** 1 Kings 17, 19

Do you ever wish God would simply show himself? That he would do a little miracle, just to prove he's there? That he'd come down and talk to you, just for a minute?

People all through history have asked God to prove himself. "Where are you? Come down and show yourself. Don't hide. We want to see you."

God showed himself like that a few times in history. During the days of Noah, when the flood happened, God showed his power. In the time of Moses, when God sent plagues on Egypt and did miracles for Israel, God proved himself nearly every day. Then in the time of Elijah and Elisha, God performed many miracles. Finally, the age of Jesus and the apostles was filled with miracles.

In this Bible story about Elijah, we see God doing a stupendous miracle. Elijah challenged the idol worshipers to a duel. When their god did nothing, Elijah called on the true God to send down fire. God answered immediately, and all the people fell on the ground. "The Lord is God!" they cried.

Why doesn't God prove himself these days? Actually, God often does prove himself. People see answers to prayer every day. We have the Bible, too, which is full of miracles. Many times people are healed in response to prayer. Don't demand that God prove himself; instead pray. The answers you see will be proof enough.

**PRAYER:** Lord, let me not demand proofs as much as study your Word as the best proof. Amen.

# Wanting the Wrong Things

**Since your vineyard is so convenient to the palace, I would like to buy it to use as a vegetable garden. I will give you a better vineyard in exchange, or if you prefer, I will pay you for it.** 1 Kings 21:2

**MAIN READING:** 1 Kings 21 • **OPTIONAL READING:** 1 Kings 20, 22

Shelby told her best friend Sarah, "Emily's comb is so cool. Maybe she'll sell it to me."

Sarah answered, "I don't think so. Emily's pretty happy with it."

Shelby approached Emily and asked her, "How much for that comb you wear in your hair?"

"Oh, I couldn't sell it," Emily answered. "It was from my grandmother."

"Come on, I'll pay $5."

"I'm sorry," Emily said. "I just can't do that. My mom would be angry."

Shelby went away angry. She wanted that comb something fierce. Then she hatched a plan. She would steal the comb when Emily was in gym class.

Have you ever wanted something like that? The Bible calls such feelings covetousness. It means longing for something that belongs to another.

That happened to King Ahab. He wanted Naboth's vineyard. When Naboth wouldn't sell, Ahab's wife devised a way to kill Naboth and take the vineyard by force. God punished Ahab and his wife severely for their sin.

Wishing for a gift isn't wrong. But wanting things that belong to others is sin. Be wary of your feelings, or you may do something evil to get what you want.

**PRAYER:** Father, help me to learn never to covet things the way Ahab did. Amen.

Week 12: Friday

# A Double Portion of God's Spirit

**When they came to the other side, Elijah said to Elisha, "What can I do for you before I am taken away?" And Elisha replied, "Please let me become your rightful successor."** 2 Kings 2:9

**MAIN READING:** 2 Kings 2 • **OPTIONAL READING:** 2 Kings 1, 3, 4

What do you want most in life? Riches? Honor? Fame? Glory? Popularity? Pleasure?

These are all nice things, and God does give them to some people. But most of us have to be happy with our lot in life. There's not much we can do to change that.

There is one thing, though, that you can ask of God. It's found in the Bible passage we're looking at today. Elijah was about to leave the earth and go to heaven. His disciple, Elisha, followed him down to the river. There, Elijah asked Elisha what he most wanted. Elisha was about to become a great prophet. Surely he could have anything he wanted, like Solomon did.

But Elisha had his mind on only one thing. He wanted a "double portion" of the Spirit that Elijah had had, as it's described in other translations. What does that mean? He wanted twice the joy, twice the love, twice the peace, and twice the power that Elijah had.

Isn't that amazing? You know what is more amazing? Elijah gave it to him, in the name of God.

If you want to ask God for something special today, think about asking for a double portion of his Spirit. Your life will never be the same.

**PRAYER:** Lord, grant to me that double portion so I can serve you doubly well. Amen.

Week 12: Saturday

# Seeing the Truth

**Then Elisha prayed, "O Lord, open his eyes and let him see!" The Lord opened his servant's eyes, and when he looked up, he saw that the hillside around Elisha was filled with horses and chariots of fire.**
2 Kings 6:17

**MAIN READING:** 2 Kings 6 • **OPTIONAL READING:** 2 Kings 5, 7, 8

An army surrounded the prophet Elisha and his servant Gehazi. It looked like no escape. Every side was taken. Spears glinted in the sunlight. Arrowheads looked bright and sharp. Swords were drawn.

What could they do?

When Gehazi stepped out of the tent that morning, he wanted to run. But there was nowhere to run. It was then that Elisha came out of the tent and looked around. Elisha could see something that Gehazi couldn't. What was it? The armies of God.

Around the mountain, standing between the foreign army and the prophet, were angels. Bright, shining, powerful angels. Later, just one of those angels would slay 185,000 men (see 2 Kings 19). And here was a whole army of them. Imagine what that army could do.

Gehazi, though, couldn't see this army. So Elisha prayed for him, and God opened Gehazi's eyes.

Did you know that angels are present by you too? You are personally protected by God. No one can touch you unless God allows it!

**PRAYER:** Jesus, help me to feel safe in you, because you are the great protector. Amen.

Week 12: Sunday

# The Devil Almost Wins It All

**When Athaliah, the mother of King Ahaziah of Judah, learned that her son was dead, she set out to destroy the rest of the royal family.**
2 Kings 11:1

**MAIN READING:** 2 Kings 11 • **OPTIONAL READING:** 2 Kings 9, 10, 12

Has the Devil ever come close to winning his war against God? He thought so, several times. When Sarah, the wife of Abraham, couldn't seem to have children, it looked like a lost cause. But God did a miracle, and Isaac was born.

Next, when King Saul pursued David and almost killed him, it appeared that the Devil had nearly won. But God preserved David.

When Jesus was crucified, the Devil thought he'd won for sure. But Jesus rose from the dead.

In today's story, Athaliah, a wicked queen, snatched the throne of David away from the rightful son. She had all the household of Ahaziah her son murdered. She wanted all the power.

God did something though. He saved one member of the family, Joash, just a baby at the time, through a faithful princess. Athaliah reigned for six years while Joash was hidden by the priests. At the right time, they brought Joash out and crushed Athaliah once and for all.

Satan thought God's kingdom hung by a thread—one little baby. But in God's world, God was in control all along. The Devil was once again driven out and God's kingdom stood firm. You can trust God that he will bring you through too.

**PRAYER:** Father, I know you will save me to the end because you love me. Amen.

Week 13: Monday

# God's Protection

**That night the angel of the Lord went out to the Assyrian camp and killed 185,000 Assyrian troops. When the surviving Assyrians woke up the next morning, they found corpses everywhere.** 2 Kings 19:35

**Main Reading:** 2 Kings 19 • **Optional Reading:** 2 Kings 17, 18, 20

King Hezekiah had a serious problem. The Assyrian army, 185,000 strong, surrounded the city of Jerusalem. There was no escape. The Assyrian commander even shouted out to the soldiers of the king standing on the ramparts that he would conquer them. He wanted them to give up now, and live.

Many people would reel in shock at such a situation. But King Hezekiah was a man of faith. He went into the temple and prayed, and then he talked to Isaiah, God's prophet. Isaiah assured Hezekiah that if he would only trust, God would save them.

Hezekiah spoke to his people. He assured them they were safe. God was about to do a miracle.

What a miracle it was too. An angel of the Lord destroyed the army. One hundred eighty-five thousand soldiers died that night, and the commander of the Assyrians escaped into the night to go back to Assyria where he was later assassinated.

The amazing thing is that this event is not just recorded in the Bible. Herodotus, a Greek historian, referred to it in his writings. He believed a "plague of rats" killed the Assyrian army.

We know the truth. God protects his people. Follow him, and he will be with you.

**Prayer:** Jesus, help me to trust in your protection always. Amen.

# Return to God's Word

**Go to the Temple and speak to the Lord for me and for the people and for all Judah. Ask him about the words written in this scroll that has been found. The Lord's anger is burning against us because our ancestors have not obeyed the words in this scroll.** 2 Kings 22:13

**MAIN READING:** 2 Kings 22 • **OPTIONAL READING:** 2 Kings 21, 23—25

Can you imagine going to church and having no Bible? No matter where you look, no one has a copy. It has disappeared.

That's what happened in the nation of Judah (the southern kingdom of Israel). God's Word was forgotten, perhaps for many years. The priests did their duties. The king listened to counsel. But God's Word was gone.

Imagine if you knew nothing about what God's Word says. No promises from God when you're down. No hope from God when you're hurting. No power from God when you need strength.

One day a priest found a copy of the Law, the Word of God, in the temple. He reported to Josiah, king of Judah at that time, what he'd found. Josiah had the priest read the book to him. When he heard it, he was startled. Amazed. Shocked. His people had ignored God's Law for too many years. He would change that immediately.

Josiah began some great reforms that saved Judah from destruction. The power of God's Word worked. Many people were saved.

God's Word has power. Without it, we cannot survive. But with it, we will live forever.

**PRAYER:** Lord, teach me to live off your Word like food. Amen.

# A Special Prayer

**He was the one who prayed to the God of Israel, "Oh, that you would bless me and extend my lands! Please be with me in all that I do, and keep me from all trouble and pain!" And God granted him his request.** 1 Chronicles 4:10

**MAIN READING:** 1 Chronicles 4 • **OPTIONAL READING:** 1 Chronicles 1—3, 5—9 (long reading, but it's mostly genealogy)

This prayer might be a good guide for anyone who seeks God's blessing. The important thing this prayer reveals is that the author of it wanted the blessing God had for him. What blessing was that? He didn't know. But he believed God wanted to bless him. He didn't demand riches, honor, fame, power, or anything like that. No, he just wanted God to bless him in whatever way God wanted to.

Think about that. Are you praying for all kinds of things in your life? But what if God has better, greater blessings in mind? What if God really wants to bless you with something incredible, but because you're always praying about something else, you've missed it?

That was the secret of this prayer. The author just asked God to bless him however he wanted. That's a great way to pray. Why? Because it lets God be God, and you the blessed one.

**PRAYER:** Father, help me to learn to pray with power. Amen.

Week 13: Thursday

# The Three Mighty Men

**David remarked longingly to his men, "Oh, how I would love some of that good water from the well in Bethlehem . . ." So the Three broke through the Philistine lines, drew some water from the well and brought it back to David. But David refused to drink it. Instead, he poured it out before the Lord.** 1 Chronicles 11:17, 18

**Main Reading:** 1 Chronicles 11

**Optional Reading:** 1 Chronicles 10, 12—14

When a football team wins the Super Bowl, the teammates carry the coach out on their shoulders.

When a smart student gets perfect grades, he wins awards.

When a wise person makes a great speech, we give her applause.

What did David do when three of his men did something incredible?

You find the story in today's reading. David, before he was king, often fought the Philistines. One day he commented how he'd love some water from the well in his hometown. Three men were listening. They barged right into enemy territory and took the water from under the Philistines' noses.

When they returned to camp, David was astounded. He probably congratulated the men on their courage and love. But then he did something that was perfect. He poured out the water as an offering to the Lord.

When someone does something well, what is the right response? Congratulate them, yes. Give them awards, sure. But first, thank God. He made it possible.

**Prayer:** Lord, may I always remember you are the one to praise. Amen.

# Three Important Parts of Prayer

**David appointed the following Levites to lead the people in worship before the Ark of the Lord by asking for his blessings and giving thanks and praise to the Lord, the God of Israel.** 1 Chronicles 16:4

**Main Reading:** 1 Chronicles 16

**Optional Reading:** 1 Chronicles 15, 17—19

How should we pray? What should we pray about? King David told the priests to pray in three specific ways:

1. Petition. That's bringing requests to the Lord. "Jesus, please do such and such for so and so." "Lord, help me study well for the test tomorrow." "God, enable me to play well in the game this afternoon." You make a request for yourself or others.

2. Thanks. A second element of prayer is thanksgiving. You thank God for answering your prayers. You thank him for helping you. You thank him for being your friend. It's not hard at all. God has done something good in your life. You thank him, just like you would your mom or dad.

3. Praise. An important dimension of prayer, this is where you let God know how great you think he is. "Lord, praise you for your love. I couldn't live without it." "Father, praise you for being the great God of the universe. You are the best." Praise is perhaps the highest form of prayer, because it's us giving God our love and adoration.

Do you use all three elements in your prayer life? Try it today. After you make a request, thank him. And after you thank him, praise him. It's a good pattern to follow.

**Prayer:** Jesus, please make my prayer life blossom. I want to learn to pray well. Amen.

Week 13: Saturday

# Giving Should Cost Something

**But the king replied to Araunah, "No, I insist on paying what it is worth. I cannot take what is yours and give it to the Lord. I will not offer a burnt offering that has cost me nothing!"** 1 Chronicles 21:24

**MAIN READING:** 1 Chronicles 21

**OPTIONAL READING:** 1 Chronicles 20, 22—24

There's an old story about a $20 bill and a $1 bill talking about their adventures. The $20 tells the $1, "I've been to Paris, France, to New York City, all over the Midwest. I've been to carnivals and great plays and I've even been used to buy a giant-screen television. You should see what I've seen."

The $1 responded, "I wish I was like you. For me, it's always the same: go to church. Go to church. Go to church."

That's funny, but it makes an important point. Many Christians find it easy to put a dollar in the offering plate. What's a dollar? A large candy bar? A hamburger? A box of pens? A Hot Wheels® toy car? We don't really worry too much about giving a dollar.

When King David was confronted with a similar situation, he knew what to do. He wanted to make a sacrifice to God. Araunah, a man of faith, offered to give him everything he needed. But David refused to take it for free. He would not sacrifice to God something that cost him nothing.

When you give to the work of God, it should cost you something. It should be a bit of a sacrifice. When we give like that, God is pleased.

**PRAYER:** Lord, help me always to give so that it costs me something. Amen.

Week 13: Sunday

# God Tests the Heart

**I know, my God, that you examine our hearts and rejoice when you find integrity there. You know I have done all this with good motives, and I have watched your people offer their gifts willingly and joyously.**
1 Chronicles 29:17

**Main Reading:** 1 Chronicles 29

**Optional Reading:** 1 Chronicles 25—28

The old song about Santa Claus says that he's "making a list and checking it twice, going to find out who's naughty and nice." Imagine if Santa could see the heart, instead of just the outside of the person. What kind of list would he have then?

Santa is a myth, but God isn't. He sees the heart. He knows what thoughts go through our minds. He knows when we wish we could kill someone. He hears it if we curse and use bad words in our heart, even if we don't say them with our tongues. He sees when we wish trouble on someone we don't like.

How can you clean up your heart? There's a simple way. Just like a garden needs water, and grows beautiful veggies when watered, so your heart needs spiritual water to grow good thoughts and kind attitudes. What is that spiritual water? The water of the Word of God. When we douse our hearts in God's Word, memorizing it and keeping it deep inside, God begins to change our thoughts. We soon have pure, friendly thoughts going through our brains, instead of muck.

**Prayer:** Jesus, help me to have beauty in my heart by learning your Word. Amen.

### Week 14: Monday

# Who Did It?

**Blessed be the Lord, the God of Israel, who has kept the promise he made to my father, David.** 2 Chronicles 6:4

**Main Reading:** 2 Chronicles 6 • **Optional Reading:** 2 Chronicles 1—5

I have a friend who started and led a fantastic ministry from about 1950 to 1990. Over those years, thousands of young people were converted. Many went on to have their own work for God. Many others grew in grace and became closer to Jesus.

After retirement, this lady decided to write a book about her experiences. She wanted those who supported the ministry to see all that God had done. She wrote the book and finally had it published. It was called "God Did It!" She wanted anyone who read the book to know her ministry wasn't her idea, or her doing. God was involved from day one. And anything good that came from it was because of God.

In the same way, King Solomon built a tremendous temple in Jerusalem. However, when it came time to show the world what he had done, Solomon took no credit. He proclaimed that God had answered prayer. God had enabled the workmen to fashion the temple. And the result was all God's doing. God did it from beginning to end.

That is the way you will always want to work in God's kingdom. Let God lead, involve him through prayer at every step. In that way, your work will last and God will be mightily pleased.

**Prayer:** Lord, help me to step aside and let you do it the way you want. Amen.

Week 14: Tuesday

# Humble Yourselves

**If my people who are called by my name will humble themselves and pray and seek my face and turn from their wicked ways, I will hear from heaven and will forgive their sins and heal their land.**
2 Chronicles 7:14

**Main Reading:** 2 Chronicles 7

**Optional Reading:** 2 Chronicles 8—11

What is the key to God's blessing? How can we pray so that God answers?

There is one way. This is not a formula, but this is what this verse shows us to do:

Humble ourselves. That is, if we recognize that we can't do anything worthwhile without God's help, God will bless. When we do things on our own, they may succeed, but they will have no worth.

Pray. Talk to God. Confess your sins. Thank him. Praise him. Pray for others. Let God know about everything that is in your heart.

Seek God's face. Cry out to him to show himself through mighty works. Let God know you will not stop until he answers.

Turn from our wicked ways. Turn from anything you know is sin. Stop doing it. End it today.

If we do this, then . . .

God will hear from heaven.

God will forgive our sin.

God will heal our land.

It's not a formula, just a wise way to pray. Are you humbly seeking God's face? Then trust that he will answer . . . in his own time.

**Prayer:** Father, I cry out to you to teach us to seek you always. Amen.

Week 14: Wednesday

# The Powerless

**O Lord, no one but you can help the powerless against the mighty! Help us, O Lord our God, for we trust in you alone. It is in your name that we have come against this vast horde. O Lord, you are our God; do not let mere men prevail against you!** 2 Chronicles 14:11

**Main Reading:** 2 Chronicles 14

**Optional Reading:** 2 Chronicles 12, 13, 15, 16

We have no power in ourselves to . . .

Please God.

Make him listen.

Gain his blessings.

Change ourselves.

Become more like Jesus.

Win a lasting victory.

Did you know that you're powerless? No one of us can do anything without Jesus. Oh, sure. We might make the soccer team. We might get good grades on our own. We might catch a bass while fishing. But ultimately, anything that's good and lasts must come from Jesus.

The prayer above was spoken by King Asa as he went out to fight. He knew God had to accomplish the victory. Without God's help, he could do nothing.

Call on God always to be with you. Then you will succeed.

**Prayer:** Lord, I ask you always to be with me and lead me. Amen.

Week 14: Thursday

# What's First?

**Then Jehoshaphat added, "But first let's find out what the Lord says."** 2 Chronicles 18:4

**MAIN READING:** 2 Chronicles 18

**OPTIONAL READING:** 2 Chronicles 17, 19—21

Steph, Shari, and Kellie stood at the bottom of the four trees, looking up. "It might be a good place to build a tree fort," Steph said.

"The trees look strong," Shari answered.

"They go pretty high," Kellie added.

"Have you seen anywhere else?" Shari then asked.

Steph and Kellie immediately said, "Let's build here."

Shari continued looking up. "Maybe we should pray about it. Or maybe we should ask my older brother. He knows about tree forts."

"Good idea," Steph answered. "Let's do it."

Shari was doing something all Christians should do before they attempt something big and new. The three kids prayed. At other times, they might have done what Jehoshaphat mentioned to his ally. He wanted to consult a prophet of the Lord before going into battle. He had to make sure God was in it.

Before you take a test . . . before you start a big project . . . before you buy a gift . . . before you give money to a cause, you should always consult God. Does he want you to do this? Is he in it? Commit your plans to the Lord, and he will give you success. Otherwise, you could easily fail.

**PRAYER:** Jesus, remind me always to pray before I do anything. Amen.

Week 14: Friday

# Do Good

**Amaziah did what was pleasing in the Lord's sight.** 2 Chronicles 25:2

**MAIN READING:** 2 Chronicles 25

**OPTIONAL READING:** 2 Chronicles 22—24

Mark and his mother drove down the street, heading for home. Suddenly, Mark saw a boy he knew from school walking along. "Give him a ride, Mom," he said.

"Who is he?" his mother asked.

"A kid from school."

Mark's mother stopped and they offered the boy a ride. He said with a smile, "Thanks. It's a long walk home."

"I forget your name," Mark said to him.

The boy responded, "Jerry Cranmer. I live up on Livingston Street."

In a few minutes, Mark's mother drove into one of the tougher sections of town. They soon found Jerry's house. The lawn was burned out. Two old rusty cars sat in the front yard. And the house looked like it was falling down. Mark said to Jerry, "See you in school."

When Jerry had gone, Mark said to his mother, "He's a nice guy. I should get to know him better."

"That's a good idea."

That was what you could call a good deed. Something done to give God glory, not just for yourself. That was what King Amaziah did. He did what was pleasing in God's sight. What good can you do today? Little things. Don't think about doing something so big the whole world takes notice. It's just little things like giving a kid a ride home.

**PRAYER:** Jesus, help me to do good everywhere I go. Amen.

Week 14: Saturday

# The Danger of Pride

**But when he had become powerful, he also became proud, which led to his downfall.** 2 Chronicles 26:16

**Main Reading:** 2 Chronicles 26

**Optional Reading:** 2 Chronicles 27—29

"You da man!" friends of Levi cried as he dribbled the basketball down the court. He'd scored over 10 points. His team was winning by 20.

"Go, Levi, go. You're the best," others shouted.

As Levi worked his way around defenders, his mind told him, "No one can steal the ball from you. You're the best. You can make any shot you want."

He wasn't watching closely, though, and as he went up for a jumper, the defender snuffed him. Then the defender grabbed the ball and sprinted down court.

A little pride can fell you. That's what happened to Uzziah. He thought he was such a great guy, such an important person, that he didn't follow God's rules anymore. He figured they didn't apply to him. In his pride, he performed a dangerous act in the temple. God punished him immediately. He became a leper for the rest of his days.

Watch out for pride. It will purr in your heart, telling you how wonderful you are, and then it will stab you in the back.

**Prayer:** Father, protect me from pride. I don't want to mess up. Amen.

Week 14: Sunday

# Giving from the Heart

**The people responded immediately and generously with the first of their crops and grain, new wine, olive oil, honey, and all the produce of their fields. They brought a tithe of all they owned.** 2 Chronicles 31:5

**MAIN READING:** 2 Chronicles 31

**OPTIONAL READING:** 2 Chronicles 30, 32, 33

Lena stared at the money in her hand. Twenty dollars. For her birthday, she'd received over $200 in money gifts. Her parents told her she should give 10 percent to the Lord. So here it was.

But that $20 sure looked like a lot of money. She could buy some nice new clothes with $20. She could go to the movies four times. She could save it and make it even bigger as she saved other gifts.

But she also loved the Lord. As the offering plate came closer to her pew, she sighed. She prayed, "Lord, help me to give with a whole heart. Help me to believe you will bless this."

The offering plate started down her row. When it reached Lena, she hesitated only a moment, then put it in. As she watched the plate continue down the row, a sudden shot of joy filled her. She had given the most money ever in her life in church. She felt good. She felt like she'd pleased the Lord.

Giving with a cheerful, happy heart is the kind of giving God loves. Is that the way you give? If not, what can you do to change your attitude?

**PRAYER:** Jesus, teach me to give with a cheerful heart. Amen.

Week 15: Monday

# Refusing to Listen

**But Josiah refused to listen to Neco, to whom God had indeed spoken, and he would not turn back.** 2 Chronicles 35:22

**Main Reading:** 2 Chronicles 35

**Optional Reading:** 2 Chronicles 34, 36

Does God ever speak through unbelievers? Can we ever listen to something said by a person who doesn't know Jesus?

Of course. All truth is God's truth, whether it comes from the Bible, a believer, or an unbeliever.

However, beware of trusting too much in those who don't love Jesus. Sometimes they will give you the right advice. At other times, run.

In this Bible story, Pharaoh Neco told King Josiah that God had spoken to him. God told Neco to fight against another king that Josiah was allied to. Neco tried to warn Josiah to go home. Josiah wouldn't listen.

How could Josiah have trusted in Neco's message? How could he have confirmed that God had really spoken to Neco? Simply through prayer, consultation with a prophet or priest, or other spiritual means.

When an unbeliever gives you advice he says is from God, be careful. It could be right, but it might not. How you can find out is simple: ask God yourself. Pray about it. Seek the wisdom and guidance of the Bible, and listen to your Christian friends.

God sometimes uses unbelievers to speak to us. Don't automatically say they're wrong. Seek the advice of others. And go to God himself. He will answer you somehow.

**Prayer:** Lord, may I always listen for your truth, no matter what the source. Amen.

Week 15: Tuesday

# Great Joy

**The Temple of God was then dedicated with great joy by the people of Israel, the priests, the Levites, and the rest of the people who had returned from exile.** Ezra 6:16

**MAIN READING:** Ezra 6 • **OPTIONAL READING:** Ezra 5, 7

Suzanne sang the songs with real gusto. When the pastor prayed, she prayed with him. And as he preached his sermon, she listened intently.

Suzanne was a new Christian. She had given her life to Jesus only weeks before. Joy carried her along. She felt lifted up constantly.

God wants us to experience joy in worship, like the Israelites did in Ezra's day. Worship shouldn't be dull and boring. We should never go to church with the attitude, "Oh, I have to do this now." No, God wants us to come before him with singing. He longs that we discover the real joy in worship.

What is worship for you? A drag? Boring? Uplifting? Fun? Empowering?

Worship is meant to be the time when the church comes to God for new strength. God wants to meet us at the time and place and bless us. When we come with that kind of attitude, we're sure to find that God is there. He listens. He responds. He speaks to your hearts.

Come with joy in your heart. Ask God to touch you deeply. Then you will experience the beauty of worship.

**PRAYER:** Father, guide me as I come to your house, so that I might learn your Word. Amen.

# Repentance

**I prayed, "O my God, I am utterly ashamed; I blush to lift up my face to you. For our sins are piled higher than our heads, and our guilt has reached to the heavens."** Ezra 9:6

**MAIN READING:** Ezra 9 • **OPTIONAL READING:** Ezra 8, 10

In church, you probably hear a lot about repentance. What is it? How does it happen? What do you do when you repent of your sins?

The word repentance means "to change your mind," or "to have a change of heart" about something. When you repent, you have a change of heart about your sins. You say, "I no longer want to act that way." "I want to go in a new direction." "I'm leaving that lifestyle behind."

God wants us to take a good look at our lives. Sometimes the Holy Spirit will speak to your heart. "Don't you think you need to stop doing such and such?" "Aren't you tired of living like that?" "Don't you see that this is bad for you?"

You're faced with a decision. Should you do something about this conviction? Of course you should. You should give up whatever is being pointed at. You should leave it behind.

When you repent of something God says is bad for you, you achieve a great victory for Christ. God wants you to repent, not because he wants to take something good away from you, but because he wants to help you become a great person.

**PRAYER:** Lord, help me to learn to repent of all the things I shouldn't do. Amen.

Week 15: Thursday

# Getting What You Want

**O Lord, please hear my prayer! Listen to the prayers of those of us who delight in honoring you. Please grant me success now as I go to ask the king for a great favor. Put it into his heart to be kind to me.**
Nehemiah 1:11

**Main Reading:** Nehemiah 1 • **Optional Reading:** Nehemiah 2—4

Shara only wanted one thing. She longed for her teacher to let her work on her art projects during recess, instead of sending her to play outside. She loved art. She enjoyed drawing and painting and sculpting. Numerous little projects sat all around the classroom. Shara was considered the class artiste! Now she wanted to practice her art even more.

Thinking about it, Shara decided to study God's Word to see if it would offer help. She came upon the story of Nehemiah and suddenly saw an answer. "God," she prayed, "give me success with my teacher today. You know all I desire. You know why I desire it. Let me stay inside and work on my art."

Shara was doing something we all do. We want something. How do we get it?

Some people manipulate, throw tantrums, shout, scream, beg, wail. Others will use money or giving gifts to get what they want. These are probably not very good ways of going about it.

Shara chose a wise course. Go to God. Ask him to get involved. Tell him exactly what you want. Then wait for the right moment. If God truly desires that you get what you want, he will grant it through the person you talk to.

What do you want? Trust God. Go to him first, and you will find him ready and able to help.

**Prayer:** Jesus, help me to remember always to go to you first. Amen.

Week 15: Friday

# God's Help

**When our enemies and the surrounding nations heard about it, they were frightened and humiliated. They realized that this work had been done with the help of our God.** Nehemiah 6:16

**MAIN READING:** Nehemiah 6 • **OPTIONAL READING:** Nehemiah 5, 7, 8

When God gets involved, sparks fly!

That's what happened to Nehemiah and his crew of Israelites. They needed to build a wall around the city of Jerusalem. It had been destroyed when King Nebuchadnezzar attacked the city in 586 B.C. God had allowed the people to be taken into slavery and exile because of their rampant sin.

But now a new day had come. The people of Israel were given a chance to return to their homeland by the new king of Persia, Cyrus. God spoke through Cyrus. He told Israel to rebuild their temple. They did this under the leadership of Ezra.

But other problems persisted. Jerusalem had no defenses and many enemies. They needed protection and help. Nehemiah left his position as cupbearer to another king of Persia, Artaxerxes, and started a building campaign in Jerusalem. Many enemies fought them psychologically (though not physically). Nehemiah didn't let up. In 52 days, the whole wall was rebuilt. It was a miracle.

But not a miracle of people. God had given his help. And that's all you ever need for a big job.

**PRAYER:** Jesus, may I always remember to seek your help in any work for you. Amen.

Week 15: Saturday

# When All Is Going Well

**But when all was going well, your people turned to sin again, and once more you let their enemies conquer them.** Nehemiah 9:28

**MAIN READING:** Nehemiah 9 • **OPTIONAL READING:** Nehemiah 10—13

Louie sat on the edge of his bed, rubbing his eyes. Another day, another time to play and have fun. Another day to learn.

Louie had it good. His parents were together and not arguing anymore. His grandparents gave him lots of money at Christmas. His little brother and sister didn't bother him too much. He had made the Little League baseball team as catcher. School had turned into a breeze. He received all As and Bs, rarely a C or anything less. The girl he liked, liked him. And everyone thought he was great. Even church didn't seem as boring.

He just didn't think it could be any better.

He should have been watching out, though. Good times are often the most dangerous of all. Like what happened to Israel: when good times came, they forgot God.

It's easy to do. When everything is perfect, why pray? Why spend a lot of time in the Bible? Why go to church that much? God is blessing you. Surely he understands.

This is a dangerous time. Be careful when good times roll. They're the best time for Satan to attack and knock you down.

**PRAYER:** Father, protect me from myself. Let me never forget you. Amen.

Week 15: Sunday

# If I Die, I Die

**And then, though it is against the law, I will go in to see the king. If I must die, I am willing to die.** Esther 4:16

**Main Reading:** Esther 4 • **Optional Reading:** Esther 1—3

Queen Esther was caught in the middle. A wicked man, Haman, had developed a hatred for her Uncle Mordecai. Because Mordecai was a Jew, Haman wanted to kill all Jews. He talked King Xerxes into declaring a special day of slaughter. Anyone could kill a Jew and take his possessions on that day.

The queen was Jewish too. But no one knew it. She could easily hide herself. But her uncle told her God may have made her queen because of this plot. Perhaps she became queen so she could help. "At any rate," he told her, "help will come. If it doesn't come from you, God will send others. But you will disappear from history."

Esther took it seriously. She had to help her people. Her problem was that the king hadn't seen her for nearly a month. To walk into the king's inner court unannounced invited death. If the king didn't admit her, he could have her executed.

That's why Esther said, "If I die, I die." She was willing to go before the king, even if it meant her death.

God granted Esther success. When Esther got involved in saving her people, everything turned around. Haman ended up being executed on the gallows he had prepared for Mordecai.

God works when we walk in faith. Look to him, and you will have success.

**Prayer:** I trust you, Lord, praying that you would lead me even when it's tough. Amen.

Week 16: Monday

# God's Intervention

**That night the king had trouble sleeping, so he ordered an attendant to bring the historical records of his kingdom so they could be read to him.** Esther 6:1

**Main Reading:** Esther 6 • **Optional Reading:** Esther 5, 7

Esther had little hope that she could win this battle alone. A man named Haman, very powerful in the Persian kingdom, had talked the king into making a law to annihilate the Jews. Esther was Jewish. She was also the queen. She approached the king in his court chamber. She invited him to a little lunch. She didn't know what she would do, but she believed God would give her something.

God did. Before the fated lunch, the king couldn't sleep one night. Probably to help him become drowsy, he asked that the court records be read to him. The reader selected a passage about the deeds of Mordecai, a Jew. Mordecai had given the king a warning about a plot against his life. The plot was foiled. But was Mordecai ever rewarded? There was no record.

Many things happened in succession the next few days. Haman became the object of rejection and execution. God had worked events so that Queen Esther, her uncle Mordecai, and the Jews were saved.

When God works in human events to make things go a certain way, we call it God's providence. God continually leads events for his own purposes. He does that for every Christian too.

Do you trust God to work as things happen around you? Do you look to him for help? He will work, and he will help you always.

**Prayer:** Lord, help me to trust that you know what you're doing in my life. Amen.

# God's Great Turnaround

**The king's decree gave the Jews in every city authority to unite to defend their lives. They were allowed to kill, slaughter, and annihilate anyone of any nationality or province who might attack them or their children and wives, and to take the property of their enemies.** Esther 8:11

**MAIN READING:** Esther 8 • **OPTIONAL READING:** Esther 9, 10

God turned it all around. A threat against the Jews was stopped. God made sure the Jews, Queen Esther, and Uncle Mordecai survived. And the enemies of the Jews were destroyed.

How had God done it? Through a mysterious sequence of normal human events God engineered the turnaround. Everything that happened in the book of Esther looks normal. Nothing seems weird or crazy. God worked through normal human situations to bring about the end he desired.

God will work in your life in the same way. Many times you won't even realize he's doing something. Often, it looks like situations have simply happened without his intervention. But God is working behind the scenes leading everything where he wants it to go.

Expect God to open doors for you. Expect him to engineer events in your life so that at times you succeed. Sometimes he will even allow you to fall or fail. He has a purpose for everything. Line yourself up with him. You can trust he will lead it to the end he prepared all along.

**PRAYER:** Father, I look forward to what you might do in my life today. Amen.

# Attacked

**Satan replied to the Lord, "Yes, Job fears God, but not without good reason! You have always protected him and his home and his property from harm. . . . But take away everything he has, and he will surely curse you to your face!"** Job 1:9-11

**MAIN READING:** Job 1 • **OPTIONAL READING:** Job 2—4

Satan wanted to hurt Job. He hated the man of God. He believed that if bad things started happening to Job, the believer would reject God and curse him to his face.

God decided to allow a little test. Was Satan right? Would Job turn on God if things went badly?

Satan attacked. Job lost his donkeys, his camels, his sheep, and his children. Satan stole them or killed them all. What did Job do? He didn't curse God. He fell to his knees and cried out, "The Lord gave me everything and the Lord has taken it away. Praise the name of the Lord!"

Isn't that amazing? How could Job do this? One reason: because he really loved God. And he understood how God works in the world. Nothing he had was really his. It was all on loan till Job died, and then God would pass it on to someone else.

How do you feel when things go wrong in your life? Could Satan be attacking you? It's possible. The important thing is that you trust God and turn to him, even when you think he has hurt you. God would never hurt you so that you lost your faith. But God will test you at times.

How will you do when God tests you?

**PRAYER:** Lord, I want to pass the test. Don't let me fail. Amen.

# Experience

**From my experience, I know that fools who turn from God may be successful for the moment, but then comes sudden disaster.** Job 5:3

**Main Reading:** Job 5 • **Optional Reading:** Job 6—8

Justin's teacher said, "In my experience, it's better to tolerate all religions. If you want to have your own, that's fine. But don't try and force it on anyone else."

Justin listened with interest. His church youth leader had been talking about this very issue. Only the youth pastor used the Bible to support his points. One thing he said that made Justin think: "If you always rely on your own experience, you will end up failing. Our experience is not the standard. The Bible is the standard."

Justin wasn't sure what to think of it. Who was right—his teacher, or the youth pastor? Was experience an important factor in any situation?

People can learn much by experience. That's the most basic way we learn. But in the teacher's case here, and in the case of Job's friend Eliphaz, experience gave them the wrong idea. It's good to learn from experience, but not good to base your life on it. The Bible is the main source we should build our lives on. Experience can mislead, as it did in Eliphaz's case. And it can also be a lie, as in the teacher's.

Trust the Bible. Learn from experience. But give the Bible the important place.

**Prayer:** Jesus, help me to be a good judge between the Bible and experience. Amen.

Week 16: Friday

# Who Am I?

**And who am I, that I should try to answer God or even reason with him?**
Job 9:14

**Main Reading:** Job 9 • **Optional Reading:** Job 10—12

Who are you?

Kid? Preteen? Fifth grader? Church-goer? Friend of God? Christian?

Each of us is many things. But Job brings up a good point in this verse. He asks who he is that he should try to reason with God. Job realized in the vast expanse of the universe he was no one. He had little reason to think that God would debate him about his problem. He didn't have much support for thinking that God would even care.

But Job believed that God did care. He believed that he did matter to God. And he believed that God would tell him the reason for his suffering.

You know what? Who are you—a nobody? No! You are somebody in God's eyes. You matter to him. You have every right to bring up any problem or situation with him. In fact, God invites you to talk out your problems with him. He will never turn you away. He may not tell you the reason you're suffering (he didn't with Job, either), but he will be with you through it.

The fact is, God wants you to come to him with everything. Hold nothing back. Let God know how you feel. Tell him what troubles you.

God will listen and answer. Maybe not the way you desire, but he will still answer. Why? For one reason: he loves you.

**Prayer:** Jesus, let me never think that you don't care about me. Amen.

Week 16: Saturday

# Please Tell Me!

**Tell me, what have I done wrong? Show me my rebellion and my sin. Why do you turn away from me? Why do you consider me your enemy?** Job 13:23, 24

**MAIN READING:** Job 13 • **OPTIONAL READING:** Job 14, 15

If things go wrong in your life, are you allowed to ask God why?

All through the book of Job, we see Job calling out to God. He wanted God to tell him what he did wrong. In the verse we're looking at today, Job felt frustrated. Why wasn't God answering? Why did God treat him like an enemy? For many pages, Job will call on God with no answers coming. God seemed to disappear from his life. Didn't God care? Couldn't God help? Why did he do nothing?

Christians ask these kinds of questions when their lives get messed up. When things go wrong, many cry out to God, "Why? Where are you? What did I do wrong?" Often, it seems that God doesn't answer.

God would answer Job, though. At the end of the book, God comes to Job and talks to him from out of a whirlwind. He asks Job many questions: "Did you create the ocean? Do you know how the stars stay in the sky? Do you know why it snows in one season and rains in another?"

Of course, Job has no answers. God never does tell him why his life went haywire. But God assures him of one thing: that he is in charge of Job's life, and he knows what he's doing. There is only one answer for Job: keep trusting God, even when you don't understand why he does what he does. He still loves you.

**PRAYER:** Father, may I find in you all the answers I need. Amen.

Week 16: Sunday

# Accusations

**How long before you stop talking? Speak sense if you want us to answer!** Job 18:2

**MAIN READING:** Job 18 • **OPTIONAL READING:** Job 16, 17

"You shouldn't have done it. Just tell me, what did you do wrong?" Uncle Bill asked Karen when she came home in tears. Many of the kids in her class were angry at her.

Karen's mother told her, "You must have insulted them or something, honey. Think! What did you do to get them upset and angry?"

And Karen's brother commented, "I always knew you would mess things up!"

Have you ever had people tell you things like that when your life goes wrong? These are the kinds of things Job's three friends were saying to him. They repeatedly told him he was suffering because he had sinned. But we know from the beginning of the book that the real reason Job suffered was because Satan attacked him. Satan was trying to get Job to curse God.

You can pray about the advice people give you. And you can be sure that God is not going to accuse you of wrongdoing if you haven't sinned. In fact, always remember: God is not an accuser. Satan is! So when you're accused, if you know of nothing wrong, then realize the accusations must be from Satan.

The Devil will do anything to destroy you. Beware of his tricks.

**PRAYER:** I believe in you, Jesus, and I know you will always tell me the truth. Amen.

Week 17: Monday

# My Redeemer Lives

**But as for me, I know that my Redeemer lives, and that he will stand upon the earth at last. And after my body has been decayed, yet in my body I will see God! I will see him for myself. Yes, I will see him with my own eyes. I am overwhelmed at the thought!** Job 19:25-27

**MAIN READING:** Job 19 • **OPTIONAL READING:** Job 20—22

Jeni stared into the coffin. Her grandfather lay still and quiet. He did look at peace, as some had already said. But Jeni knew the truth. She believed her grandfather was at peace because he was with Jesus. One day both of them would be united in heaven. The whole family would rejoice because all had become believers in the last few years.

As Jeni stepped away from the coffin, one of her teachers nodded to her. "I'm so sorry about your grandfather," Mrs. Lipinski said.

"It's OK. I know where he is," Jeni said.

"You know where?"

"In heaven. With Jesus."

"You really believe that, huh?" Mrs. Lipinski asked.

"Yes. Ever since I was little."

Mrs. Lipinski smiled. "I wish I had a belief like that. But I don't."

She turned away to another teacher who had come to the funeral.

You'll meet many people in the world who don't believe in life after death. Many are not happy. Many live with great fear. But your witness can help them. Remember—your redeemer, Jesus, lives. And you will live with him forever because of it.

**PRAYER:** Lord, I praise you that you conquered death and rose from the dead. Amen.

# Tested Like Gold

**But he knows where I am going. And when he has tested me like gold in a fire, he will pronounce me innocent.** Job 23:10

**Main Reading:** Job 23 • **Optional Reading:** Job 24—26

What happens when you put gold into a furnace?

At first it melts slowly, until it's a shiny liquid. Then, any impurities rise to the surface. Good gold refiners take the impurities, the "dross," and strip it away from the pure gold. Fourteen-carat gold is less pure than 18-carat. Twenty-four carat gold is the purest of all, having no impurities at all in it. If someone gives you a 24-carat gold ring or pin, they spent some big bucks on it.

How can the refiner tell when the gold has lost all impurities? When he can see his face in the reflection of the pure gold. The melted gold acts as a mirror. The purer the gold, the clearer the image.

God puts us into the fire sometimes, too. His purpose: to refine us. To get rid of impurities. When God tests us, bad stuff rises to the surface. Our anger. Our hatred. Our lying. As he tests us, he rids us of those impurities. We no longer want to live in them. In the end, we emerge pure and innocent.

God wants to make you the purest gold possible, 24-carat. Next time he tests you, perhaps you should say, "I am becoming purer by the minute." And it will be true.

**Prayer:** Father, I praise you that you refine me each day. I want to become pure. Amen.

Week 17: Wednesday

# God's Friendship

**In my early years, the friendship of God was felt in my home. The Almighty was still with me, and my children were around me.**
Job 29:4, 5

**Main Reading:** Job 29 • **Optional Reading:** Job 27, 28, 30—32

How do you "feel" the friendship of God, like Job says in the verse for this day?

There are many ways. God's blessings on your life and family are one means. The fact that your family prays and your dad or mom takes you to church is another. When you talk to God yourself, you're showing you're his friend, and he is yours. When you read the Bible, you're also showing you reverence him and want to learn from him.

One of the best ways to show God is your friend, though, is to talk about him like he is.

"Well, the Lord spoke to my heart the other day and . . ."

"Yes, God blessed my dad with a new job just last week . . ."

"Sure, God is watching over me. I don't have to be afraid of anything."

When you talk like this around your friends, they soon get the message. God is real to you. He's there, watching, leading, helping. He's not someone "out there." He's not just the man upstairs or the guy I pray to. No, God is an important part of your life. When you show others how important he is to you, they figure out pretty soon that you and he are friends.

**Prayer:** Father, thank you for being my friend. I value that more than anything. Amen.

Week 17: Thursday

# God Speaks

**But God speaks again and again, though people do not recognize it. . . . He whispers in their ear and terrifies them with his warning.**
Job: 33:14, 16

**Main Reading:** Job 33 • **Optional Reading:** Job 34—37

Job's three friends, Eliphaz, Zophar, and Bildad, fired everything they had at the suffering man. They told him he had hidden his sin. If he would only admit what he'd done wrong, he would be made well. The argument went on for so long that it takes 30 chapters of the book of Job to record it. Finally the argument was over, but Job hadn't budged from his original position. "I have done nothing wrong. Why is God doing this to me?"

A fourth man sat by saying nothing. His name was Elihu. He was younger than the others, but his youth didn't prevent him from being wise. As the others fell into silence, Elihu spoke. He offered some wisdom to Job that we find here, in this verse.

He tells Job God does speak, over and over, but people don't hear. He "whispers" in their ears. He warns them at times. God's words are everywhere—in nature, in the world, in the heart. He counsels Job to stop demanding that God sit down and talk and to start listening to his heart.

That's not bad counsel. Sometimes the best thing to do when you hurt is to start listening. Ask God to speak, and he will. He will tell you what you need to know. Just quiet yourself enough to hear.

**Prayer:** Jesus, make me a listener for your voice. Amen.

Week 17: Friday

# I Have Some Questions

**Who is this that questions my wisdom with such ignorant words? Brace yourself, because I have some questions for you, and you must answer them.** Job 38:2, 3

**Main Reading:** Job 38 • **Optional Reading:** Job 39, 40

God finally speaks to Job. He appears in a whirlwind. Out of the storm, his voice rattles out over the five men who sit on the ground. But God speaks only to Job.

What do you think God said? What would you expect?

"Oh, I'm sorry, Job, that all these bad things have happened. I'll fix it right away."

Or maybe, "Hey, Job, what do you want to know? Ask anything."

Perhaps, "Look, Job, I know things are bad right now. But they'll get better. Give it time."

Or try this: "Hey, things could be a lot worse, Job, my friend. You could be dead!"

You know what? God said none of the above. Instead, he started asking Job impossible questions. "Where were you when I created planet Earth?" "What keeps the earth from caving in? What makes you able to stand on its surface?" And so on and so on.

Why did God do this? For one reason: God wanted Job to rethink all he was saying. He longed that Job recognize his wisdom. He was trying to get Job to see that the man could trust him with everything, because he was capable and perfectly wise.

Has God said that to you when things go wrong? "Trust me. Just trust me. I know what I'm doing." If so, then why not trust him?

**Prayer:** Jesus, help me to trust you for everything. Amen.

# I Repent!

**I had heard about you before, but now I have seen you with my own eyes. I take back everything I said, and I sit in dust and ashes to show my repentance.** Job 42:5, 6

**MAIN READING:** Job 42 • **OPTIONAL READING:** Job 40, 41

How would you like to hear these words from someone you had a fight with: "I was wrong!" "I'm sorry—I didn't mean it!" "Please forgive me. I didn't know what I was talking about."

You'd feel like the person had finally come to his senses—right? You'd sense that things between you were brightening.

I suspect that's how God felt with Job when he uttered the words of today's story. Job admitted to God that all his yelling and shrieking were wrong. He now saw that God loved him, cared about his situation, and didn't intend to look like an enemy. Job realized that God was wise and loyal and would never hurt him personally.

It's hard sometimes to make such an admission. You're proud. You want to be right. Saying you're wrong is like giving up.

But sometimes that's exactly what we must do. With a parent. With a brother or sister. With a friend. With God. Admit they were right and you were wrong. Just say it. Get it out.

Once that is done, then you can really talk. Then you can go back to being friends. Then you will be free from anger!

**PRAYER:** Father, thank you for helping me see the truth. Amen.

# Do Not Follow

**Oh, the joys of those who do not follow the advice of the wicked, or stand around with sinners, or join in with scoffers.** Psalm 1:1

**Main Reading:** Psalm 1 • **Optional Reading:** Psalms 2—7

There are three stages to sin. When we decide to do wrong things with others, it usually happens at three levels.

Stage one: You listen to the bad advice of a friend. He says something is OK when it's not. Stealing. Lying. Drugs. Drinking. It can be any number of things. But he talks you into trying something you know is sin. That's what Psalm 1 means by "following the advice of the wicked."

Stage two: After you've done wrong, suddenly you're one of them. You "stand around" with them. You talk. You make jokes. Everyone laughs. All the bad guys and girls are suddenly your best friends. According to Psalm 1 you've gone further into sin: You're now "standing around with sinners."

Stage three: At this point, you start to make fun of those who won't sin like you have. The goody-goody kids. They refuse to do the things you do. So you mock them. You laugh at them. You put them down. You have, according to Psalm 1, "joined in with scoffers."

Have any of these things happened in your life? Are you listening to wicked advice? Or standing around with bad people? Or making fun of good people? Watch out. You're in great danger. Turn around, and return to Jesus.

**Prayer:** Help me, Jesus, to always turn away from sin. Amen.

Week 18: Monday

# Your Name Is Majestic

**O Lord, our Lord, the majesty of your name fills the earth! Your glory is higher than the heavens.** Psalm 8:1

**MAIN READING:** Psalm 8 • **OPTIONAL READING:** Psalms 9—15

How great is God? Why do we call him majestic?

Think about these things:

God is all-powerful. He can do anything. He created the universe out of nothing. He made mankind—with our eyesight, our ears, our ability to feel and touch, all of it—by simply speaking some words.

God knows everything about each of us. He knows how many hairs are on our heads. He knows everything we do. Nothing is hidden from him.

God lives everywhere. He's in China right now and also the U.S. He's in your heart and mine. And he's not divided up. His whole person is in all places.

God is perfectly holy. He can never sin. He can never do anything wrong. He could never tell a lie, or steal, or curse.

God loves us completely. His love is everlasting. He will never change.

God is gracious. He gives gifts constantly and blesses his people. He will never stop giving us every good thing.

No wonder he's called majestic. He's the greatest.

**PRAYER:** Lord, you are majestic, and I worship you. Amen.

# All Good Things from You

**I said to the Lord: "You are my Master! All the good things I have are from you."** Psalm 16:2

**MAIN READING:** Psalm 16 • **OPTIONAL READING:** Psalms 17—22

Uncle Buddy showed Jimmy, his nephew, around the huge house.

"This is the kitchen," he said.

He led Jimmy into another room. "This is the game room." It had every game imaginable—video games, pinball machines, and even a single bowling lane.

Jimmy stared into the living room. Beautiful couches, a giant screen TV. Everything anyone could want. "This is the living room."

Finally, Jimmy exclaimed, "This is the coolest house I've ever seen!"

Uncle Buddy laughed. "Well, the truth is, Jimmy, I didn't do any of this on my own. God gave me the brains to think it up, the money to buy it, and the friends and family who can share it with me. It's all from God. So you should thank him, not me."

Did you ever realize everything comes from God? Your brains. Your family. Your place in the world. Without God, you have none of it. That's a good reason to thank God for what you have right now, isn't it?

**PRAYER:** Father, thank you for giving me good gifts. I praise you for them. Amen.

Week 18: Wednesday

# God Is My Shepherd

**The Lord is my shepherd; I have everything I need.** Psalm 23:1

**Main Reading:** Psalm 23 • **Optional Reading:** Psalms 24—26

Sunday morning, Tim's mom called him to breakfast. "We've got church today, honey," she called, "so get going."

Tim hated to admit it, but he didn't much like church. It was boring. He rarely learned anything new. And he had no real friends there.

How might someone like Tim come to see church in a different way?

One way would be to understand what's supposed to happen in church. Why do we go? Is it to hear a sermon? Is it to sing some songs? Is it to worship God?

All these things. But there's something else you may have missed. Remember the Twenty-third Psalm? The first verse is quoted above.

God is a shepherd. Jesus was called the good shepherd. What precisely does a shepherd do? He feeds his sheep, waters them, protects them, and doctors them when they hurt. Those are the kinds of things that are supposed to happen in a church. We feed on the Word of God. We're given water when we thirst, so that we feel refreshed for the day ahead. When we're afraid, God comforts us. And when we need healing, God gives us soothing words and friendship through people and the Bible.

When you go to church with the idea of meeting with God, it changes everything. It might even make you want to be there!

**Prayer:** Lord, help me learn to enjoy church the way it's supposed to be. Amen.

# Wait

**Wait patiently for the Lord. Be brave and courageous. Yes, wait patiently for the Lord.** Psalm: 27:14

**MAIN READING:** Psalm 27 • **OPTIONAL READING:** Psalms 28—31

Sometimes you've just got to wait.

Wait for summer so you can play ball.

Wait for winter so you can ice skate.

Wait for your birthday so you can get that big present you want.

Wait to graduate from high school.

Wait to find a wife or husband.

It seems like we're always waiting.

You also have to wait for God to fix things in your life. God wants us to learn to be patient when things go wrong and we pray for his help. We need to learn to wait when we want something badly but God's not ready to give it to us.

The psalm in the lesson today tells us to "wait patiently" for God. God will act. God will bless us. God will help us. At the right time. There's never a wrong time with God. All time is the right time for him, and he will do what you need when the time is best.

Stop worrying. Leave your needs in the hands of God. He will meet them when he's ready.

**PRAYER:** Jesus, let me learn to wait for you, even when I feel impatient. Amen.

Week 18: Friday

# Misery

**When I refused to confess my sin, I was weak and miserable, and I groaned all day long.** Psalm 32:3

**MAIN READING:** Psalm 32 • **OPTIONAL READING:** Psalms 33—36

Carla lay on her bed, groaning.

"What'sa matter, Car?" asked her sister, Shellie.

"I feel bad."

"Why?"

"I don't know."

Carla felt as if someone had sucked the strength right out of her. She shook when she walked, and she couldn't seem to get enough air. She thought she might be sick.

But she knew she wasn't.

"I did something," she finally admitted.

"What?" Shellie asked.

"I cheated on a test in school. Now I feel horrible."

"Then go, confess it to the teacher, and get it straightened out. She'll forgive you, even if she flunks you. But that's better than this."

Carla knew her sister was right. She told the teacher the next day. Suddenly, she felt new, alive, and free. "God's no longer on my case," she said with happiness.

It's true. Sin will make you feel more than guilt. Sometimes, sick feelings assault you. A heaviness overwhelms you. Sadness grips your heart.

But admit the sin, take care of it, and all is well again.

**PRAYER:** Jesus, may I never conceal sin from you. Help me to confess everything. Amen.

# Don't Envy the Wicked

**Don't worry about the wicked. Don't envy those who do wrong. For like grass, they soon fade away. Like springtime flowers, they soon wither.** Psalm 37:1, 2

**MAIN READING:** Psalm 37 • **OPTIONAL READING:** Psalms 38—41

Josie gazed at the girl in the third seat up on the row of desks across from hers. Jasmine Winslow wore the coolest clothes, Josie thought. Jasmine always bought what was right in style. She was the coolest person in the whole class.

When Jasmine got up to answer a question the teacher put on the board, Josie watched her all the more. Jasmine walked so cool. Jasmine knew all the answers. Jasmine just shone. Next to Jasmine, Josie was like a wilted dandelion. No one noticed her.

The one thing that made a difference to Josie was that Jasmine wasn't a Christian. In fact, she often put down kids who went to church. Josie rarely talked to her, but she knew Jasmine sometimes said nasty things about other girls who believed in Jesus.

Still, it wasn't much comfort. Jasmine was cool, and Josie wasn't even chilled. She was lukewarm at best.

What was happening here? It's something all of us do at one time or another. We envy someone who has nicer clothing, better CDs, a bigger bedroom. It can really be anything. What matters is we wish we had what that person has.

God warns us in this psalm, "Don't be envious. Don't worry about what others have." Why? God will bless you in his time. Trust him for that.

**PRAYER:** Father, let me not be envious. Let me be satisfied with your gifts. Amen.

# Thirsting for God

**I thirst for God, the living God. When can I come and stand before him?**
Psalm 42:2

**MAIN READING:** Psalm 42 • **OPTIONAL READING:** Psalms 43—45

Have you ever thirsted for God?

You know what thirst is, right? You come home from a hot day. You've been running around outside, playing your heart out. First, it started in the back of your throat. Then your tongue felt dry. Soon, it seemed your mouth was on fire and your body felt weak. You needed water. Water! Water! Water!

This psalm pictures thirst well. It talks about a deer darting around in the woods, looking for a stream. The deer has been running, running, running. Maybe a hunter is after it. Maybe a bear or a mountain lion. It needs water. It cries out. "Please find me water soon, or I'll die."

Thirst for God is like that. You want to know him. You want to be near him. You want him to work in your life. You feel pangs deep in your chest. You hurt inside because you need him so badly.

That's thirst. When you thirst for God, you realize how much you need him. You cry out in the night, "Give me yourself, Lord!" You seek him at every turn. You can't think about anyone else but him.

That's thirst. Are you thirsty for God? Cry out to him. Ask him to come to you and satisfy your thirst. Ask him to be your running stream of refreshment.

**PRAYER:** Lord, I see you. Be near to me. Fill my heart with your blessings. Amen.

# God Is a Refuge

**God is our refuge and strength, always ready to help in times of trouble.** Psalm 46:1

**MAIN READING:** Psalm 46 • **OPTIONAL READING:** Psalms 47—50

You're lying in bed. All is quiet. Only you and your thoughts.

You hear a sound. It's different. Strange. What was it?

You peek up, surveying your room. Suddenly, you see him. He's sitting in your desk chair, staring at you. Two bright beady eyes cloaked deeply in black robes. Fangs. He wants to . . .

Oh, it's only the way your clothes are piled on your chair.

Another sound.

More alarms.

Will you ever get to sleep?

This world is full of scary stuff. If you have ever watched a movie with some horrifying elements—a murder, a vampire, a werewolf—you know how it can leave you with nightmares.

Scarier still is being on a dark street, alone, with some thugs following you. Or separated from your family in a strange place, not knowing which way to turn.

What do you do under such conditions? This Scripture for today is an answer. "God is our refuge." He will help. He will speak to your heart.

Go to him, and find true comfort until the scare is over.

**PRAYER:** Lord, praise you that you are a true and sure refuge in this world. Amen.

Week 19: Tuesday

# A Clean Heart

**Create in me a clean heart, O God. Renew a right spirit within me. Do not banish me from your presence, and don't take your Holy Spirit from me.** Psalm 51:10, 11

**MAIN READING:** Psalm 51 • **OPTIONAL READING:** Psalms 52—54

So many things go on in our hearts. Kind words. Nasty thoughts. Hopes. Fears. Encouragements. Worries. Desires to help. Desires to kill.

It all goes back to the beginning. When Adam and Eve sinned in the Garden of Eden, they plunged the world into sin. Everyone born from then on had a sinful nature. That means we're born with a natural desire to sin, to do wrong things, to defy God. No matter how hard we try, we can't escape this influence.

That is, until we become Christians. God gives us a new heart. The old one is still there, lurking in the darkness. But the new one takes over. We begin to experience good, kind, wholesome thoughts. We learn to pray, to read God's Word, to do good wherever we go.

But the old heart is still there. King David knew that when he wrote Psalm 51. He wrote this after his sin with Bathsheba. He knew his old nature had taken over and done dastardly things. That's why he prayed, "Create in me a clean heart." He wanted God to clean him up, make him new inside, forgive him.

Do you want a clean heart? Go to God. He's the specialist in cleaning up the seat of the soul.

**PRAYER:** Father, praise you for cleaning up my heart. I feel so much better. Amen.

Week 19: Wednesday

# I Will Sing

**But as for me, I will sing about your power. I will shout with joy each morning because of your unfailing love. For you have been my refuge, a place of safety in the day of distress.** Psalm 59:16

**Main Reading:** Psalm 59 • **Optional Reading:** Psalms 56—58

Ever feel like simply singing — belting out a song for the Lord?

One of the things that will happen in your spiritual life is a desire to sing. God's Spirit will work inside you and show you the joy of praising God in song. Your heart will resound with a hymn or a contemporary tune. You will feel lifted up. God will refresh your spirit.

God enjoys singing—any kind. Even if you're not very good at it. Singing shows . . .

. . . joy. You're feeling good in God's presence.

. . . love. You want to be close to God.

. . . peace. You sense God is with you and all is well with your world.

. . . divine happiness. The real kind, not the passing kind.

God wants you to sing to him, whenever you feel good in his presence. Let him fill your heart with the joy of the music. Ask him to come to you and make music in your soul.

**Prayer:** Lord, let me make music with my soul at all times. Amen.

# Meditating

**I lie awake thinking of you, meditating on you through the night. I think how much you have helped me; I sing for joy in the shadow of your protecting wings.** Psalm 63:6

**Main Reading:** Psalm 63 • **Optional Reading:** Psalms 60—62

We used to hear a lot about meditation.

There was transcendental meditation—or TM—which involved saying a mantra or special word over and over. It's not biblical meditation.

There's Buddhist meditation, which involves emptying your mind of everything so that you're supposedly at peace. But that's not biblical meditation.

There's doctor's medication. Oh, wait, no, that's medicine. Meditation is what we're talking about. Sorry.

Real meditation involves several things:

Talking to God with your heart. Praying, really. Just turning over thoughts and ideas in your mind and sharing them with God.

Asking questions of the Spirit of God. Real meditation means speaking to the Spirit. Ask him questions. Expect answers.

Turning over in your mind phrases and words from the Bible. Think about "love," or "God's greatness," or "Jesus' sacrifice." Let your mind go free and consider all the ideas behind these thoughts.

Meditation isn't difficult. David, in the psalm we're looking at today, did it as he lay on his bed. He turned to God, talked to him, asked him questions. God responded. It was a time of learning, a time of drawing near to God.

**Prayer:** Jesus, let me draw near to you through meditating on your Word. Amen.

Week 19: Friday

# What He Did for Me

**Come and listen, all you who fear God, and I will tell you what he did for me.** Psalm 66:16:

**MAIN READING:** Psalm 66 • **OPTIONAL READING:** Psalm 64, 65, 67

Have you ever given your testimony? In church? At school? To a friend?

This verse shows us what giving a testimony is all about. What is that? Praising God. Telling others of his wonders in your life. Speaking the truth to unbelievers about what God is doing in the world.

When King David thought about the greatness of God and how many things he had done in his life, he had to tell everyone. Can you imagine the king talking to his generals? Do you see him speaking with a shepherd boy about what he learned about God when he was a shepherd?

Giving your testimony is an important part of Christian living. Being able to tell others what you have found in Christ will feed your own soul. You'll feel built up and encouraged in the love of God.

How do you give a testimony? Just a few thoughts:

1. Tell something about what God has done in your life.
2. Leave in important details. "I prayed this. . . . God answered this way."
3. Don't forget to make it fun. Dramatize a little, without fabricating. Just tell the truth, but get into it.

Now go and find someone you can tell about your latest discoveries in Christ. That will not only please the Lord, but energize you!

**PRAYER:** Jesus, lead me in giving my testimony. May I never back down. Amen.

# Pray for the King

**Long live the king! May the gold of Sheba be given to him. May the people always pray for him and bless him all day long.** Psalm 72:15

**Main Reading:** Psalm 72 • **Optional Reading:** Psalm 68—71

Kerri's mother stopped by her bedroom and found Kerri kneeling by her bed. A sheet of paper lay on the bedspread. Kerri fervently prayed. Her mother said, "Honey, what are you doing?"

"Oh, I'm praying," Kerri said.

"That's great. What are you praying about?"

"Well, at church last Sunday we learned how we should pray for our leaders. So I'm praying for the president, our state senators and congressmen, people in the government, our leaders in church. All sorts of leaders."

"Really?" Her mother picked up the list. "Wow! This is really something. You're praying about all these people?"

"Yeah. It's kind of fun. I never thought I'd like it. But I feel like I'm really helping the world."

"That's beautiful. Keep up with it, honey. God will bless you and our country."

What Kerri was doing was something so important we should never miss it. God wants us to pray for our leaders, just like today's psalm says, "Pray for the king." They need God's help and direction. Without God, they will surely fail.

So get on your knees. Ask God to help the president and any others you can think of. It's a matter of life and death!

**Prayer:** Father, help me to keep praying about our leaders always. Amen.

Week 19: Sunday

# I Desire You

**You will keep on guiding me with your counsel, leading me to a glorious destiny. Whom have I in heaven but you? I desire you more than anything on earth.** Psalm 73:24, 25

**Main Reading:** Psalm 73 • **Optional Reading:** Psalm 74, 75

Robert studied the verse over and over. It spoke of God being a rock and a refuge. He tried to think of all the things he knew of like that. The big rock down by the end of his driveway. Mt. Rushmore, where four presidents' faces were carved into the rock. A castle he'd visited.

Robert went over and over the verses, thinking about them and praying.

When he finished, he found his father in his office. "Dad, I learned something today," he told him. His dad listened as Robert talked on and on about what he was learning from the Bible.

As Robert walked to school, he found himself praying for his friends. "Help Jon to believe in you, Lord. And Doug and Jimmy."

In school at his desk, Robert listened to the teacher, and then said to God in his heart, "What can I pray about for her?" God gave him a few ideas.

What was Robert doing? He was "desiring God" like today's verse speaks about. To desire God is to want a closer, more intimate relationship with him. Desiring God is putting him first in your life.

Do you desire more of God? Tell him so, and then watch him work. You will be amazed.

**Prayer:** Lord, I desire a closeness to you more than anything else in life. Amen.

# Remembering the Past

**When the Red Sea saw you, O God, its waters looked and trembled! The sea quaked to its very depths.** Psalm 77:16

**MAIN READING:** Psalm 77 • **OPTIONAL READING:** Psalms 76, 78

Grandpa Jordan turned to Andre. "You know when I was a kid, we made snow forts as high as the eaves of the house. We had snowball battles like the Great War. We had a lot of fun in those days."

"Did your mom make you go to church?" Andre asked.

"Oh, of course. Mom believed in Jesus. Why, she would invite the whole neighborhood over on a Sunday afternoon for pie after church. Have somebody give a talk. That's how I became a Christian."

"What happened?"

"Oh, this one guy came through. About six feet eight inches tall. Basketball player. He gave a talk. Told us about the battle of Jericho. It was thrilling. Then he told us, 'When God blows his horn for all of us to come heaven, are you going to be ready?' Put the fear in me for sure. So I told Jesus I wanted him to be my Savior."

The past. The stories. Old people. Young people. That's what today's verse is talking about. Telling the old stories.

Do you like talking about the past? There's one thing God wants us to do when we have such talks—to remember him and the things he's done in our lives. Do you remember? Are you telling the stories? It's a way to interest others in Jesus.

**PRAYER:** Lord, thank for all the great stories of the faith. They encourage me. Amen.

Week 20: Tuesday

# He Won't Withhold Any Good Thing

**For the Lord God is our light and protector. He gives us grace and glory. No good thing will the Lord withhold from those who do what is right.** Psalm 84:11

**MAIN READING:** Psalm 84 • **OPTIONAL READING:** Psalms 79—83

"I sure would like to make my baseball team," Gordon said at dinner when his dad asked for prayer requests.

"Do you think we should pray about something like that?" Dad asked. "It seems kind of trivial."

Mom jumped in. "Well, I was just reading in the book of Psalms this morning in my quiet time and I found a verse. Psalm 84. It said God will withhold no good thing from his children. Gordon's a child of God. So why shouldn't he pray about it?"

Dad nodded. "Is that what you think, Gordon?"

"I thought we could pray about anything," Gordon said. "Isn't it OK to pray about things you'd really like?"

Why not? God doesn't always give us what we want, but we should feel free to bring anything to him. He cares about us enough to provide us with good things, perhaps even a spot on the local baseball team!

God answers prayers in many ways. Sometimes he says yes, sometimes no, and sometimes wait. But God always answers. Don't hold back any prayers from God. God is the God of big things and little things, so pray away.

**PRAYER:** Father, praise you that you hear all my prayers, no matter how small. Amen.

Week 20: Wednesday

# Love, Truth, Righteousness, and Peace

**Unfailing love and truth have met together. Righteousness and peace have kissed!** Psalm 85:10

**Main Reading:** Psalm 85 • **Optional Reading:** Psalms 86—88

The two girls argued and fought. Finally, Sal said to her friend, "OK, I'll let you copy my homework. But it's the last time."

"Thanks," Angie answered. "Now you're helping me."

When Sal thought about it, she realized she had decided to cheat on the homework because she just wanted peace. She wanted to be done with it. She wanted Angie to stop making her do something she knew was wrong.

Angie was back the next week. "Just this last time," she told Sal. "All I need is your math homework. I don't get it. It's hard. Please?"

Sal gave in again because she didn't want an argument.

Can there be real peace without righteousness? The verse for today puts them together. Actually, real peace only happens in the world—between family members, between friends, between countries—when both are doing the right thing. Righteousness—doing right, doing good, not breaking God's laws—is necessary. Otherwise, the peace is just one giving in to another. And that means one will feel hurt and used, even if she says nothing about it.

You can't have love without truth, otherwise it's just sappy foolishness. You can't have peace without righteousness. Otherwise, it's just giving in to demands. Work for all four, and you will have a God-honoring situation.

**Prayer:** Jesus, help me always to strive for what is best, not just what works for the moment. Amen.

# Make the Most of Your Time

**Teach us to make the most of our time, so that we may grow in wisdom.** Psalm 90:12

**MAIN READING:** Psalm 90 • **OPTIONAL READING:** Psalms 89, 91, 92

Every person on Earth has the same amount of time today. Twenty-four hours.

How we each use it, though, is another matter.

When you're young, time doesn't seem like such a big deal. You always have time. If not today, the weekend. But as you grow, you'll find you'll want to cram more into your day. Planning your day will help. Someone once said, "If you fail to plan, you plan to fail." When you think through your days and plan things, they often go better.

How do you plan your day and use your time wisely?

1. Make a "to do" list. What do you need to do today? Homework? Go to school? Play some ball after school? Write it all down. Then figure out what times you can do each.

2. Write things down on a calendar. A doctor's appointment? A test coming up? Put it on your calendar. Then you won't forget it.

3. Figure out the things you really want to do this year, and write them down. This is called making priorities. What things are important to you? Making the basketball team? Getting good grades? Write your goals down and talk to God about them.

When you've planned things, they usually get done. Oh, and don't forget to pray about them too. Ask God to help you make sure they happen.

**PRAYER:** Lord, I pray that I might use my time wisely, to please you. Amen.

Week 20: Friday

# God's Unfailing Love

**Who will protect me from the wicked? Who will stand up for me against evildoers? Unless the Lord had helped me, I would soon have died. I cried out, "I'm slipping!" and your unfailing love, O Lord, supported me.** Psalm 94:16-18

**MAIN READING:** Psalm 94 • **OPTIONAL READING:** Psalms 93, 95, 96

Many enemies lurk out there, trying to destroy us. Who?

For one, the Devil. He wants to make you slip up. He will keep you from Jesus. He will try to stop you from reading your Bible and praying. He'll do anything to mess up your life.

For another, the world. What do we mean by the world? All the influences out there that try to get our attention. Television. Movies. Magazines. Video games. Friends. Drug dealers. Bad guys and girls. All of these will want to steal your time. If you don't watch out, you will have wasted your life doing stupid things for fun, things that have no real meaning.

For a third, your own self. Sometimes this is called "the flesh." It's your old nature, the person who ruled your life before you became a Christian. Even though as a Christian, the flesh has been overwhelmed by your new nature, he's still there. Still trying to trip you up by doing wrong things.

These enemies all want to stop you from having a real relationship with God. They want to mess up your life. But remember, you have an important person on your side too. God and his "unfailing love." He will protect, and lead, and strengthen you. When these enemies attack, turn to him, and he will help you overcome them.

**PRAYER:** Jesus, let me be watchful, so I don't give in to my enemies. Amen.

Week 20: Saturday

# Thankfulness

**Enter his gates with thanksgiving; go into his courts with praise. Give thanks to him and bless his name.** Psalm 100:4

**MAIN READING:** Psalm 100 • **OPTIONAL READING:** Psalms 97—99

What's there to be thankful for? Everything that's good in your life, and even some of the things that are bad.

Start with your family. Your parents, your brothers and sisters. Thank God for their love and care in your life.

Next, thank God for your school. Your teachers. Your principal. Your friends. Thank him for the grades you get. Thank him for helping you learn. Thank him for the brain he gave you and the body.

After that, thank God for our country. For freedom. For safety. For good leaders. For our president and others in the government.

Thank God for your body—your eyesight, and ears, and nose, and ability to talk. Thank him for health and good feelings. Thank him if you're healthy. Tell him thanks for all the great things you can do with your body—run, leap, jump, fix things, move.

These are just a few starter ideas. There are many more things you can begin thanking God for. Remember that, ultimately, anything good in your life is from him.

So start thanking him today.

**PRAYER:** Father, I thank you for reminding me to give thanks for everything. Amen.

# Refuse to Look

**I will refuse to look at anything vile and vulgar. I hate all crooked dealings; I will have nothing to do with them.** Psalm 101:3

**MAIN READING:** Psalm 101 • **OPTIONAL READING:** Psalm 102

John stood with several of his friends in the parking lot. They were about to go to the beach. Suddenly, a man walked up to them with a bundle of magazines. "Want to buy some of the good stuff?" he asked and waved a magazine with pictures of naked men and women on the cover.

John gaped, astonished that someone would be this bold. His friend Benjamin grabbed him. "Let's get out of here!" he cried.

John knew he was right. He shouldn't look at those pictures. He happened to remember the verse that we're looking at today. Don't "look at anything vile or vulgar." Not in a movie. Not on television. Not listening to certain music on the radio.

All over the world, nasty images vie for your attention. Some rap songs tell us to kill people. Some movies show tremendous violence and also nudity.

What are we to do? Turn away. Get out of there. Don't look. Fight your curiosity and refuse to let those images get imprinted on your mind.

If you don't, you will have to live with them there for the rest of your life.

**PRAYER:** Lord, help me to watch my eyes and ears and reject bad things. Amen.

Week 21: Monday

# Our Sins—Gone!

**He has removed our rebellious acts as far away from us as the east is from the west.** Psalm 103:12

**Main Reading:** Psalm 103 • **Optional Reading:** Psalms 104, 105

I know Jesus died for our sins," Chad said to his dad. "But what did God do with them?"

His father smiled. "For one thing, he buried them in the deepest sea, according to Micah 7:19."

"That's pretty deep," Chad commented.

"He did more than that, though. He also refuses to remember them anymore. And he has also blotted them out, like correction fluid covers a bit of typing. He said that in Isaiah 43:25. He also swept them away like a morning mist, he says, in Isaiah 44:22. You know how the sun burns off a mist in the morning? That's what God did with your sins."

"Boy, God has sure done a lot to get rid of them, hasn't he?"

"Yes," Chad's father said. "But the best one is found in Psalm 103:12. There, God says he has removed your sins as far as the east is from the west."

"That's infinity!" Chad said. "I learned that in school."

"You're right. God has made sure your sins will never come back to haunt you."

"Maybe I ought to thank him then."

And maybe you should too.

**Prayer:** Lord, thank you that you have gotten rid of all my sins. Amen.

# Speak Out!

**Has the Lord redeemed you? Then speak out! Tell others he has saved you from your enemies.** Psalm 107:2

**Main Reading:** Psalm 107 • **Optional Reading:** Psalms 106, 108, 109

"Too many Christians are like the Arctic River," the evangelist cried. "They're frozen over at the mouth!"

It's true. Many Christians never tell one person about Jesus or their faith in him. They're either afraid someone will get mad at them. Or worried it might jeopardize getting something else they want. Or maybe they just don't care.

Do you care about lost people? If so, speak out, as the verse in this reading says.

Speak up about what God has done for you. What prayers has he answered this month? What protection has he given your family? What blessings have you received?

Speak up about Jesus' death on the cross, and his resurrection. Tell your friends the good news, which is what gospel means. It's good news that we no longer have to fear God. We don't have to worry about judgment. We will never go to hell . . . if we trust Jesus.

Speak up about what you believe is right. If someone starts spouting off about something he did wrong—a lie, a theft, a person he hurt—tell him the truth: God is against such people. And if God is against them, what chance do they have?

Yes, it's time to speak up. Don't be afraid. God will be with you. And you will help some people find salvation.

**Prayer:** Father, help me never to shut up when I should speak up. Amen.

Week 21: Wednesday

# At God's Right Hand

**The Lord said to my Lord, "Sit in honor at my right hand until I humble your enemies, making them a footstool under your feet."**
Psalm 110:1

**MAIN READING:** Psalm 110 • **OPTIONAL READING:** Psalms 111—115

Do you ever wonder when Jesus will come back? When the world will be made right? When all the enemies of God's people are thrown into prison? When only good and kindness and love remain?

The day will come. Jesus will return. He will sit on his throne at the right hand of God the Father. Every nation will come and worship him. Every person will bow his knee to Jesus. All the world will praise him for all he's done.

Jesus' day is coming. So don't worry about the future. God will take care of you. He will lead you through any trouble. He will be with you when you face down an enemy. And he will protect you, even from yourself, when you're tempted to do wrong.

The verse today is the most quoted Old Testament verse in the New Testament. It appears in the Gospels and in the letters of Paul. Every saint of every age has longed for the day when Jesus will reign forever. It will be a day of real peace. Every wrong will be righted. And we will reign with Jesus forever.

Do you look forward to that day? It is coming. Be ready. And all will be well for you and your family.

**PRAYER:** Jesus, I hope that you will come quickly, because I want to be with you. Amen.

Week 21: Thursday

# God Hears and Answers

**I love the Lord because he hears and answers my prayers. Because he bends down and listens, I will pray as long as I have breath!** Psalm: 116:1, 2

**Main Reading:** Psalm 116 • **Optional Reading:** Psalms 117, 118

God answers every prayer. It's just that he doesn't always answer with a yes.

What are the possible ways God can answer our prayers?

1. He can say, "Yes, I will do what you ask." Maybe you need some money, or a new shirt, or you're sick and need healing. Many times, God answers such prayers through normal means. He doesn't do a miracle. But it's an answer, just the same.

2. He can say, "No, I will not grant that request." If you ask for super powers, or to be elected president, God may say no. You may also ask for healing for a friend or for some other blessing. God has his reasons, and he may say no.

3. He might say, "No, not right now. Maybe later." You have to wait for this answer. God wants you to grow up a little. He wants to prepare you so when he answers, you'll be able to appreciate it.

4. He could say, "Maybe, if you take certain actions first." This is a tough one. You have to do something before God will answer. He may want you to start tithing or witness to a friend. It could be anything. God sometimes answers in this way.

God always answers our prayers. Sometimes he will even answer, "No, but I have something else for you which is better," too. And that's the best answer of all.

**Prayer:** Lord, I know you will answer, so I'm going to keep praying. Amen.

# How to Overcome Sin

**I have hidden your word in my heart, that I might not sin against you.** Psalm 119:11

**MAIN READING:** Psalm 119:1-16

**OPTIONAL READING:** Psalm 119:17-64

The bad habit was just too strong. Marie couldn't overcome it. It held her life in its hands, and she knew it would always be there.

But then one day God spoke to her about the bad habit. "You can win over this. But you need to start doing some things that will help you."

God showed her the things she had to do. (1) Get involved in church and helping with the youth group. (2) Start praying with real fervency, refusing to quit. (3) Begin reading her Bible and memorizing God's Word.

That's a crucial one, that number three. The verse we're looking at today, Psalm 119:11, shows us the secret of overcoming sin. It's treasuring God's Word in our hearts. Letting it sink deep into our souls so that it becomes an important part of our life. Treasuring it so that it becomes important to us, something we want to do. Hiding it away so we can pull it out when temptation strikes.

The secret to winning over sin isn't so hard. Bad habits aren't that hard to break. It's a matter of mind and heart over sin. Get your mind on God's Word and obey it from your heart. Then you will see that bad habit run!

**PRAYER:** Lord, help me fight off sin through using your Word every day. Amen.

Week 21: Saturday

# A Lamp in the Darkness

**Your word is a lamp for my feet and a light for my path.** Psalm 119:105

**MAIN READING:** Psalm 119:104-112

**OPTIONAL READING:** Psalm 119:65-103, 113-176

You're out camping. The night is starless, cloudy, dark. You can't see anything out there in the woods. You hear startling noises—a bird, some skittering, a chatter of a squirrel, a howl, and a growl. What's out there? Is it something that could hurt you?

What do you do? You could sit in your tent and worry. Or you could pick up your knife, grab your flashlight, and check it out.

That's what you do. You crawl out of your sleeping bag. You draw out your sharpest hunting knife. And then you grasp your flashlight.

A second later you're out of the tent. Where do you shine the light? You could shine it in the trees, weave it around to see if you can spot something. But if you do any walking, you'll shine the light at your feet. So you can see where you're stepping. What you want to avoid. That rock over there. That fallen branch. This little hole in the ground. You step around each because you've seen them with your flashlight.

The verse for today, Psalm 119:105, shows us the same idea, except it lights the path of our lives. With God's Word, we can see where to go, what to do in dangerous situations. With God's Word in our hearts, we know what God says about many subjects. We can follow it, even when we're a little frightened or confused.

Use the lamp of God's Word, and no night will ever scare you again.

**PRAYER:** Lord, help me to use your Word as light in my life today and always. Amen.

Week 21: Sunday

# God Never Sleeps

**He will not let you stumble and fall; the one who watches over you will not sleep. Indeed, he who watches over Israel never tires and never sleeps.** Psalm 121:3, 4

**Main Reading:** Psalm 121 • **Optional Reading:** Psalms 122—126

If something bad happens to you in life, does that mean God wasn't looking? That he didn't know what was happening? Or that he was napping, or asleep, or just wasn't on his guard?

This psalm points out that God never sleeps. He is always watchful. He is always there. He never grows tired or worn out or even bored. He's as fascinated with your life as if you were the only person on planet Earth.

Wherever you go, God is there. He is vigilant, like a careful sentry. He stands guard over your life like an army protecting a king. He will not let anything touch you that he doesn't see can help you in some way. Even the bad things he sometimes lets come into your life—those things he will use for good in your life. Nothing is wasted. No matter how ridiculous or worthless something seems, God can make it turn out for good in your life.

A little boy once prayed, "God, please take care of yourself. Because if anything happens to you, we're all done for!"

God doesn't have to take care of himself. He's always perfect. And he's with you. So stop being afraid and step out in faith to do all that he calls you to today.

**Prayer:** Jesus, help me to trust in your love, no matter where you take me. Amen.

# God Has to Be There

**Unless the Lord builds a house, the work of the builders is useless. Unless the Lord protects a city, guarding it with sentries will do no good.** Psalm 127:1

**MAIN READING:** Psalm 127 • **OPTIONAL READING:** Psalms 128—132

Without God," Grandpa said, "life is a fearful walk through dangerous territory with no to help in sight or over the hill." Terri listened to her grandfather talk about his experiences, but she thought about what he'd said. Was life really that way?

She decided to test it out. The next morning, she asked her friend Ashleigh if she was ever scared. She knew Ashleigh wasn't a Christian, though Terri had talked to her many times about Jesus. "I guess kind of all the time," Ashleigh said. "Tests in school scare me. Walking home in the dark scares me. Cars passing by with men in them scare me sometimes."

Terri next asked her next door neighbor, Mrs. Franks, about it. Terri's mother had often talked to Mrs. Franks about the Lord, but the old lady said she had her own beliefs. "Does life ever seem scary to you, Mrs. Franks?" Terri asked as she sipped a lemonade.

"Oh, it's kind of humdrum most of the time. But dying. That's scary. Don't know what happens then."

Over and over, with everyone she talked to, she learned that people were scared. Why was life like that? Then it hit her. It was like that for one reason: to make people want Jesus. "That's it," Terri said. "I'll tell them Jesus is the answer to all our fears."

And so can you.

**PRAYER:** Lord, praise you that you are with me and I don't have to be scared. Ever. Amen.

# Harmony

**How wonderful it is, how pleasant, when brothers live together in harmony!** Psalm 133:1

**Main Reading:** Psalm 133 • **Optional Reading:** Psalms 134—138

Jeremy's dad shouted at his mother, "I don't care what we need. I wanted that money."

Jeremy's mother stood in a corner of their little kitchen, cowering. "Please get control of yourself, Bill!"

Jeremy lay in bed in his room, scared. His dad was in a mood again, and he guessed that his mom had spent too much of the little money they had. It seemed Mom and Dad always screamed about money.

That night, Jeremy prayed for the hundredth time about the situation in his family. God gave him an idea and the next day he went to a friend's family. He told them everything. His friend's father came by the house one night and talked to Jeremy's father. They began spending time together. Over the course of a year, things began to change. Jeremy saw a change in his dad. One day, his dad went to church. In time, he also became a Christian, and things got much better.

Is there peace and quiet in your home these days? Talk to God and he will give you ideas to try. Talk to a counselor or a friend. Get your parents some real help. A home doesn't have to be this way, and with God's help it can change.

**Prayer:** Father, I pray that you would bring peace to my home today. Amen.

Week 22: Wednesday

# Wonderfully Complex

**Thank you for making me so wonderfully complex! Your workmanship is marvelous—and how well I know it.** Psalm 139:14

**Main Reading:** Psalm 139 • **Optional Reading:** Psalms 140—144

I bet you never thought of yourself that way. "You're wonderfully complex!" Not something a guy says to a girl, or a father to a son. "You're handsome." Or, "You're very smart." Or, "You are so good at sports." But, "You're wonderfully complex"? No way.

But it really is quite an incredible thing. Think of how God made you. Your eyes, your ears, your mouth. That you can form words when you talk. That you can taste the ginger in a ginger snap! Isn't that amazing?

What about the way you swing a bat? Or how you can sew a perfect seam in a new dress? Aren't these skills that make you "wonderful" in others' eyes?

How about your heart? Your lungs? Your kidneys? How they all work together so well, and keep you in good health? Who made all that happen? It just didn't come about by coincidence, did it?

God has made you "wonderfully complex." That means you're amazing, startling, stunning, beautiful, perfect. Even if you have a disability, even if you're not good at some things, that doesn't diminish it. God made you the way you are for a purpose, and that's the most beautiful part of it. God was very careful when he made you. Everything came together just like he wanted.

Isn't it time to thank him for you?

**Prayer:** Jesus, praise you for making me the way you did. I like it. Amen.

# I Will Meditate

**I will meditate on your majestic, glorious splendor and your wonderful miracles.** Psalm 145:5

**MAIN READING:** Psalm 145 • **OPTIONAL READING:** Psalms 146—150

Do you ever sit down and think of all the great things God has done in your life?

You may not have seen a miracle, like a person who is blind regaining his sight, or a disabled man being able to walk. But there are miracles all around you. God made them happen. What are they?

Think of the sun. It rises every day. It warms the earth. It makes the flowers and fruits grow and gives us the seasons. Without the sun, we would be little more than a cold speck of mud.

Think of your backyard. What adventures are out there? A dog? A cat? A neighbor friend? A garden? A swing set? A trampoline? Do you know that God planned for you to have these kinds of things from the very beginning? He planned for you to live right where you are and have the family you have before he ever made the earth.

Finally, think of your friends. People like you. Some would give their lives for you, or their kidney, or heart, if you needed it. There is no one like you, and no one like any of your friends. They're all unique, God's gifts to you.

No wonder the psalmist said to meditate on these things. We need to look at life as a gift of God.

**PRAYER:** Lord, thank you for giving me life. I want to live it for you. Amen.

# Get Taught How to Live

**Don't be impressed with your own wisdom. Instead, fear the Lord and turn your back on evil. Then you will gain renewed health and vitality.**
Proverbs 3:7, 8

**MAIN READING:** Proverbs 3 • **OPTIONAL READING:** Proverbs 1, 2, 4

You know what I hated about church growing up? They always seemed to be telling me how I should live. I wanted to do things my way, but the church said, "Do it God's way." I wanted to go off and have fun, but the church said, "Listen to God and his Word." I wanted to make friends with some of the bad guys. The church said, "Be careful what friends you make. They could lead you astray."

At the time, I didn't like it. But after I became a Christian I saw the wisdom of learning right from wrong. I learned what was wise and what was foolish. I found out how to live right and how to avoid evil.

We all like to do things our way much of the time. Many times, that's fine. But many other things—honesty, gentleness, truthfulness, friendship—have rules that are meant to help us not make big mistakes.

Going to church helped. You may not like all the things they tell you at church to do or not do. But be careful that you don't stray from the truth. God gives us truth to keep us happy and healthy. He's not against fun. He's against sin.

**PRAYER:** Lord, let me begin to find in church the answers to the problems I have. In Jesus' name. Amen.

Week 22: Saturday

# A Lesson from the Ants

**Take a lesson from the ants, you lazybones. Learn from their ways and be wise! Even though they have no prince, governor, or ruler to make them work, they labor hard all summer, gathering food for the winter.** Proverbs 6:6-8

**MAIN READING:** Proverbs 6 • **OPTIONAL READING:** Proverbs 5, 7, 8

Do you ever think it might be good to be like an ant? King Solomon noticed these little insects and studied them. He saw that they worked in teams. He found out they plan their lives around the seasons. He discovered that they were right smart little creatures.

Would you like to be like an A-N-T?

A is for Active. Get active. Get out there doing something. Plant a garden. Put together a model. Play a game. Shoot some hoops. Do something for heaven's sake. Don't waste your time on foolish things—like watching too much television. Give your life to what really matters—building friendships and building the kingdom of God.

N is for Nurturing. Do you work with your family to help everyone get along and be happy? Do you do things for your mom, your dad, your brothers and sisters, to let them know you love them? Nurture good relationships. Nurture the people around you. That means building them up with encouragement and love.

T is for Trustworthy. Can people count on you? Do they know you will do what you say you will do?

ANTs are Active, Nurturing, and Trustworthy. Are you like that too?

**PRAYER:** Lord, teach me to build those qualities that make life fulfilling. Amen.

Week 22: Sunday

# Dishonesty Versus Right Living

**Ill-gotten gain has no lasting value, but right living can save your life.**
Proverbs 10:2

**MAIN READING:** Proverbs 10 • **OPTIONAL READING:** Proverbs 9, 11, 12

Julia saw the wallet lying open on the counter. Her mom had gone upstairs.

Looking into the wallet, she saw that her mother had plenty of $1 and $5 bills. Surely she wouldn't miss a couple of them.

Snatching two $1 bills, Julia slipped them into her pocket and then closed the wallet. It lay just like she found it.

What could she buy with $2? Not much, but maybe some fun. Play the video games down at the local hangout. Buy a couple of candy bars. Pay for some cheap earrings.

When her mom walked into the kitchen, Julia quickly sat down. "What's the matter?" her mother asked. "You look like you've seen a ghost."

"Nothing. Just worried about a test tomorrow." Did she look that guilty?

All afternoon Julia fretted about her crime. Would her mother see that some money was missing? Would she be caught? By nightfall, Julia was a nervous wreck. Was $2 worth this much trouble?

Did you know that God will speak to your heart about sin? He will convict you and talk to you about making it right. If you do nothing about it, he may even let you become miserable.

In the end, Julia confessed to her mom what she had done. She promised never to do it again. And suddenly she felt at peace. Yes, honesty had saved her life.

**PRAYER:** Jesus, help me to be honest, no matter how strong the temptation. Amen.

# Listen to Discipline

**A wise child accepts a parent's discipline; a young mocker refuses to listen.** Proverbs 13:1

**MAIN READING:** Proverbs 13 • **OPTIONAL READING:** Proverbs 14, 15

"Sammie, I'm grounding you because I love you."

I've heard that before, Sammie thought.

"You did a bad thing and there have to be consequences."

Why? Sammie wondered. Why can't you just forgive me?

"I do forgive you, but there is a price to be paid for that kind of behavior."

Why a price? Why not just yell at me? Does it have to be grounding?

"This hurts me more than it hurts you."

Yeah, right. Sammie turned his face to the bed as he lay alone in his room, thinking about all the things he was missing because he was grounded.

"I'm sorry I have to punish you, but it's necessary sometimes."

Through his frustration, Sammie thought, One day, when I'm a parent, I'll never ground my kid.

Ever have those thoughts while being disciplined? Has your mom or dad said similar words? Discipline is never fun, for kid or parent. But without it, for some reason, we never really learn. God had it right all along. We need discipline to get the message into our hearts and into our lives.

**PRAYER:** Lord, I don't want to be disciplined, but I'm glad my parents care enough to do it when it's necessary. Amen.

# Commit It to the Lord

**Commit your work to the Lord, and then your plans will succeed.**
Proverbs 16:3

**MAIN READING:** Proverbs 16 • **OPTIONAL READING:** Proverbs 17, 18

First, I'm gonna get a paper route," Alison told her mom. "And then I'm going to give a tenth of everything I earn to the Lord."

"Sounds like a great idea to me," Alison's mom commented. "But maybe you should commit it all to the Lord first."

What did the Lord have to do with it? Alison wondered. It was just a paper route. She'd use the money to make her room look nice. She'd buy great dolls for her doll collection. And nice stationery to write notes to friends on.

"I like your idea," her mom answered. "But first let's just talk to the Lord about it."

Talk, talk, talk! Alison mused. We need action. "And then I'm gonna . . ."

Great plans. Do you ever have them? You sit on your bed and think. You see all these great things in your mind. You've got it all laid out.

And then—poof! It's all gone as you go downstairs to make a peanut butter and jelly sandwich.

How do you gain success with all your grand plans? You commit each plan to the Lord first. That means you invite God to be part of it. You ask God if this is what he wants for you. You allow God to shape it and guide it so that you become a player in his hands.

That way you will have success with the plans you have.

**PRAYER:** Father, let me always remember to put my plans in your hands. First! Amen.

Week 23: Wednesday

# Don't Go Too Fast

**Zeal without knowledge is not good; a person who moves too quickly may go the wrong way.** Proverbs 19:2

**Main Reading:** Proverbs 19 • **Optional Reading:** Proverbs 20, 21

Don't throw caution to the wind," says one old proverb.

This verse from Proverbs 19:2 gives us the same idea. When it says, "zeal without knowledge," it's talking about the passion of finding something new. You've got an idea. A subject for a paper. A little invention. A new play for the ball team. You go out there and start telling everyone about it. And then someone says, "But that won't work. You can't do . . ."

And you're feeling a little humiliated. What is the solution to the passion of the moment? "Knowledge." Think it through. Look at possible objections. Figure out the negatives of your great positive idea.

The proverb continues on that the person who moves too quickly may go the wrong way. Sometimes a little "intelligence" in the army sense is necessary. Check out the terrain. Study where you want to go. If you have the right information, you can succeed. But without it, you will surely fail.

Caution. It's a spiritual attitude. You're careful. You look to the Lord for help and direction. You proceed carefully. And in the end, you succeed.

**Prayer:** Jesus, help me to be careful when I work on a new project. Amen.

Week 23: Thursday

# Filled with Foolishness

**A youngster's heart is filled with foolishness, but discipline will drive it away.** Proverbs: 22:15

**MAIN READING:** Proverbs 22 • **OPTIONAL READING:** Proverbs 23, 24

"I'm better than you are—bleah!"

"You are such a dope."

"Let's see who can throw a rock the farthest."

"I bet I can burp louder than you."

Ever been in one of those conversations? If you're like me, you probably have. I remember many a spitting contest when I was a kid.

But a lot of it is foolishness.

Worse is when you get involved in doing bad things. The Bible calls sin and evil "foolishness" in some verses. It's foolish because it's worthless and it hurts other people.

How can you avoid foolishness? By accepting the discipline of your mom and dad when you do something that they say is foolish. When we're disciplined, we learn quickly. We also learn not to do the same thing again.

Respect your parents' attempts at disciplining you. Even if you don't like the discipline, even if it hurts sometimes, it's to help you become a better person. Sometimes our hearts are full of foolish ideas. But godly discipline will take it out of our hearts. In its place we will find wisdom.

**PRAYER:** Lord, praise you for giving me parents who care. Thank you. Amen.

Week 23: Friday

# Don't Take the Best Places

**Don't demand an audience with the king or push for a place among the great. It is better to wait for an invitation than to be sent to the end of the line, publicly disgraced!** Proverbs 25:6, 7

**MAIN READING:** Proverbs 25 • **OPTIONAL READING:** Proverbs 26, 27

"What're you doing sitting here, Jared?" Louie asked his friend. "You're supposed to be sitting over there, by Rick."

"But this is the best seat," Jared complained. "That's why I saved it for Barrie. Now get out!"

Has that ever happened to you? You have to slink off, your tail between your legs, because you tried to take a seat saved for someone else.

Solomon saw a good solution to the problem. Don't try to hog the best seats—at birthday parties, at ball games, at special events. Sit somewhere that maybe no one else wants. Then, when the host notices you there, he can call you up to a better spot.

Sometimes people refer to it as "don't toot your own horn." It means, don't try and make like you're more important than you are. Let others talk about your great achievements. Let others praise you. Then, when people hear it, they're more apt to receive it.

**PRAYER:** Lord, teach me to be humble and not always put myself first. In Jesus' name. Amen.

Week 23: Saturday

# Bold as Lions

**The wicked run away when no one is chasing them, but the godly are as bold as lions.** Proverbs 28:1

**Main Reading:** Proverbs 28 • **Optional Reading:** Proverbs 29

Are you bold? Are you willing to step in, speak up and say what you believe without flinching?

Boldness is an important quality in the Bible. Bold people get things done. They witness to others. They start projects and see them through. They give their opinion when it's needed. They're not afraid of what others think.

Why are they this way? For one reason: they're godly, like the verse in Proverbs 28:1 says. What does godly mean? It means "like God." It's a statement about character. When we say someone is godly, we usually mean he's like Jesus—honest, friendly, kind, daring, bold.

Do you want to be a godly person? There's only one way to become that way: learn from Jesus. Take him into everything you do. Invite him to be part of any project you start. Make sure when you start something new, he's involved. For instance, a godly person won't go into certain kinds of movies because he knows Jesus wouldn't attend them. She doesn't use certain words—cuss words—because she knows Jesus wouldn't use them. He never acts dishonestly.

If you want to be bold—tough, strong, fearless—then let Jesus work in you. He will shape you into a godly person who will go anywhere, do anything for the kingdom of God.

**Prayer:** Lord, make me more bold so that I can serve you wherever I am. Amen.

Week 23: Sunday

# Defend the Poor

**Speak up for those who cannot speak for themselves; ensure justice for those who are perishing.** Proverbs 31:8

**Main Reading:** Proverbs 31 • **Optional Reading:** Proverbs 30

"What I think Ruth is trying to say is that she doesn't want you guys pushing her around anymore," Bethanne said to the two girls. They had made life miserable for Ruth by picking on her and putting her down. Ruth wasn't the type who would fight back. She didn't know how to deal with mean people. As a result, mean people often knocked her around.

"Who are you?" one of the girls asked. "Her bodyguard?"

"No, I'm just a friend," Bethanne answered. "Stop treating her badly, or you have to answer to me."

"Oh, I'm really scared," the other girl said, glowering. "What will you do—beat us up?"

"Listen," Bethanne said, "I'm not very big. But I have a big sister who plays lacrosse. She bangs people around all the time. Stop pushing Ruth around, or I'll get my big sister involved."

The two shook their heads with disgust, but then they walked away. They both knew about Bethanne's big sister.

Speaking up for defenseless people is part of what it means to be a Christian. Help the poor. Encourage the weak. Warn the mean and unruly. You don't have to be a superhero to help someone in need. All you need to do is speak up.

**Prayer:** Jesus, may I always be willing to help hurting people. Amen.

Week 24: Monday

# Meaning in Life

**I also tried to find meaning by building huge homes for myself and by planting beautiful vineyards.** Ecclesiastes 2:4

**Main Reading:** Ecclesiastes 2

**Optional Reading:** Ecclesiastes 1, 3, 4

Where do you find fulfillment in life? When does your life start to mean something? What can you do to have an impact on your friends, your family, your church?

Many young people don't even consider these questions. It's just school, home, church, and play—different activities, but nothing incredible. Some kids find great fulfillment in hitting a home run, cooking a great meal, helping Dad work on the car. King Solomon, though, struggled with real meaning. When does your life start to count for something?

He tried pleasure—drinking until he was drunk and seeing lots of women. He tried building great monuments to himself—gardens, vineyards, a temple, a palace. He built up his army. He read books and grew in wisdom and knowledge. None of it satisfied for long.

In the end, Solomon came to one conclusion: there is only one thing that makes life meaningful—faith in God and doing what he wants you to do.

Solomon found out the truth about life. How about you? Where are you finding your real satisfaction in life?

**Prayer:** Jesus, help me to find my greatest joy in life in you. Amen.

# Ears Open, Mouth Shut

**As you enter the house of God, keep your ears open and your mouth shut! Don't be a fool who doesn't realize that mindless offerings to God are evil.** Ecclesiastes 5:1

**MAIN READING:** Ecclesiastes 5

**OPTIONAL READING:** Ecclesiastes 6—8

Ali chattered away as she and her friends stepped into the worship center of her church.

"Shhhh!" someone said. Ali ignored her.

"Oh, and what about Brian? He's cute, isn't he?" Ali was saying.

"We'd better be quiet," one of Ali's friends said. "We're in church now."

Sometimes you can walk into church and act like it's no different from anything else. But it is different. You come to worship God. You are there to meet with him and learn from him. Being quiet is a good idea. Close your mouth and open your ears.

Beware of talking too much in church. Beware of chatting when the minister is preaching, or the music team is singing. God is not easily offended. But to regard him the same as everything else is offensive. God is the creator. He's ruler of the universe. You don't come before him as if he were one of the kids down at the video store.

Saying something to God, making him a promise, or asking him for something is also serious business. God doesn't take it lightly. He answers every prayer, even dumb ones. He's listening to you when you come into church. Are you listening to him?

**PRAYER:** Father, teach me true reverence in all I do! Amen.

# Do It Well

**Whatever you do, do well. For when you go to the grave, there will be no work or planning or knowledge or wisdom.** Ecclesiastes 9:10

**Main Reading:** Ecclesiastes 9

**Optional Reading:** Ecclesiastes 10—12

Matt pushed the lawn mower along, his mind spinning with fury. Why did he have to do this now when his friends were getting together a ball game? Who cared if the lawn was done anyway? No one noticed.

He jerked the lawn mower back and forth around the garden beds. Spots of grass stuck up in places. By the edges, he missed several tufts. But who cared? What did it matter? No one would notice.

He wheeled the machine into the backyard and began there. Again he missed places. Again, his thoughts seethed with anger.

When he was done, he ran off to play with his friends, leaving the lawn mower in the middle of the yard. When his dad arrived home, he called Matt and walked him through the yard. "You missed there and there. That needs a little edging. You'll have to do some clipping there."

Matt complained, "Dad, what is the big deal? It's just a lawn."

His father stared at him. "And when you become an adult and you have a family and a job, what will you say? 'What's the big deal? It's only a job. It's only my wife. It's only my kids.'"

Matt hung his head. His father said, "Whatever you do, do it well. Then God is pleased. That's all that matters. Because if God is pleased, so am I."

**Prayer:** Lord, help me always to do the best I can, even when I don't want to. Amen.

Week 24: Thursday

# Mine Forever

**My lover is mine, and I am his.** Song of Songs 2:16

**Main Reading:** Song of Songs 2

**Optional Reading:** Song of Songs 1, 3, 4

Have you ever thought that you belong to Jesus? And that he belongs to you?

We are united with Jesus in a very special way. Not just friends, not just disciples, Jesus has made us part of his body. He owns us, and we own him.

That may sound a little strange, but it's true. Jesus' commitment to each of us is not just a piece of paper. It's not just words. No, Jesus is responsible to God the Father for us. He answers to God about what we do with our lives. He must report to God the Father about how we're progressing, what we're learning. Jesus is so committed to you that he died for you. He will never let you go.

Have you ever worried that Jesus could become so sick and tired of you that he'd drum you right out of the church? Have you ever thought that Jesus could change his mind about you?

He never could. Because you're part of him. For him to disown you would be like cutting out his heart. He couldn't do it.

"Jesus is mine and I am his," Solomon might have said in the Song of Songs. It's true of a wife or husband, and it's true of a Christian with the Lord. Jesus will keep you close, if you let him. He will never let you go.

**Prayer:** Lord, I praise you that I'm safe with you. Forever. Amen.

Week 24: Friday

# Drink Deeply of His Love

**Oh, lover and beloved, eat and drink! Yes, drink deeply of this love!**
Song of Songs 5:1

**MAIN READING:** Song of Songs 5
**OPTIONAL READING:** Song of Songs 6—8

Do you ever savor something someone said to you? Like a grandfather might say, "I love the way you are a good friend to those you love." Or a mom, "You look so beautiful today."

What do we do with such encouraging words? If you're like me, you repeat them in your mind. You think about them all day. You turn them over and over, enjoying them again and again.

When Solomon told his lover to "drink deeply of this love," that was what he was talking about. Savor the words Jesus has spoken in Scripture. Let them turn over and over in your head. Like, "The Lord is my shepherd." Or, "I will never leave you or forsake you." Those are great words. When we drink them in and let them color our thoughts and our hearts, we are drinking of his love. We let his words sink deep down into our souls so that we learn to love them.

Are you thirsty? Are you drinking of God's love for you? Do you let his words sink in deep? Do you let them swirl around in your mouth like a spoonful of ice cream?

God wants to shower you with his love. He wants to make you feel like you matter to him. Because you do!

---

**PRAYER:** Lord, may I always drink your love deeply. In Jesus' name. Amen.

# Talk About That Sin

**"Come now, let us argue this out," says the Lord. "No matter how deep the stain of your sins, I can remove it. I can make you as clean as freshly fallen snow. Even if you are stained as red as crimson, I can make you as white as wool."** Isaiah 1:18

**MAIN READING:** Isaiah 1 • **OPTIONAL READING:** Isaiah 2—4

Angel refused to talk about it. She had lied to her mother. Now she lay on her bed, crying. She just wanted to disappear.

Her mom stepped into her room. "Angel, let's talk about this. I don't want to punish you if I don't have to. I want to forgive you and be done with it. Just tell me why you lied."

Angel buried her head in her pillow. "I don't want to talk about it!" she cried into the pillow.

Her mom set her hand on Angel's shoulder. "If you don't talk it out, it'll fester inside you like a wound. You won't feel any real happiness till you've dealt with it."

Angel lay very still, then sat up. "I'm sorry. I was afraid you'd be mad, so I lied."

"Honey, you never need to be afraid to tell the truth to me. I'll always understand."

Finally, the story spilled out. One of her friends threw a party and Angel wanted to go. But it was Saturday night, a time when church held youth group. When her parents went out for dinner, Angel snuck out to the party.

As the truth came out, the pressure inside her went away. Soon she felt much better. Her sin truly was removed, like God had said it would be.

**PRAYER:** Lord, may I always be willing to come to you to talk about my sins. Amen.

Week 24: Sunday

# God Is Holy

**Holy, holy, holy is the Lord Almighty! The whole earth is filled with his glory!** Isaiah 6:3

**Main Reading:** Isaiah 6 • **Optional Reading:** Isaiah 5, 7, 8

Imagine the moment. Several majestic creatures—seraphim—stand around God's throne, fluttering their six wings. They are all crying out, "Holy, holy, holy is the Lord Almighty!"

All the angels stand before the throne in awe. God is great. God is all-powerful. God is the greatest of all.

Why did the seraphim say "holy" three times? Why not just once? There is no other characteristic of God, even love, that is spoken three times in Scripture. Why holy?

Perhaps they wanted to emphasize the importance of this trait. God is holy, utterly separated and removed from evil. He can't even want to sin, let alone do sin.

Perhaps the creatures speak the word three times because God, though one essence, appears as three persons. "Holy to the Father, Holy to the Son, and Holy to the Holy Spirit," might be what they meant.

They may also say it three times because it's God's greatest trait of all, not just important, but the one thing that makes him unique and utterly perfect.

God's holiness is a great truth. It means he would never sin against you, never change his mind about you, never ask you to do something wrong. We can hide in God's holiness, for it protects us from all evil.

**Prayer:** Lord, I thank you that you are holy, holy, holy. I trust in your holiness to protect me from myself forever. Amen.

# A Child Is Born to Us

**For a child is born to us, a son is given to us. And the government will rest on his shoulders. These will be his royal titles: Wonderful Counselor, Mighty God, Everlasting Father, Prince of Peace.**
Isaiah 9:6

**MAIN READING:** Isaiah 9 • **OPTIONAL READING:** Isaiah 10—12

Who is Jesus?

You know the answer. "Why he's the Savior of the world. He's the Lord of lords and King of kings. He's the Son of God."

True, but a little different slant registers in Isaiah 9:6, the verse for today. Here we see four aspects of Jesus' character.

He's the Wonderful Counselor. Like a mentor or friend, Jesus gives us the "out of this world" counsel that helps us in tough situations. His advice always rings with truth. It always helps. It always gives us the power to endure.

He's the Mighty God. That's "Almighty." He can do anything. No problem worries him. No tough spot throws him. He always knows how to handle everything.

He's the Everlasting Father. He'll be around forever. He never changes, never grows old, never gets tired. Like a good father, he is tender, compassionate, loving.

He's the Prince of Peace. He brings peace to any situation we'll let him into. He gives us peace in the depths of our hearts. He offers us peace in our relationships, if we'll only trust him.

**PRAYER:** Jesus, may I always trust in your counsel, leadership, and friendship. Amen.

Week 25: Tuesday

# I Will Punish

**I, the Lord, will punish the world for its evil and the wicked for their sin. I will crush the arrogance of the proud and the haughtiness of the mighty.** Isaiah 13:11

**MAIN READING:** Isaiah 13 • **OPTIONAL READING:** Isaiah 14—16

"What's the matter, Brian?" James asked his friend.

"Oh, things are going bad again," Brian said.

James knew Brian had much trouble at home with an alcoholic father.

"What kind of things?"

"Joe Crumb is threatening to beat on me again. I wish he'd just go away."

"I'll help you, if I can. But maybe we ought to pray about it first."

Brian agreed, but said, "You pray, I don't know how."

James prayed for his friend and hoped for the best.

Do you ever feel like your enemies are closing in? They'll hurt you or mess you up in some way and you can't do a thing about it?

Be patient. One day, God will deal with the evil of the whole world. Everyone who does evil things will be punished. None will escape.

It's a great idea until you realize that if you don't believe in Jesus, you'll be one of the ones who is punished. Have you trusted Jesus? Do you believe? Make it firm today if you haven't before. It's a matter of your eternity.

**PRAYER:** Father, I trust that you will deal with all evil people at the end. Amen.

Week 25: Wednesday

# God Fears No One

**Look! The armies rush forward like waves thundering toward the shore. But though they roar like breakers on a beach, God will silence them. They will flee like chaff scattered by the wind or like dust whirling before a storm.** Isaiah 17:12, 13

**MAIN READING:** Isaiah 17 • **OPTIONAL READING:** Isaiah 18—20

Is God ever afraid? Does he ever look down at the armies of Earth—with their tanks and their machine guns and their missiles—and cringe in fear?

Never! God is so powerful that if he speaks one little word, those armies will run. No one can stand up to him. He is the greatest of all.

What does this mean for me? It means you never have to be afraid, either, if you're on God's side. God is with you. God stands with you. He is by your side always, and will go before you to pave the way. He's the biggest guy on the block, and no one can stand up to him.

Whenever you are afraid, turn to a verse like the one for today. Remember that God is the most powerful person of all. He can help you through any difficulty. He will win over any enemy. It might appear at times that he hasn't helped, that you've lost the battle. But God is always there. Sometimes he lets the enemy gain some ground for a certain purpose. But in the end, if we trust him, he will see us through. He will never allow his child to be destroyed.

**PRAYER:** Jesus, I trust that you will be there whenever I face trouble. Amen.

# Fallen Angels Punished

**In that day the Lord will punish the fallen angels in the heavens and the proud rulers of the nations on earth.** Isaiah 24:21

**MAIN READING:** Isaiah 24 • **OPTIONAL READING:** Isaiah 21—23

Have you ever had these thoughts when you stand in the store looking at game CDs, or DVDs, or something else you might purchase?

"Why don't you go to the checkout desk? When the checkout person isn't looking, swipe the CD over the magnetizer. Then you can walk out with it."

Or, "Just stick it under your jacket. No one will notice."

Or, "Watch how they check you out. Then figure out a way to do the same thing yourself."

Thoughts like that come to all of us at one time or another. Where are they from? I have no doubt they're from the forces of darkness. These are demons, tempters, fallen angels who want to trip us up. They will suggest many evil things to you. Lie. Cheat. Steal. Hate. Cuss. Hit. Hurt others. It can be any of a multitude of things. They will taunt you. They will put you down if you don't do what they say.

Watch out. These beings are trying to destroy you. But guess what? A day is coming, according to today's verse, when all those beings will be judged.

God has let evil beings live right now for his own reasons. But one day, they will be judged, never more to tease or taunt or tempt.

**PRAYER:** Lord, thank you for watching over me and protecting me from evil angels. Amen.

Week 25: Friday

# Perfect Peace

**You will keep in perfect peace all who trust in you, whose thoughts are fixed on you!** Isaiah 26:3

**MAIN READING:** Isaiah 26 • **OPTIONAL READING:** Isaiah 25, 27, 28

Erin read today's verse with great interest. "Perfect peace." What is that?

You know what perfect peace is not. You turn fearful, crazy, angry thoughts over and over in your mind. You let them make you feel bad things—hatred, rage, inferiority. Thoughts like . . .

When you do poorly on a test: "You are such a fool. I don't think anyone is as stupid as you."

When you strike out in an important baseball game: "You are the worst player on the team. Go home and don't show your face again."

When you ask a question and everyone turns around to look at you like you're the dumbest person in the world. "Who doesn't know the answer to that one? What's wrong with you?"

God can tame those thoughts for you. He can rid you of them, if you ask him. Call out to him and ask him for his perfect peace. But God won't just zap you with it. Memorize his Word and think about that. That's a sure way to get his peace into your heart. Think about the great things of God. Thank him for his blessings.

Soon, your mind won't be shouting those horrible things. It will be silenced by God's perfect peace.

**PRAYER:** Lord, put your perfect peace in me so I can live in joy. In Jesus' name. Amen.

# Lip Honor

**These people say they are mine. They honor me with their lips, but their hearts are far away. And their worship of me amounts to nothing more than human laws learned by rote.** Isaiah 29:13

**Main Reading:** Isaiah 29 • **Optional Reading:** Isaiah 30—32

Doug muttered the words as the rest of the congregation sang. "Amazing grace, how sweet the sound . . ." It wasn't very sweet to Doug. He was bored and wanted to get home to play video games.

The pastor's prayer was even worse. Did the guy ever end? Why did he just go on and on? When the prayer was finished, Doug said, "Amen," like everyone else, but it was just a knee-jerk reaction. He felt nothing.

The sermon, though, that was the kicker. Man, could that pastor go on. Why didn't he just say it and be done with it? Why did he have to say it and say it and say it again?

The service finally ended and Doug blew a sigh of relief.

Worship is a time to focus on God. But many people, like Doug, find it boring and meaningless. Worship is not a time to be entertained. It's when we meet with God and he speaks to us. But too many people treat worship just like today's verse says—honoring God "with their lips, but their hearts are far away."

Is that you? Are you giving God lip service, but no real worship? Make an adjustment. God is not pleased when we just go through the motions.

**Prayer:** Father, teach me not to give lip service, but to give lip praise. Amen.

Week 25: Sunday

# The Coming Day

**The lame will leap like a deer, and those who cannot speak will shout and sing! Springs will gush forth in the wilderness, and streams will water the desert.** Isaiah 35:6

**Main Reading:** Isaiah 35 • **Optional Reading:** Isaiah 33, 34, 36

The day is coming. Every hurting person will be comforted. Every dying soul will find new life. Every person committed to Christ will leap and sing and shout for joy. Jesus will come back! We will live in a God-honoring, righteous place where evil will never come again.

Isaiah 35 is a perfect chapter to remind us of what God's going to do. Flowers will grow in the desert. No one will ever be tired again. All will rejoice. All will praise. All will lift their voices in thanksgiving to God.

Do you look forward to that day? Do you hope it will come soon?

Why not pray today, "Lord, please come quickly. Save us out of this world. Don't wait for a better day. Come today, if possible. I will wait for you and long for you all my days. You are my Lord and my friend. I want to be with you forever!"

**Prayer:** Jesus, praise you that you are coming again. I look forward to it. Amen.

# Healing

**Think of it—the Lord has healed me! I will sing his praises with instruments every day of my life.** Isaiah 38:20

**Main Reading:** Isaiah 38 • **Optional Reading:** Isaiah 37, 39

More than any other prayer request, the main thing we pray about nowadays is for healing. For relatives. For friends. For ourselves.

Sometimes it seems that God rarely answers this prayer. Sometimes Christians stricken with cancer never get well. Occasionally, friends with burns, heart attacks, or other ailments never recover. In other situations, people remain disabled, or broken for the rest of their days.

Doesn't God care?

Actually, when you think about it, God heals many more times than he doesn't. Think of all the times in your life you became sick. God healed you all those times, didn't he?

Other times, people are healed and we simply forget the circumstances. It's the ones who aren't healed whom we think about.

But God can't be put into a box. Many times he doesn't heal because of reasons only he has. The important thing is that, as Christians, we are healed from sin. We will live with him forever, never to die again. That's the real healing for all of us, and the one he never refuses.

---

**Prayer:** Jesus, bring your healing when possible, and if not, bring a heart of thanks. Amen.

# Mount Up with Wings Like Eagles

**But those who wait on the Lord will find new strength. They will fly high on wings like eagles. They will run and not grow weary. They will walk and not faint.** Isaiah 40:31

**Main Reading:** Isaiah 40 • **Optional Reading:** Isaiah 41—43

John Wesley, an evangelist of the 17th century, preached over 40,000 sermons in his long life. He rode over 250,000 miles on horseback visiting people to preach to.

Dwight Moody, a preacher of the 19th century, spoke to millions about Jesus. He is said to have led over a million souls to the Lord.

Billy Graham is the greatest of them all. He has preached to millions, if not billions of people. Countless numbers have accepted Jesus through his witness.

What strengthens these men? What gives power to any of us?

It's God. These verses in Isaiah 40 point out the source of power. God gives those who wait on him the strength to mount up with wings like eagles. God is the source. He gives the ability, the words, and the wisdom to build his kingdom.

Do you ever feel weak? Maybe you need rest. Maybe you need a good night's sleep. Or maybe you need power from God.

Call out to him and he will give it. He never turns away from his beloved children.

**Prayer:** Father, give me your power. Make me mount up like an eagle for you. Amen.

Week 26: Wednesday

# Swept Away Your Sins

**I have swept away your sins like the morning mists. I have scattered your offenses like the clouds.** Isaiah 44:22

**MAIN READING:** Isaiah 44 • **OPTIONAL READING:** Isaiah 45—47

Josh stood before the minister. He hadn't wanted to do it. But his friends talked him into it. Drugs. Marijuana. He'd tried it. He'd gotten high. But he didn't feel good about it. He felt filthy inside.

"What do I do?" he asked his minister.

"Ask for God's forgiveness, repent, and don't do it again. It's that simple," the kind man said.

"But won't God make me pay somehow?" Josh asked. "Won't he punish me?"

"There are consequences for sin, yes," the minister said. "But many times, God simply overrides them. The important thing is to get it right with the Lord now."

Josh nodded. "Can you help me?"

"Sure, let's pray."

The minister led Josh in a straightforward prayer for forgiveness. He helped Josh to ask for God's strength and new resolve not to give in to the temptation again. Josh suddenly realized how blessed he was. He had a God who cared. He had a Lord who would not hold it against him. He had a friend in Jesus who would stand with him no matter what.

"I feel free," Josh said when they were finished.

"That's what God does best—setting people free," the minister said.

**PRAYER:** Lord, I want to be set free from sin. Forgive me, for all of it. Amen.

Week 26: Thursday

# Your Name on My Hand

**See, I have written your name on my hand.** Isaiah 49:16

**MAIN READING:** Isaiah 49 • **OPTIONAL READING:** Isaiah 48, 50, 51

Does your grandmother have your picture in her wallet? Does your dad or mom carry that school photo with them always? Are you a little embarrassed when they take it out to show to friends and acquaintances?

But wouldn't you be sad if they didn't care? If they didn't have anything from you as a reminder that you belong to them?

God has a wallet too. Not a real wallet, but a collection he keeps for ready reference. When angels ask him about you, God holds up his hand. Your name is written on it. Your name, in blazing letters of fire, shines on his palm. It's a big palm too. Big enough for every name of every Christian of all time.

Your name is written on God's hand. Did you know that? It really is. God is proud to show others that you belong to him. Every time he shakes a hand, or gestures with his hand to his angels, they see your name. You are special to God in that way.

Did you know God is proud to be your friend, your Lord, your God? Did you know God's chest puffs up with joy when he speaks about you to others? You are in his thoughts every minute of every day. Just like your mom or dad, or your grandparents. God feels about you like your parents do about you—only bigger!

**PRAYER:** Lord, thank you that I'm always in your thoughts. Amen.

Week 26: Friday

# God Laid the Guilt on Him

**All of us have strayed away like sheep. We have left God's paths to follow our own. Yet the Lord laid on him the guilt and sins of us all.**
Isaiah 53:6

**Main Reading:** Isaiah 53 • **Optional Reading:** Isaiah 51, 52, 54

Try to imagine the ceremony. A young Jewish man named Elkanah has sinned against his parents. He knows he has to make it right before God.

He goes to the flock and purchases a lamb. He grabs his donkey and, with a tether to the lamb's head, he leads the animal to Jerusalem. The journey is long. He passes many worshipers on the way, others going to the temple to sacrifice animals because of their sins.

After several days, he arrives in Jerusalem. He leads the lamb to the temple. There he stands in line with many other people holding lambs, doves, bulls, and other animals. Soon it is his turn. The priest takes the lamb. By now Elkanah has grown fond of the lamb. It prances about and baas when he brings it feed. He has spent hours playing with it. The priest knows nothing of this.

Elkanah tells the priest his sin. Then he sets his hand on the lamb's head. His sin is transferred to the lamb. The priest then kills the lamb and sets its body on the altar.

Elkanah goes home. He is forgiven. But at a price. In some ways, his heart is heavy. He liked that lamb. He even gave it a name: White-tail. But now it's gone, because he sinned.

God gave the Jews that ceremony to prepare them for the real Lamb: Jesus.

**Prayer:** Lord, thank you for sending Jesus to die for me. Amen.

Week 26: Saturday

# God's Thoughts

**"My thoughts are completely different from yours," says the Lord. "And my ways are far beyond anything you could imagine. For just as the heavens are higher than the earth, so are my ways higher than your ways and my thoughts higher than your thoughts."**
Isaiah 55:8, 9

**MAIN READING:** Isaiah 55 • **OPTIONAL READING:** Isaiah 56—58

What thoughts God must have!

He knows every person who has ever lived and lives now. He knows when they get up and when they go to sleep. He knows what they think about. He has counted the number of hairs on their head. He hears their prayers—all day.

He sees all that happens on our planet. He has seen the earthquakes, the tornadoes, the hurricanes. He sees the people huddled in their homes, hoping the storm will not destroy them. He hears their little cries.

God has witnessed every sin that was ever committed. He has heard all the excuses people make for their terrible deeds. He has watched souls slip into hell after death because they never trusted him. And he weeps for them. He has also ushered countless souls into his heaven.

What does God think about?

Everything, everyone, every which and where and why and how. His thoughts could never be contained in an encyclopedia. If they were written for one day, all the books in the world wouldn't be enough.

On top of all this, God thinks of you. Every second. Forever.

**PRAYER:** Father, praise you that you know me, and think of me always. Amen.

# Cut Off

**But there is a problem—your sins have cut you off from God. Because of your sin, he has turned away and will not listen anymore.** Isaiah 59:2

**Main Reading:** Isaiah 59 • **Optional Reading:** Isaiah 60—62

Do you ever look at the flowers your mom brings in from the garden?

Beautiful. Study the stem. It's cut off from the roots of the flower, isn't it? No nourishment can get through. It's dead.

Has your dad or an uncle ever pruned back the branches on a tree in his yard? Note that branch lying on the ground. Cleanly sawed off, maybe some wetness came through on the stump. That's water, or sap. Nourishment. But now it's cut off. It's dead and will never live again.

Have you ever known a person with an amputated limb?

Have you ever seen a fish lying out of the water, flopping around, unable to breathe?

These are things that have been "cut off." Their source of life is gone. They cannot survive.

In the same way, sin cuts us off from God. We cannot experience his Spirit, his life. We're dead. We may not feel that way. We may just feel empty, or sad, or unfulfilled. But that's what it means to be dead inside.

There's only one way to live again. Become reconnected to your source—God. Have you reconnected? Have you given yourself to him?

If not, why not do it today?

---

**Prayer:** Jesus, praise you that you are the source and hold back from no one. Amen.

Week 27: Monday

# Forgotten!

**Look! I am creating new heavens and a new earth—so wonderful that no one will even think about the old ones anymore.** Isaiah 65:17

**MAIN READING:** Isaiah 65 • **OPTIONAL READING:** Isaiah 63, 64, 66

"I don't want to go to heaven," Lucy said to her mom.

"Why?" her mother answered. "Why would you think such a thing?"

"I like it here on earth. I want to live here forever. I like oranges and apples and cheeseburgers. I like playing at the beach. I like my friends. I don't want to go to heaven."

"Darling," her mother said, "what makes you think those things won't be there? Do you think God would create such things and just let them disappear?"

"Well, no, but . . . I just hope it's not too different."

"Actually, it's going to be very different. But in a good way," her mom said. "God's going to do greater things than he's ever done before. The original things will probably be there. But all sorts of new, amazing things will be there too."

"Really?"

"Honey, heaven will be incredible. So incredible that you'll forget about anything you have down here. It will be so much better in comparison."

Do you ever worry about what heaven will be like? How it will be different from things now? You can stop! God plans to blow our socks off with the new one!

**PRAYER:** Jesus, I look forward to your new heaven and earth. It will be incredible. Amen.

# Too Young?

**"O Sovereign Lord," I said, "I can't speak for you! I'm too young!"**
Jeremiah 1:6

**MAIN READING:** Jeremiah 1 • **OPTIONAL READING:** Jeremiah 2—4

You're just a young kid. You don't know anything."

"Oh, listen to the kid—acting like he's seen everything in the world!"

"Hey, shut up and listen, kid. You don't know what you're talking about."

Ever hear those kinds of words from adults, parents, grandparents? If you're like I was, you probably hear it a lot. When you're young, just a kid, you don't know nearly as much as an adult. You don't have the experience. You haven't been to most places. You haven't even been married and had a family. How can you know anything?

That doesn't matter, though. If God wants you to speak up, speak up. Don't worry about what others say.

That's the problem Jeremiah had. In our verse for today, we see Jeremiah telling God he was too young and didn't know how to speak. God assured Jeremiah that he'd be with the young man. Then he could speak up wherever he was. He didn't have to hesitate ever again.

God loves you no matter how old you are. He will employ you in his kingdom work too. Never think you're too young to speak up for God. He uses many different kinds of people, and he surely wants to use you.

**PRAYER:** Father, let me never be afraid to speak up for you and your work. Amen.

# God Searching

**Lord, you are searching for honesty. You struck your people, but they paid no attention. You crushed them, but they refused to turn from sin.** Jeremiah 5:3

**Main Reading:** Jeremiah 5 • **Optional Reading:** Jeremiah 6—8

God searches the world. Did you know he's looking down at everyone and he's searching for a certain kind of person: an honest person.

Many people aren't honest. They tell lies. They hurt others. They cheat on tests. They say things they don't mean and which they know they shouldn't. It's amazing that God doesn't just turn away and go off on his own, never to look down upon us again.

But God is a God full of hope and expectation. He's always looking, watching, searching for people. He wants them to believe in him and follow him. He wants them to be the people of heaven. He wants honest people because he wants a heaven that is honest. No more lies. Everyone doing the right thing. Would you be amazed to see such a world?

It's coming. God's going to create a heaven and earth where honesty reigns. It will be a perfect place forever.

What does God see when he looks down at you? Does he see an honest person? Does he see someone who will make a good citizen of heaven?

It's up to you to be that kind of person. But trust the Lord—he'll work in you to make you that way if you ask.

**Prayer:** Lord, I want to be honest. Help me never to cheat anyone. Amen.

Week 27: Thursday

# Not Your Own

**I know, Lord, that a person's life is not his own. No one is able to plan his own course.** Jeremiah 10:23

**MAIN READING:** Jeremiah 10 • **OPTIONAL READING:** Jeremiah 9, 11, 12

It must have been awful to be a slave before the Civil War," Josie said to her friend, Cindy. "I can't imagine being whipped or something."

"What gets me," Cindy said, "is being owned by someone. Not to be able to do anything you wanted, but always having to do what they wanted. That doesn't sound like fun at all."

"That's what worries me about God," Josie answered. "We belong to him, too, don't we? He owns us, doesn't he?"

Have you ever thought about Christian faith that way—that God owns you? That you belong to him?

The difference between you and the slaves of America before the Civil War is that God is the perfect master. He never beats us. He never makes demands. He has made us part of his family. Yes, we belong to him, but in a good way. We're princes and princesses. We're part of a royal family, and we can never be taken out of it. God will lead us, but he won't force us to do what he wants. He longs that we do his will willingly and joyfully.

That's a big difference. God wants to fulfill you. And when you are fulfilled, he is fulfilled too. He is happy to see you succeed, with joy in your heart and love in your soul.

**PRAYER:** Lord, praise you that I belong to you and can never be taken away. Amen.

# No One Loves Me

**Then I said, "What sadness is mine, my mother. Oh, that I had died at birth! I am hated everywhere I go. I am neither a lender who has threatened to foreclose nor a borrower who refuses to pay—yet they all curse me."** Jeremiah 15:10

**MAIN READING:** Jeremiah 15 • **OPTIONAL READING:** Jeremiah 13, 14, 16

Joni lay on her bed, weeping. "What's wrong?" her sister Kellie asked.

"Nothing. Just go away."

"What happened? Tell me. I won't tell anyone."

For a second, Joni thought about it. Then she said, "Brad broke up with me today."

Joni wasn't allowed to date yet, but sometimes kids "went together" in school when they liked each other.

"Brad's a jerk," Kellie commented.

"You're right about that. But now no one likes me. Everyone hates me because of Brad," Joni said.

"I like you," Kellie said quietly.

Have you ever felt as if everyone hated you, no one cared about you? That's how Jeremiah felt, as the verse for today says. He was God's prophet. God sent him to warn Israel and help them become good people. But everyone hated him.

It was a sad day. But later, God did something that Jeremiah never forgot. God told him that, although his people hated him, God loved him.

That was enough.

**PRAYER:** Jesus, even if no one else ever loved me, I know you love me. Amen.

# Heartsick

**The human heart is most deceitful and desperately wicked. Who really knows how bad it is? But I know! I, the Lord, search all hearts and examine secret motives. I give all people their due rewards, according to what their actions deserve.** Jeremiah 17:9, 10

**MAIN READING:** Jeremiah 17 • **OPTIONAL READING:** Jeremiah 18—20

I'd like to really stomp Mike, Ned told himself. He's such a dope. Why do we have to be friends?

On the other side of the room, Mike glanced at Ned. He had similar thoughts. Ned is such an idiot, he heard his mind say. I hope he falls off his bike and breaks a bone!

All through class, the two ex-friends thought hateful things about each other.

It probably happens every day you're at school. Kids are jealous of each other. Young people hate and put down each other in their minds. Youth think awful things about others—their teaches, their families, even their friends.

Why is it like this inside our hearts? For one reason: sin has made our hearts sick. Look at the verses for today from Jeremiah 17:9, 10. They tell us the heart is sick, a liar, wicked. It thinks terrible things about decent people. It cusses on the inside. It shrieks evil ideas against everyone.

There is a way to overcome it, though: through Jesus. God knows our hearts and through Jesus he can clean them up and make them new.

**PRAYER:** Father, thank you for working in my heart. I praise you for your love. Amen.

Week 27: Sunday

# The Righteous Branch

**"For the time is coming," says the Lord, "when I will place a righteous Branch on King David's throne. He will be a King who rules with wisdom. He will do what is just and right throughout the land."**
Jeremiah 23:5

**MAIN READING:** Jeremiah 23 • **OPTIONAL READING:** Jeremiah 21, 22, 24

Do you ever wish our world was different? That hatred, racism, bigotry, and people putting down each other would end? Do you ever want a place to live that's warm and friendly, with no arguing, no yelling, no curses in the night?

All of us probably long for a new world. We know we're not sinless. We know we don't always do the right thing. But we wish for a world where everyone was sinless, where everyone did the right thing always.

Do you know what? God says such a world is coming. He will one day put Jesus on the throne of the world. We don't know exactly what this will involve, but he will rule righteously. He won't steal from the treasury. He won't take bribes from the rich people. He will lead us with perfect wisdom.

Do you want such a world to come? Then, pray, "Come, Lord Jesus." For only through him and with him can such a world ever be.

**PRAYER:** Jesus, I say come quickly. I want you to be my ruler. Amen.

Week 28: Monday

# There's Always Hope

**The Lord gave me every word that I have spoken. But if you stop your sinning and begin to obey the Lord your God, he will cancel this disaster that he has announced against you.** Jeremiah 26:12, 13

**Main Reading:** Jeremiah 26

**Optional Reading:** Jeremiah 25, 27, 28

The people of Israel sinned uncontrollably for years. Finally, God had had enough. He would punish them severely. Exile. Slavery. Abandonment. Through Jeremiah he warned the people that doom would descend upon them.

But in judgment, God feels the need to offer mercy. He may hate how we're leading our lives. He may be disgusted by what he sees us doing. But, though he knows punishment and discipline may be the only way to turn us around, he always offers mercy and grace. "Repent, all will be well. You will not be harmed!"

He did this same thing in the book of Jonah. When Jonah walked to the city of Nineveh and pronounced God's judgment against it, God remained merciful. The people repented, and God didn't destroy the city.

Like a loving, compassionate parent, God never enjoys disciplining his children. He wants them to thrive, to grow, to become righteous, godly people. But sometimes that is not possible. In such cases, he must discipline us. Even then, though, he offers mercy.

Are you in a disciplining time? Is God working on you because of your sin? Repent. Turn back. Do what's right. And God will stop the discipline.

**Prayer:** Jesus, may I always remember you are merciful. Amen.

Week 28: Tuesday

# God's Plans

**"For I know the plans I have for you," says the Lord. "They are plans for good and not for disaster, to give you a future and a hope."**
Jeremiah 29:11

**MAIN READING:** Jeremiah 29 • **OPTIONAL READING:** Jeremiah 30—32

God has a plan for your life.

It includes everything you will ever do. It takes into account your personality, your gifts, your dreams, and hopes. His purpose is to fulfill you as a person. God wants to make you the best you you can be. He longs to bless your life in ways that you would never want to miss. He plans to do good in your life, and not evil.

That doesn't mean his plan won't allow bad things to happen. It doesn't mean he will answer every prayer you ever have with a resounding yes. It doesn't mean you won't go through some hard things. It doesn't mean you aren't free and can't do what you really want to do. But it does mean that when your life ends, you will be able to look back and say, "God, you did all things well."

How do you connect with God's plan for your life? Just walk with God. Every day. Every hour. Pray to him. Talk to him. Learn from him. Let him work in your life. Let him lead you. He will lead you into what I often call the great adventure. The great adventure is the life God has planned for you.

Life is difficult at times. At other times, it's wonderful. God gives us each a wonderful mix of things in life that keeps it interesting. You will never be bored in the hands of God.

**PRAYER:** Father, let me enter into your plan for my life with delight and hope. Amen.

Week 28: Wednesday

# Ask Me

**Ask me and I will tell you some remarkable secrets about what is going to happen here.** Jeremiah 33:3

**MAIN READING:** Jeremiah 33 • **OPTIONAL READING:** Jeremiah 34—36

If you could ask God anything, what would you ask him?

"Why did you let my grandpa die?"

"Why did my dog run away?"

"Why did I strike out in that championship baseball game?"

"Why aren't all my prayers answered?"

These are questions all of us have at times. God promises in today's verse in Jeremiah that he will answer all such questions. Maybe not this minute. Maybe not even this year. But over time, God will answer all your questions. Some, he will wait till you're with him in heaven to answer. Others will wait until you're an adult.

But God's invitation is always the same. "Ask me and I will tell you." He wants you to know. To be informed. Not to be afraid. Not to be in the dark and worried about the future. God wants you to feel safe and secure in his grasp.

Every prayer you pray will someday be answered. Maybe not with a yes, but it will be answered. God keeps a running list. He never forgets one, even though you may have forgotten about it. Why? Because he loves you.

**PRAYER:** Lord, teach me never to hold back a question from you, because I know you will answer. Amen.

Week 28: Thursday

# Stuck in a Well

**So the officials took Jeremiah from his cell and lowered him by ropes into an empty cistern in the prison yard.** Jeremiah 38:6

**Main Reading:** Jeremiah 38 • **Optional Reading:** Jeremiah 37, 39, 40

Have you ever suffered?

Maybe you have faced a terrible disease in your life. Maybe you've been paralyzed or otherwise disabled. Maybe you've been hurt by your family or others.

All of us suffer at times. In today's verse, we see Jeremiah, one of God's greatest prophets, thrown into a well. He was imprisoned. It was damp down there, cold. Often he felt hungry. At times he thought he might die.

He had many questions too. He wondered why God had allowed this to happen to him. He cried out to God for help, and no help seemed to come. For days and days. Jeremiah wept so much, he nearly gave up.

But God remained with him. God never left his side. God never forgot about Jeremiah. Later, he sent people who would free him. God took care of Jeremiah, fed him, and made him feel safe again.

Bad things still happened, though. Jeremiah suffered deeply for his faith. His words to the king incited anger and hatred. But he continued to speak them. Because they were God's words.

You may suffer at times in this life. God does not say everything will always be perfect. But one thing you can be sure of: God is there with us. He suffers with us. And he will rescue us at the right time. Just like he did with Jeremiah.

**Prayer:** Lord, I don't like to suffer, but I know you will always be with me in it. Amen.

Week 28: Friday

# Show Us What to Do

**Please pray to the Lord your God for us. As you know, we are only a tiny remnant compared to what we were before. Beg the Lord your God to show us what to do and where to go.** Jeremiah 42:2, 3

**Main Reading:** Jeremiah 42 • **Optional Reading:** Jeremiah 41, 43, 44

The people had been destroyed. Multitudes were taken into slavery. All looked lost. Israel would never be a nation again.

Or would they?

When the people saw how great a disaster came upon the sinful leaders of Israel, they recognized their mistake. God was not to be toyed with. God could not be cheated, or lied to. He knew the truth, and he would punish when it was necessary.

But there is something anyone can do in the midst of such a situation: pray.

That's what the people asked Jeremiah to do: pray. Pray for the people. Pray for the nation. Ask God what he wanted them to do. Cry out to God for help and strength and mercy.

You know what? God heard. In 70 years, Israel would be returned to their land. They would come back to rebuild the temple under Ezra. They would fix the broken walls of Jerusalem under Nehemiah. Israel would return to greatness.

Prayer is power. Prayer opens the ear and heart of God. Pray today. Pray this minute. Pray all the time. Remember to pray in your darkest hour and your highest moment. Pray, for God hears, and he will help and answer.

**Prayer:** Jesus, I praise you that you always hear us, even when we cry out of trouble. Amen.

Week 28: Saturday

# Don't Be Discouraged

**But don't be discouraged. I will bring great disaster upon all these people, but I will protect you wherever you go. I, the Lord, have spoken!** Jeremiah 45:5

**MAIN READING:** Jeremiah 45 • **OPTIONAL READING:** Jeremiah 46—48

Baruch worked as Jeremiah's scribe. He wrote down Jeremiah's words on a scroll and delivered it to the king. Baruch was a good man. He stayed faithful. He never turned on his friend Jeremiah. He gave his best at all times.

What do you think Baruch thought when he saw the destruction come upon the people? Did he think he would be crushed with them?

Of course. What would you think? But God was faithful. He knew about Baruch, that he was a godly, committed believer. God knew where he was at all times and wanted to comfort him. So he gave Baruch some strong words through Jeremiah: "Don't be discouraged!"

It's so easy to be discouraged. Trouble looms on the horizon. The economy is bad. Your parents are worried about money. You have a tough teacher in school this year who never has any mercy. And your best friend just moved away to another state.

What do you do? Like he encouraged Baruch, God wants to encourage you. Don't be discouraged. God is still with you. He won't give up on you. He will guard you and lead you through this tough time. Be strong. Look to God, and he will answer in might and power.

**PRAYER:** Father, no matter how bad it gets, I will always trust you. Amen.

Week 28: Sunday

# Our Redeemer

**But the one who redeems them is strong. His name is the Lord Almighty. He will defend them and give them rest again in Israel.**
Jeremiah 50:34

**MAIN READING:** Jeremiah 50 • **OPTIONAL READING:** Jeremiah 49, 51, 52

Enemies on every side! Nowhere to go! Every turn is a trap, every road an ambush!

Ever feel like that? No matter where you look, the world looks dark and lost. The book of Jeremiah is a book full of darkness and despair. Bad things happened to Israel because of their sin. Events went against them. Powerful enemies conquered them. They put the people into slavery and wouldn't let go.

But never underestimate the power of God. In Jeremiah 50:34 we see God's answer to powerful enemies: "Your redeemer is strong." What is a redeemer? It's a person who pays for your freedom. It's like you are a slave, and a very rich man comes and buys you out of slavery, then sets you free.

That's exactly what Jesus did when he died on the cross. He bought us all out of our slavery to sin and set us free to obey him. He made us new people and gave us new hearts. Those new hearts want to honor and follow him.

Your redeemer is strong. No matter how dark the clouds around you, look to God. He will fight for you. He will get you out of trouble. He will redeem you so that you are truly free forever.

**PRAYER:** Jesus, thank you that you set me free. Amen.

Week 29: Monday

# Broken

**Lord, see my anguish! My heart is broken and my soul despairs.**
Lamentations 1:20

**MAIN READING:** Lamentations 1 • **OPTIONAL READING:** Lamentations 2

Do you ever feel like crying when you see a decent person doing something evil?

A father who drinks to excess and can't control it.

A friend who speaks abusive words, putting down others.

A schoolmate who has gotten involved in drugs or witchcraft.

People do dastardly things. Sometimes, when we see them acting in ways that are wrong, we weep. Why? Because we don't want to see them hurt. We don't wish that they destroy themselves. We long that they see success in their lives.

Jeremiah is often called the weeping prophet because he wept so much over Israel's sins. He saw destruction, terror, and pain on every side. All it did was make him weep more. Jeremiah felt pain when he saw his friends and neighbors destroy themselves. He didn't wish danger or pain on anyone.

Is that your heart? It's OK to weep about those you care for. But even more to weep for those you may not know who are hurting themselves or others.

God knows your heart. Pray for those who sin. Ask God to have mercy. And sometimes, weep. It's the only thing left to do when words fail.

**PRAYER:** Jesus, I weep for the souls of those who sin. Help them to repent. Amen.

# God's Faithfulness

**The unfailing love of the Lord never ends! By his mercies we have been kept from complete destruction. Great is his faithfulness; his mercies begin afresh each day.** Lamentations 3:22, 23

**Main Reading:** Lamentations 3 • **Optional Reading:** Lamentations 4, 5

Lamentations is one long lament. A lament is a long poem or song that expresses grief or sadness. Jeremiah lamented the way his people had gone. He wept for them going into slavery. And he felt pain that some of his closest friends had died.

But in the middle of this long poem, a ray of light shines. Jeremiah remembers that though the world is in trouble, though sin is rampant, there is much to rejoice about. God's goodness. God's greatness. His faithfulness to us even when we are unfaithful.

God is unique in all of human history. He remains loyal even when his people desert him. He hangs in there, even when we sin and curse him. He sticks with us, even when we act as if he doesn't exist.

Jeremiah saw that faithfulness of God, and he worshiped. God truly was worth serving and loving. He would be there for Jeremiah, and even the sinful people of Israel, no matter what. Anyone who cried out to him for mercy would get it. All who asked him for help would find him flying to their side.

God just can't stop loving us.

**Prayer:** Father, thank you that you are faithful even when I'm not. Amen.

# Fantastic Things

**From the center of the cloud came four living beings that looked human, except that each had four faces and two pairs of wings.**
Ezekiel 1:5

**MAIN READING:** Ezekiel 1 • **OPTIONAL READING:** Ezekiel 2—4

Ezekiel saw strange things. Marvelous beasts in the sky. Each had four faces and four wings. The creatures weaved back and forth. They went forward, then back, then to the side. They looked like spinning wheels inside of spinning wheels.

Was Ezekiel drunk? Was he high on drugs?

No, God pulled back the curtain of heaven and let Ezekiel see something no person has ever seen. Ezekiel witnessed the living creatures who hover over God in worship. They're called cherubim, and they're angelic creatures. Not all angels look human. Some are fantastic like these. And these cherubim were some of the greatest angels of all. They defended and protected God's holiness. No one who wasn't loyal and good could come near.

God created many other creatures besides those on Earth. One day we will see all his creative handiwork. Would you like to ride on the back of a flying angel? Would you like to caress the coat of a cherub? Would you like to warm in the fire of a seraph (an angel burning with fire)?

There is much to look forward to. Ezekiel gives us only a glimpse. But one day we will see all that we've imagined God can do, and even more.

**PRAYER:** Jesus, I look forward to the day when your true creative powers are unleashed forever. Amen.

Week 29: Thursday

# God's Jealousy

**Then at last my anger will be spent, and I will be satisfied. And when my fury against them has subsided, all Israel will know that I, the Lord, have spoken to them in my jealous anger.** Ezekiel 5:13

**MAIN READING:** Ezekiel 5 • **OPTIONAL READING:** Ezekiel 6—8

Sheila crossed her arms and stared across the room. The new girl, Addie, was playing up to her boyfriend, Nathan. And Nathan was paying attention. Sheila said some nasty things to her friends and they all laughed. But Sheila was hot.

When Addie walked back to her seat, Sheila walked over to Nathan. "Have a good time, Nate?"

"What? What's wrong now?" the young man asked.

"I saw you with her. Laughing. Talking. I may just break up with you right now for it."

"I was just messing around. Come on, Sheila, don't get so mad!"

What was Sheila experiencing? Jealousy. Whenever someone attempts to take something that belongs to us, we can become jealous. We want to protect our relationship. We don't want someone to destroy it.

Did you know God can become jealous too? When Satan, or evil people, or others lead one of his children astray, he becomes angry. He doesn't want anyone to hurt his relationship with that person. He will fight to protect it.

God is never jealous in a bad way. But watch out when someone tries to take what is his.

**PRAYER:** Lord, thank you that you will always protect our relationship. Amen.

Week 29: Friday

# A Sanctuary

**Therefore, give the exiles this message from the Sovereign Lord: Although I have scattered you in the countries of the world, I will be a sanctuary to you during your time of exile.** Ezekiel 11:16

**Main Reading:** Ezekiel 11 • **Optional Reading:** Ezekiel 9, 10, 12

Sanctuary. A protected place. A place we can go and be comforted when we are afraid. A temple that God uses to keep his children safe.

God is our true sanctuary. No matter what mistakes we make in this life, God will always offer us a safe place in his heart. He will never allow us to be destroyed if we cling to him.

In the Old Testament, God speaks of cities of refuge, places where a person who accidentally killed someone could go. In this city of refuge, they were protected. No one could touch them.

The temple was a similar kind of refuge—a sanctuary. Do you think of the worship center of your church as a sanctuary? Perhaps your parents or pastor even calls the main room where you meet to worship a sanctuary. Why? Because it's a protected place where God can meet with you privately and safely.

Even when Israel had been taken into slavery, God promised to remain their sanctuary. All they had to do was turn to him for protection, and he would give it.

**Prayer:** Lord, praise you that you are my sanctuary, my quiet place of worship. Amen.

# Fame and Beauty

**But you thought you could get along without me, so you trusted instead in your fame and beauty.** Ezekiel 16:15

**Main Reading:** Ezekiel 16 • **Optional Reading:** Ezekiel 13—15

Are you a popular person in your school? Are you a good-looking guy or girl?

You need to be careful. Good looks and popularity can make you forget God. They can lead you to think you're really something and you don't need him.

God calls such lack of respect idolatry. Such people give their time and money to the wrong people, the wrong things. That is what Israel did. They took the good gifts God had given them—homes, money, food—and used them for idolatrous practices.

As the above verse shows, your fame and fortune and popularity are gifts from God. Not everyone gets them.

What gifts do you have from God? Your brain, your abilities and talents, your good looks, your position as president of your class? All these are from God. Never forget who gave them to you, and God will continue to give such gifts.

**Prayer:** Father, I thank you for my gifts and abilities. Let me never forget they're from you. Amen.

Week 29: Sunday

# Death of the Wicked

**"Do you think," asks the Sovereign Lord, "that I like to see wicked people die? Of course not! I only want them to turn from their wicked ways and live."** Ezekiel 18:23

**MAIN READING:** Ezekiel 18 • **OPTIONAL READING:** Ezekiel 17, 19

The news reported tonight about a suicide bombing. The reporter said that the terrorist wanted to murder innocent people in order to make a political statement.

Many people would like to see someone like that really pay for his sin. They believe the electric chair, gas chamber, or firing squad are too easy on them. They want to see such people suffer real pain for what they've done to others.

How does God feel about wicked people? Does he enjoy seeing them killed, or beaten up, or sent to their deaths?

From today's verse in Ezekiel we learn that God takes no pleasure in the death of wicked people. Yes, justice may be served. Yes, God is angry with their wicked deeds. But their death and sentence to hell gives God no real joy. He weeps for every soul that turns away from him.

Justice is good. When wicked people pay a penalty for their sins, the world is a better place. But no one should rejoice in the suffering and punishment of the wicked.

How much better that they repent and learn the truth.

**PRAYER:** Jesus, I pray that many wicked people in this world will turn to you. Amen.

Week 30: Monday

# Pleasing to Me

**When I bring you home from exile, you will be as pleasing to me as an offering of perfumed incense. And I will display my holiness in you as all the nations watch.** Ezekiel 20:41

**Main Reading:** Ezekiel 20 • **Optional Reading:** Ezekiel 21—23

What happens when your mom or dad disciplines you?

If you're like I was, you often feel closer to them. The spanking or time out doesn't make us feel good. But afterwards, we often feel a sense of rightness about it. We deserved what we got, and we respect our parents all the more for taking responsibility. I remember watching a young parent discipline his daughter. After it was over, he held her in his arms and she looked content and happy, despite her tears.

The same thing happened to Israel when God disciplined them through exile. After the discipline was over, God promised there would be greater closeness and intimacy. They would please him. He would display them before the world as his beloved children.

Discipline never seems nice when it happens. But it leads to several wonderful things that many would not want to lose: There's new respect for God. New love also floods your soul. In the end, you experience joy because you are released and renewed.

**Prayer:** Father, let me see your discipline as a good thing, not just a punishment. Amen.

Week 30: Tuesday

# A Bare Rock

**I will make your island a bare rock, a place for fishermen to spread their nets. You will never be rebuilt, for I, the Lord, have spoken!**
Ezekiel 26:14

**MAIN READING:** Ezekiel 26 • **OPTIONAL READING:** Ezekiel 24, 25, 27

Tyre was one of the great cities of the ancient world. It sat as an island just off the coast of Phoenicia not far from Israel. Magnificent buildings studded the landscape. It was a land of power and wealth.

But the people of Tyre made the mistake of attacking Israel and committing foul deeds. God spoke in judgment against them. He prophesied that Tyre would become a waste. It would become little more than a large rock for fishermen to spread their nets on.

Has this prophecy come true?

Yes. In the fourth century before the birth of Christ, Alexander, the Greek military conquerer, attacked Tyre. Since it was an island city, Alexander had no way to lay siege to its walls. He had an idea, though. He stripped the land on the coast of every rock, boulder, and brick. He had his men throw the materials into the sea and built a jetty so his men could cross over to the island. Then he besieged it, sacked it, and utterly destroyed the city. Today, Tyre no longer exists. Fishermen use the rocks to spread their nets.

God's prophecy came true exactly as written, just as all the other prophecies of Scripture either have come true, or will in the future.

**PRAYER:** Father, praise you that you give us precise prophecies that have come true so we may trust you all the more. Amen.

Week 30: Wednesday

# Satan's Destruction

**Your great wealth filled you with violence, and you sinned. So I banished you from the mountain of God. I expelled you, O mighty guardian, from your place among the stones of fire.** Ezekiel 28:16

**Main Reading:** Ezekiel 28 • **Optional Reading:** Ezekiel 29—31

What happened to Satan, the enemy of God? How did he become the evil angel who wants to destroy God?

Ezekiel 28 offers a prime look at this angel. It tells us many things about Satan and how he became evil. It tells us he was covered with gemstones, a walking light show. He was beautiful, the greatest of all angels, and a cherub, one of the angels closest to God. He walked among the "stones of fire" and inhabited the "mountain of God." We don't know exactly what these words mean, but they signify Satan's power and prestige.

But something went wrong. Ezekiel says the great angel was filled with pride because of his wealth. He thought he was better than God and deserved the worship of other angels. He led a rebellion that took away a third of all the angels from heaven. Those who joined him became demons.

Pride is a dangerous thing. When we begin to think we're important, that we deserve this or that because of our position, we're in great danger. God opposes the proud. If they persist, he will destroy them.

**Prayer:** Lord, keep me from thinking I'm more or better than I am. Amen.

# Turning Around

**The good works of righteous people will not save them if they turn to sin, nor will the sins of evil people destroy them if they repent and turn from their sins.** Ezekiel 33:12

**Main Reading:** Ezekiel 33 • **Optional Reading:** Ezekiel 32, 34, 35

What is repentance? What does it mean to repent of your sins?

You have probably heard this word numerous times in worship. Many people are confused about exactly what it is. Is it necessary for salvation? Does it come before faith, or when we believe?

Repentance means to "change your mind" or to "turn from one thing to another." Thus to repent means to change your mind about your actions [sins] and to follow a new path. When we repent, we are agreeing with God that sin is wrong and following him is right.

Some think repentance comes before belief. Others say it happens after you've expressed faith in Christ. Whether you repented before you believed, or after, doesn't really matter. That you repented is what does matter. We continue to repent of sins all our lives.

God wants us all to change our minds about sin. He wants us to say, "I will no longer do that anymore," because we've seen the truth and agree with it.

Have you repented of any sin today? What sin are you committing that you need to change your mind about?

**Prayer:** Lord, show me what sins I need to change my mind about. Amen.

# A New Heart

**I will give you a new heart with new and right desires, and I will put a new spirit in you.** Ezekiel 36:26

**Main Reading:** Ezekiel 36 • **Optional Reading:** Ezekiel 37—39

I can't do it," Lorayne complained to her mother about doing her homework every day after school. She wanted to play. "It's too hard."

"All you have to do is choose to do the right thing, honey," her mother answered. "Now go do it."

"I may be doing it on the outside," Lorayne cried, "but I'm playing on the inside."

Our hearts, how stubborn they are! Obeying from the heart is difficult for many of us. We can make our bodies do what they should, but inside we may be seething with anger and wishing for something else. How do you make your heart want to do what's right or best?

That's God's job. He has to give us that new heart and mind that he speaks of in today's verse. God puts that new heart within us that desires to obey him and do his will. We can force ourselves to do something, but to change our hearts is more difficult. God can change us on the inside if we ask, though.

That's the best kind of obedience—obedience from the heart. That's the kind of obedience God really wants from us.

**Prayer:** Lord, work in my heart to make me willing to obey everything you say. Amen.

Week 30: Saturday

# Tell Them Everything

**He said to me, "Son of man, watch and listen. Pay close attention to everything I show you. You have been brought here so I can show you many things."** Ezekiel 40:4

**MAIN READING:** Ezekiel 40 • **OPTIONAL READING:** Ezekiel 41—44

Imagine that you're looking over Ezekiel's shoulder as he writes the words of his book of prophecy. What do you think the prophet did as he wrote? Did he chew the end of his stylus (writing instrument)? Did he stop and think as he wrote? Did God dictate the words to him so that he just wrote down what God said, not really thinking about it?

What we're talking about here is the inspiration of Scripture. How did the Bible come to be the Word of God if men wrote it?

Scripture teaches in many places (see 2 Timothy 3:16, 17 and 2 Peter 1:20, 21) that God's Word came to us through men who wrote it down. But God did not dictate or speak the words like a manager would to his secretary. Instead, the writers of the Bible were "carried along" by the Holy Spirit. Their thoughts and ideas were planted in their hearts by the Spirit. What came out was their words led by the Spirit. Thus, what we have is God's Word through the hearts of men.

Why did God use people to do this? Because he loves us and wants us to know that we are partners with him. He's not just shouting down at us from the clouds. No, he speaks to each of us through the heart.

**PRAYER:** Father, praise you for giving me your Word that I might learn the truth. Amen.

Week 30: Sunday

# The Lord Is There

**From that day the name of the city will be "The Lord Is There."**
Ezekiel 48:35

**MAIN READING:** Ezekiel 48 • **OPTIONAL READING:** Ezekiel 45—47

These words were found chipped in the rock of a prison cell wall: "God is here."

We don't know who carved those words into the stone. We don't know what he thought, or what his crime was. But sometime during his imprisonment he must have come to believe in God. He experienced God's presence as he sat in his cell day by day with nothing to do but pray and think.

When Ezekiel wrote these words at the end of his book, he must have shouted with joy. For so long, God had not been with Israel. Their sins caused a separation between them and God. God withdrew and did not speak to them as he once did. Instead, he punished them.

But Ezekiel promised that one day all this would change. God would come down and touch us all through his presence. His love would flow into our hearts. His friendship and grace would bless our days. His patience would endure with us when we made mistakes. And his Spirit would fill us to overflowing. We would experience his perfect and eternal presence.

What a gift—to have God "there" with us wherever we are. If you are a Christian, God is with you. God is there in your house, your bedroom, your classroom. He is there because he loves you. He is there because he wants to be your greatest friend.

**PRAYER:** Jesus, let me know your presence in my life. Amen.

# Obedience to God's Will

**But Daniel made up his mind not to defile himself by eating the food and wine given to them by the king. He asked the chief official for permission to eat other things instead.** Daniel 1:8

**Main Reading:** Daniel 1 • **Optional Reading:** Daniel 2—4

Obeying God. It's hard. But it's always worth the effort.

Daniel and his three friends, Shadrach, Meshach, and Abednego, were taken from their homeland Israel far away to Babylon. There, because they were handsome, intelligent young men, they were brought into the palace to be trained to serve the king. They ate the best food. They wore the nicest clothing. They were select.

But Daniel noticed a problem. In the Law of Moses, God told his people they couldn't eat certain foods. Many of these foods were on the Babylonian menu. To defy the king invited death. But to disobey God invited worse things.

Daniel talked to the man in charge of training the young men. He explained his position. The man told him they'd try an experiment for 10 days. If, after 10 days of eating the Hebrew diet, the young men looked as good as the others, they could continue.

God blessed Daniel and his three friends. After 10 days, they looked healthier than any of the other young men.

Sometimes obeying God will mean you go against the rules of school, or the government, or even your family. But choose to obey him anyway. He will bless you for your efforts.

**Prayer:** Lord, may I always obey you, even if others think it's dumb or wrong. Amen.

Week 31: Tuesday

# A Plot by Daniel's Enemies

**Daniel answered, "Long live the king! My God sent his angel to shut the lions' mouths so that they would not hurt me, for I have been found innocent in his sight."** Daniel 6:21

**MAIN READING:** Daniel 6 • **OPTIONAL READING:** Daniel 5, 7, 8

Let's set a trap for Manuel," Stephen told his two friends. "When he comes in, I'll get him to come over to this desk. I'll get him talking, and you guys get on your knees behind him. I'll shove him backwards and he'll topple onto the floor. Everyone will think it's funny."

"Why are we doing this to him?" Dave asked. "What's the big deal?"

"He's always telling everyone about Jesus and stuff. I hate it. I want to humiliate him. Make him stop."

The boys pulled their prank. Manuel fell over the backs of the two helpers. Everyone laughed. But that didn't stop Manuel from witnessing. God led him to speak up all the more. And several other kids became Christians.

Similar to Manuel's situation, Daniel also had enemies. They didn't like it that he worshiped the living God. They conspired against him and had him thrown into the lions' den. But God was with Daniel and protected him. In the end, Daniel was saved, and all his enemies were slain.

God probably won't kill any of your enemies. But he will strengthen you to face them. Don't back down to their taunts or put-downs. God is with you.

**PRAYER:** Father, I will continue to do all I can to make known your truth. Amen.

# God Keeps His Promises

**O Lord, you are a great and awesome God! You always fulfill your promises of unfailing love to those who love you and keep your commands.** Daniel 9:4

**Main Reading:** Daniel 9 • **Optional Reading:** Daniel 10—12

I prayed and nothing happened," Celia told her friend, Jenna. "I just don't know why God won't answer. I even quoted a Scripture."

"What Scripture did you use?" Jenna asked.

"The one Jesus said in the Sermon on the Mount—'Ask, and you shall receive.' I asked, but I didn't receive."

Jenna didn't know how to answer, but she finally said, "Maybe you just have to wait for awhile, or maybe God really is saying no."

The problem Celia wrestled with is a common one. Does God always keep his promises? If you look at what Daniel prayed in today's verse, you see the truth: God does keep his promises. But he doesn't keep them on our timetables.

Daniel's countrymen had been taken into slavery into Babylon. Undoubtedly, many of them repented and cried out to God for hope and relief. For many days and even years, nothing happened. But God's promise was that in 70 years, they would be sent back to Israel.

It happened just as God said. God does keep his promises. He just doesn't answer them all at the same time. Sometimes we have to wait.

**Prayer:** Lord, I believe you keep your promises, and I'm counting on it. Amen.

Week 31: Thursday

# Removing the Weapons

**I will remove all weapons of war from the land, all swords and bows, so you can live unafraid in peace and safety.** Hosea 2:18

**MAIN READING:** Hosea 2 • **OPTIONAL READING:** Hosea 1, 3, 4

Are you ever afraid of war? Of terrorists? Or nuclear weapons?

When I was a kid your age, we used to have "bomb drills." Russia and the U.S. both had nuclear weapons and there was much fear that Russia would use theirs on us. As a result, when the bell rang, we all paraded into the hallways, sat down, and put our heads between our knees. This was meant to protect us from a real bomb.

Today, the nuclear threat isn't as great. But terrorists and others have made daily living somewhat fearful. Do you ever worry about such things?

We live in a dangerous world. Being prepared for the worst is something all of us must do. God will protect us, but that doesn't mean bad things won't happen. Many of the people who died on September 11, 2001, were Christians. God loved them, but he let them die just the same.

The great hope for Christians, though, is that when we die we go to heaven to be with Jesus. We will live forever with him. No matter what happens in this world, one day Jesus will reign over all. He will destroy every weapon of destruction, like Hosea said in today's verse. No one will ever need to be afraid again.

**PRAYER:** Lord, I will not be afraid, for you are with me. Amen.

Week 31: Friday

# Return to the Lord

**Come, let us return to the Lord! He has torn us in pieces; now he will heal us. He has injured us; now he will bandage our wounds.**
Hosea 6:1

**Main Reading:** Hosea 6 • **Optional Reading:** Hosea 5, 7, 8

Does your dad spank you sometimes? Does your mom discipline you at times? Do you get punished for doing bad things?

All of us, when we're young, go through such things. But what happens when your dad or mom comes home from long trip? Don't you run to them in the airport or driveway? Don't you grab them around the waist and hug them and kiss them?

If you love your mom or dad, you probably feel that way about them. Even though they do punish you at times, you love them more than anyone else.

This was what happened in the days of Hosea. We read in today's verse that though God punished Israel for their sins, the people still returned to God. For them, it was better to be on God's side and get disciplined now and then, than to be against God and lose everything.

When we do wrong, one of the first things God wants is that we return to him. Don't run away. Don't hide. Don't freeze God out. Don't ignore God as if you hate him.

Instead, run to him. Grab him around the waist and hold on for all you're worth. Because it's better to be with him than against him.

**Prayer:** Lord, praise you that you always call out to me to come back, no matter what I've done wrong. Amen.

# The Hard Ground of the Heart

**Plow up the hard ground of your hearts, for now is the time to seek the Lord, that he may come and shower righteousness upon you.**
Hosea 10:12

**MAIN READING:** Hosea 10 • **OPTIONAL READING:** Hosea 9, 11

Have you ever met a person with a hard heart?

Sometimes their faces look mean. The set of their lips is almost a snarl. Their eyes blaze with hatred. You know deep down inside they listen to nasty, ugly thoughts. They don't like anyone, especially God. They just want to be left alone and not have anyone make their lives tougher than they already are.

On the other hand, some people who have hardened hearts seem perfectly happy. Their lives are good, but they don't want anything to do with God.

A hard heart is a serious problem. Such people are often miserable to be around. They never have anything good to say. They make all kinds of excuses for their wrong behavior. But then they condemn and judge everyone else.

There is a cure for a hard heart. Go to God and ask for a new, righteous heart. He will give it to the person who asks. He will remove the "heart of stone" from your breast, and give you a "heart of flesh."

God takes no pleasure in people who hate him. He doesn't want to destroy them. He wants to come near, make them friends, and give them new life.

God will always hear the prayer of a repentant person. But the person who refuses to give up his hard heart will stew in his misery forever.

**PRAYER:** Lord, I praise you that you have given me a new heart. Amen.

# Depending on God

**So now, come back to your God! Act on the principles of love and justice, and always live in confident dependence on your God.**
Hosea 12:6

**MAIN READING:** Hosea 12 • **OPTIONAL READING:** Hosea 13, 14

It was the day of the mile run. Alisha hated this particular race. Her chest always burned with pain at the end of the mile run. She couldn't keep up. Everyone passed her. She was the slowest one in the group, and some kids laughed at her. She just didn't have the stamina to run hard and long.

The day of the race, her mom put a little note in her lunch box. At lunchtime, shortly before gym class, Alisha read it. "Honey, I know how you dread this race. But don't worry about winning. Just 'live in confident dependence' on God (Hosea 12:6). He will get you through this."

The time of the race came. Everyone lined up. Alisha's heart already pounded. The gun sounded and she started off, slogging along, not really trying to go too fast because she knew she'd need her strength for later. As she ran, she prayed. "God, I'm depending on you. I'm depending on you. I'm depending on you."

At the first turn, most of the kids were well ahead of her. By the second lap, Alisha's chest was hurting. But she continued praying her prayer. "I'm depending on you, God."

In a few more minutes, it was over. Alisha completed the race. Her chest hurt. She wanted to fall to the ground. But she'd made it. "Thanks, God," she said as she followed everyone in for the shower.

**PRAYER:** Jesus, remind me always to depend on you for strength and power. Amen.

# God Pours Out His Spirit

**Then after I have poured out my rains again, I will pour out my Spirit upon all people.** Joel 2:28

**MAIN READING:** Joel 2 • **OPTIONAL READING:** Joel 1, 3

Have you ever been in the middle of a drought? Grass all dried up and yellow. Corn in the fields hanging and wrinkled. Cattle thin. Farmers going broke. Reservoirs nothing but mud.

Rain is essential to a nation. Without rain, crops will not grow. Without crops, animals and people won't eat. Without water, they'll go thirsty and eventually die.

A drought can be a hard time to live through.

Many people live their lives without God, as if in a drought. They're unhappy, unsettled, fearful. They may not know what's missing, but they know something is missing, and it hurts. They may become bitter and complaining, eventually going to their graves sad, broken people.

God has a remedy for a spiritual drought: his Spirit. He sends the Holy Spirit into our lives, and the Spirit of God releases joy, love, peace, and hope back into our hearts. We can run and leap again. Dance. Thrill to the music. Live in the presence of God.

How do you get God's Spirit into your life? By becoming a Christian. When you accept Christ, he puts his Spirit within you. You can release the Spirit in your life through obedience to God's Word. As you learn to walk with Jesus, the Spirit will become active.

The drought in your life will end. And you'll be dancing in the puddles.

**PRAYER:** Lord, I want you to release the Spirit in my life. Fill me up. Amen.

# Show and Pretense

**I hate all your show and pretense—the hypocrisy of your religious festivals and solemn assemblies.** Amos 5:21

**Main Reading:** Amos 5 • **Optional Reading:** Amos 1—4

Have you ever thought worship can be a lot of show and pretense?

People smiling, but it's a put on. People singing, but without real verve. People praying, but it doesn't sound real. They're just putting on a show for God. They're going through the motions. They're not really experiencing the presence of God because they don't really care about God.

What do they care about? What others say about them. What others see. How other people comment on how spiritual they all are.

This was the problem Jesus had with the Pharisees. When they gave their money in the temple, they made a big show of it. When they prayed, they stopped on street corners and bowed their heads. Everyone who passed thought they were such giants of faith. When they fasted, they let everyone know how important they were.

God hates show and pretense. He wants the real thing. He wants you to come to him in worship, prayer, and giving because you want to, because you love him, not to impress others.

Are you trying to impress other people with your spirituality? Stop! God doesn't want anymore of that. Give him your heart, and suddenly everything will make sense.

**Prayer:** Father, keep me from hypocrisy. Let me be a real worshiper in spirit and truth. Amen.

# Restoring Israel

**In that day I will restore the fallen kingdom of David. It is now like a house in ruins, but I will rebuild its walls and restore its former glory.**
Amos 9:11

**MAIN READING:** Amos 9 • **OPTIONAL READING:** Amos 6—8

Long ago, God made this important prophecy. Many people today believe it came true when Israel became a nation in 1948 after nearly 2,000 years of exile from their land. What happened?

During World War II, Germany murdered many Jews in the gas chambers of their concentration camps. Over six million Jews died, as well as nearly six million other innocent people. The world felt so badly about what Germany had done to the Jews, that they were very sympathetic to their returning to the land of Israel, at that time called Palestine. Jews flocked to Palestine where the British were in charge.

In 1947, war broke out between the Arab nations and the Jews. Eventually, by 1948, the Jews had taken most of their land back. The United Nations recognized them as a new country. Israel was a nation again—after 2,000 years of wandering.

Many believe that Israel's becoming a nation again is a key moment in prophecy. They believe Jesus' coming is the next big event in human history.

We don't know what will happen. But you can be sure of one thing: God kept his promise to Israel. It took 2,000 years. But he kept it, like God always does.

You can trust God. He never forgets any promise he's made.

**PRAYER:** Lord, I praise you that you restored Israel. I pray now that they might become believers in your Son. Amen.

# The Second Chance

**Then the Lord spoke to Jonah a second time: "Get up and go to the great city of Nineveh, and deliver the message of judgment I have given you."** Jonah 3:1

**Main Reading** Jonah 3 • **Optional Reading: Obadiah;** Jonah 1, 2, 4

Jonah was one angry man. God gave him a mission: go to Nineveh and tell them I'll destroy their city because of their sin.

Jonah didn't want to go to Nineveh to warn them. He was afraid they would repent, and God would relent and not destroy them. So he ran. In the opposite direction. It took a huge storm on the sea and three days in the belly of a great fish to wake him up to what he was doing. God got his attention, and Jonah decided to obey God.

When the fish spit Jonah up on land, God's word came to Jonah a second time. Same mission. Same message. God gave Jonah a second chance. When you read the book, you'll see Jonah was still pretty angry about everything. But the fact is, God didn't destroy Jonah or his ministry because of his sin. God gave him a second chance.

Do you ever feel as though you've sinned and messed up your life?

It could be stealing, drugs, problems in school, disobedience to your parents, running away. Many young people go through hard times. But God is the God not only of the second chance, but the third chance, the fifth chance, the hundredth chance. Never think God will give up on you.

**Prayer:** Father, praise you for the many chances you've given me in life. Amen.

Week 32: Friday

# Let Us Go Up

**Come, let us go up to the mountain of the Lord, to the Temple of the God of Israel. There he will teach us his ways, so that we may obey him.** Micah 4:2

**MAIN READING:** Micah 4 • **OPTIONAL READING:** Micah 1—3

Shakira wanted to learn God's Word. But she found understanding some of the statements she found in the Bible puzzling. Many times, she simply did not know what a verse meant.

She went to her Sunday-school teacher and asked her what to do. The teacher said, "You've got to start letting God teach you."

The teacher opened her Bible to 1 John 2:27 and showed Shakira how the Spirit lived in her heart. "The Spirit will open your mind and teach you if you let him," the teacher said. "When you don't understand something next time, pray and ask God to give you wisdom. He will. I guarantee it."

The next time Shakira had a problem with a verse, she stopped and prayed like the teacher had said. It didn't happen immediately, but later several ideas came into her mind. She suddenly saw the answer she needed. Again, she bowed in prayer. She thanked God for his Spirit, the "teacher," who was now her personal tutor.

God wants to teach you personally, like today's verse says. The Spirit lives in you and one of his great duties is to lead you into all the truth. Talk to him. Ask him for his guidance. He will fill your mind with new ideas and thoughts that will make the Bible live, and he will give you wisdom for applying it to your life.

**PRAYER:** Lord, thank you for your Spirit, my teacher. Let me learn from him every day. Amen.

Week 32: Saturday

# What God Wants from Us

**The Lord has already told you what is good, and this is what he requires: to do what is right, to love mercy, and to walk humbly with your God.** Micah 6:8

**MAIN READING:** Micah 6 • **OPTIONAL READING:** Micah 5, 7

Have you ever felt like God wants too much from you? He has so many rules. And the Bible—what a big book! He expects you and me to do all that? And then there's obeying our parents, and listening to our teachers, and loving our enemies. All of it can make you feel like it's too much. How can God expect us to do all of that?

Well, actually, God never makes you do all of it at once. He usually has you doing one thing at a time. But today's verse gives us insight into what God wants. There are three things we should put first in our lives:

Do what is right. Many times you simply know what the right thing is when a situation occurs. You don't have to pray about it, or think a lot. It's not that hard.

Love mercy. When others hurt you, God wants you to be merciful. Forgive. Don't take revenge.

Walk humbly with God. To walk humbly means not to think you're someone great or important. You're just happy God is your friend, and having him there with you is the greatest thing in all of life. You don't make demands of God. You don't throw a fit when a prayer isn't answered the way you want.

It's really not that hard. Do these things, and God says all will be well.

**PRAYER:** Jesus, help me to walk with you all my days and not be proud. Amen.

# God Knows You

**The Lord is good. When trouble comes, he is a strong refuge. And he knows everyone who trusts in him.** Nahum 1:7

**Main Reading:** Nahum 1 • **Optional Reading:** Nahum 2, 3

Did you realize that God knows you? He knows who you are. He knows what you think. He knows what dreams you have. He knows where you are at every moment. And he knows if you're trusting him and walking with him. God knows everything.

Nahum, the book you're reading today, is not a happy book. It's a record of God's anger with his people for their disobedience. But one thing Nahum reminds us of: even if everyone else is doing wrong, God sees you and knows when you do what's right.

Does that comfort you? Do you ever feel like no one notices when you do something nice for someone? Don't be mistaken. God knows. God sees. He knows everything you've ever done, and one day he will reward you for your goodness.

The people of Israel could easily have thought, What's the use? No one cares if I help out so and so. No one knows if I do some good around here.

God wanted to assure them he knew and saw it all.

He assures you of the same thing. Never think just because no person notices the good you're doing, that God doesn't. He knows all about it, and he is very pleased.

**Prayer:** Lord, help me to do good, knowing you're watching even if no one else is. Amen.

Week 33: Monday

# Reverence

**But the Lord is in his holy Temple. Let all the earth be silent before him.** Habakkuk 2:20

**MAIN READING:** Habakkuk 2 • **OPTIONAL READING:** Habakkuk 1, 3

Are you reverent? Do you show respect for God in church, in your home, in school?

Habakkuk, in today's verse, shows us what true reverence is. It's coming before God in silence. What does that mean? When we approach God, a thoughtful silence is the first order of the day. Think about what you're doing. Consider whom you're standing before. Don't just blather along about nothing. Look deeply at what you have to say, and say it well.

Reverence isn't all silence, though. There is a time to speak, and a time to sing, rejoice, and enjoy God too. Part of reverence is simply enjoying God. A famous question and answer guide about Christian faith asks, "What is the chief end of man?" In other words, what's our main purpose in life? The answer is, "To love God and enjoy him forever." Put some emphasis on that word enjoy. God wants us to enjoy him. He longs that our relationship with him not be boring, doing the same old thing all the time, but a source of exhilaration and happiness. God desires that we have a good time with him.

Sometimes that means simply being quiet before him. Other times it means whooping it up.

**PRAYER:** Lord, I want to enjoy you all my days. Amen.

# God Rejoices Over You

**For the Lord your God has arrived to live among you. He is a mighty savior. He will rejoice over you with great gladness. With his love, he will calm all your fears. He will exult over you by singing a happy song.** Zephaniah 3:17

**MAIN READING:** Zephaniah 3 • **OPTIONAL READING:** Zephaniah 1, 2

Have you ever seen two loving brothers have a reunion after a long time apart? Have you ever been there when a soldier came back from battle? Or a friend from the mission field? Have you met a friend stepping off a plane, running to greet him with a shout of joy?

That's what Zephaniah says God feels when he sees us coming to him. God rejoices over us with shouts of joy. He wants to "sing a happy song" over us. God doesn't only love you. He's not only about leading you and helping you and making your life better. No, sometimes God just wants to let you know he thinks you're the greatest. He wants to enjoy you, and tell the world, "Hey, look at my kid here! Isn't he great?"

If God feels that way about you, what does it say about his nature and character? He's not twiddling his thumbs and hoping you'll pray to him today. No, he's a warrior who whisks you up and plants kisses on your face when he returns from battle.

God not only loves you, he likes you. Get it?

**PRAYER:** Father, praise you that you enjoy being with me. That's great encouragement. Amen.

# I Will Shake the Nations

**I will shake all the nations, and the treasures of all the nations will come to this Temple. I will fill this place with glory, says the Lord Almighty.** Haggai 2:7

**Main Reading:** Haggai 2 • **Optional Reading:** Haggai 1

Do you ever read the news and wish that you could take some of those world leaders and just shake them? "What are you doing? Are you crazy with these weapons? Don't you know how many people you can hurt with this kind of attitude?"

The world is a dangerous place. Many deadly people lurk in dark places just waiting to pounce on the innocent. God protects us much of the time. He will be with us in whatever troubles we face. And one day he will shake the whole world. He'll make us wake up. "Hey," he'll cry, "listen up. This is God. I'm the ruler of the universe. You haven't been listening to me much lately. But now I'm going to make you listen. No more killing. No more lying. No more stealing and hurting people. From now on it's going to be different. Because from now on, I'm in charge."

Wouldn't you love to see God do that? Well, one day he will. He'll sit on his throne and he'll deal with every bad guy out there. He'll stop the mouths of every evil person in existence. And then he'll rule with perfect justice and righteousness.

It's a day worth waiting for, and worth looking for.

**Prayer:** Lord, hurry and come back. I want to see you make this world a different place. Amen.

Week 33: Thursday

# By My Spirit

**This is what the Lord says to Zerubbabel: It is not by force nor by strength, but by my Spirit, says the Lord Almighty.** Zechariah 4:6

**MAIN READING:** Zechariah 4 • **OPTIONAL READING:** Zechariah 1—3

Zerubbabel was a great leader. He had many fantastic ideas about how to make things happen in the Jewish kingdom. He wanted his people to live in peace. He longed that the temple be revered. He strode through the city, declaring all the things his people should do to honor God.

But one day, God spoke to him. Zerubbabel was doing all these things, and they weren't having much of an effect. He was pretty frustrated. People weren't listening. They didn't apply what he said.

So God told Zechariah the prophet in today's verse what he intended to do. He informed Zerubbabel, "Look, champ. It's not all about strength and power. You can plan and you can do all you want, but the real power is with me. When I'm on your side, things will happen. Trust me, because it's all by the power of my Spirit, not by the power of your words, or your soldiers, or your priests."

Zerubbabel took it to heart. He went out and started doing things on the basis of God's Spirit, not his ideas. And God led him. God got the people in shape. The temple was built, the wall was fixed, and everything went well again for the first time in centuries.

**PRAYER:** I remember, Lord, that it is not me who makes things happen, but you. Amen.

Week 33: Friday

# Do You Think of Me?

**And even now in your holy festivals, you don't think about me but only of pleasing yourselves.** Zechariah 7:6

**MAIN READING:** Zechariah 7 • **OPTIONAL READING:** Zechariah 5, 6, 8

Chrissy sat in church drawing. She doodled all over the church bulletin. Then she made a list of some friends she wanted to invite to her birthday party. Later on, something she heard the pastor say made her think of a test she had on Monday. She began working out problems in her head. She sure wanted to pass that test!

When the congregation sang, Chrissy just continued with her own thoughts. She was happy about something her friend Julie had said to her, and she savored that for awhile. Then she remembered something else she wanted to do that week. She wrote it down on her list.

Finally, church was over. She skipped out, glad to be free.

Is that how church goes for you? You don't really pay much attention? You mess around and listen to your own thoughts?

The Jews of Zechariah's day did the same thing. Church (or synagogue for them) was boring. Why listen? It was the same old stuff anyway.

But church isn't just about listening. As today's verse says, it's about your thoughts. Thinking of God. Saying good things to God. Talking to him in your heart.

When you let your thoughts focus on God, your church experience will change. Soon, you'll be glad to be there, because it's there you get to meet with God.

**PRAYER:** Jesus, I pray that my thoughts might begin to focus on you, not on everything else as I sit in church. Amen.

Week 33: Saturday

# Your King Comes to You

**Rejoice greatly, O people of Zion! Shout in triumph, O people of Jerusalem! Look, your king is coming to you. He is righteous and victorious, yet he is humble, riding on a donkey.** Zechariah 9:9

**MAIN READING:** Zechariah 9 • **OPTIONAL READING:** Zechariah 10, 11

There are over 300 prophecies in the Bible about Jesus' first coming. Today's verse, from Zechariah 9:9, is one such prophecy. It speaks about Jesus' coming into Jerusalem in triumph just before he was crucified.

All the city was expectant. Jesus had been doing miracles in the country. He talked in the synagogues each day. And his talks were incredible. He had so much insight. He spoke such gentle, healing words. People hung on everything he said.

Now they knew he was coming to Jerusalem. How would they know if he really was the king who would save Israel? How would they be able to prove he was the Messiah they all longed for?

There was one sure way. The prophets told us how he would come, in Zechariah 9:9. He would ride on a donkey. He would be humble. He wouldn't march in with an army.

Everyone lined up at the gate to see if this was the way Jesus would enter Jerusalem. Sure enough, he came riding on a donkey. He truly was humble. And he came with just a few men, no conquering army.

The prophecy fit. If anyone was unsure, this was a final proof. Jesus came to town just like the prophet predicted 400 years before.

**PRAYER:** Lord, thank you that you give us prophecy so we can see the truth. Amen.

Week 33: Sunday

# One God for All

**And the Lord will be king over all the earth. On that day there will be one Lord—his name alone will be worshiped.** Zechariah 14:9

**Main Reading:** Zechariah 14 • **Optional Reading:** Zechariah 12, 13

Don't all the religions in the world confuse you sometimes? There's Christianity. There's Buddhism. The Muslims. And Hinduism. Confucianism in China. Shintoism in Japan. There are many newer faiths too. Jehovah's Witnesses. The Mormons. Baha'i, and New Age. Even the Satanists.

What does it all mean? Are these all legitimate ways to find God?

One way to tell the truth is simply to see the difference. All other religions besides Christianity have mankind trying to climb up and meet God. Christianity is God coming down to meet us and save us.

Christianity also offers us hope. There's forgiveness for sins. In many religions, you have to work to get forgiveness. In Christianity, we gain it by faith. There's the hope of rising from the dead. Few other religions have such a hope. And in Christianity, there's the promise of eternal life—living with God forever in heaven. It's all free.

All other religions involve working for heaven or nirvana, or whatever. You have to do this, and then maybe you'll get there. But Jesus offers salvation and eternal life in heaven if we'll just give our lives to him.

God will reign, as today's verse says. And the truth will shine. Everyone will know he is God. On that day, there will never be confusion about religion again.

**Prayer:** Lord, I praise you for showing me the truth of Christianity. Amen.

Week 34: Monday

# The Unchanging God

**I am the Lord, and I do not change. That is why you descendants of Jacob are not already completely destroyed.** Malachi 3:6

**MAIN READING:** Malachi 3 • **OPTIONAL READING:** Malachi 1, 2

Could God ever change his mind about you? Could he decide one day that he no longer wants you to be his child? Could he throw you out of his kingdom and send you to hell, just because he decided he didn't like you anymore?

Could God reverse all his promises in the Bible one day? Could he simply say, "Everything I said in the Bible is now over. I'm starting something new"?

Might God one day flip everyone in the universe on his head? Everyone who was in hell suddenly goes to heaven? And everyone in heaven goes to hell?

These are questions many Christians worry about. The main one is, "Can God change for some reason?" If he could, we would all be in great danger. Human beings change all the time. Seasons change. The world changes. But does God change?

No! As Hebrews 13:8 says, "Jesus Christ is the same yesterday, today, and forever." God cannot change. He is perfect, and perfection cannot be changed.

In today's verse, Malachi assures the people of Israel that God doesn't change. Ever. Under any conditions.

You can rely on his promises, on his Word, on his character, on him—forever!

**PRAYER:** Lord, I praise you that you are perfectly trustworthy forever. Amen.

# Born of a Virgin

**Now this is how Jesus the Messiah was born. His mother, Mary, was engaged to be married to Joseph. But while she was still a virgin, she became pregnant by the Holy Spirit.** Matthew 1:18

**MAIN READING:** Matthew 1 • **OPTIONAL READING:** Matthew 2, 3

Only one person in all of history never had a human father: Jesus. The Holy Spirit came upon Mary, and Jesus became her Son. Joseph, who was Mary's husband-to-be, and who would later become the father of other children of Mary's, was not Jesus' father. God was.

Why did God bring Jesus into the world this way?

The main reason is that Jesus had to be both human and divine. If Joseph had been his father and Mary his mother, Jesus would have been completely human. He would have had a sin nature. He would have been no different from us. If he ever paid for any sins, it would be for his own.

But the Holy Spirit played the role of Jesus' father. Mary gave Jesus his human side. The Spirit of God gave Jesus his divine side. Jesus was both human and divine. He was human because he had to die for the sins of humans. He was divine because he had to be perfect to die for the sins of the whole world.

Over the years, you'll probably hear many things about Jesus being born of a virgin. Some people will say it's impossible. Or that it's a lie. Don't believe it. Jesus, to be truly Jesus, had to be born of a virgin. Because of that fact, you can have eternal life, go to heaven, and walk with him in this life through believing in him.

**PRAYER:** Jesus, praise you that you came to us in the best way possible. Amen.

# Tempted by the Devil

**"I will give it all to you," he said, "if you will only kneel down and worship me."** Matthew 4:9

**MAIN READING:** Matthew 4 • **OPTIONAL READING:** Matthew 5, 6

Does Jesus know what it's like to be tempted?

Does he know how it feels to have to eat your dinner but want to eat that candy bar instead? Does he understand how you sometimes want to hit someone to shut them up? Does he know anything about how you want to mess around instead of cleaning your room?

You bet. Jesus knows what it's like to face every kind of temptation. Why? Because he faced them all during his life. In today's reading, we see Jesus being tempted by the Devil. The Devil tried to get Jesus to sin by three methods. He suggested Jesus make stones into bread. Jesus was hungry. But God had told him to fast.

When that failed, Satan took Jesus to the highest point of the temple. He told Jesus to jump off because God's Word said angels would catch him. This would be an easy way for Jesus to prove he was the Son of God. But the Father had other ways for Jesus to do that, so Jesus refused.

Finally, Satan offered Jesus everything in the world, if he would just worship him. Jesus told Satan to go away.

Food. Fame. Fortune. Those were the things Satan tempted Jesus with. Are they things you also face? Jesus knows what it's like. Go to him when you're tempted, and he will show you the way through it.

**PRAYER:** Father, help me to remember to ask Jesus for his help when I'm tempted. Amen.

Week 34: Thursday

# By My Spirit

**Do for others what you would like them to do for you. This is a summary of all that is taught in the law and the prophets.** Matthew 7:12

**MAIN READING:** Matthew 7 • **OPTIONAL READING:** Matthew 8, 9

Jeri knew Sami had taken her favorite game. Now she wanted it back. But she also knew Sami would lie and say she hadn't taken it. So Jeri decided maybe she should just fight it out with Sami and get the game by force.

The only problem was, Sami was a good fighter. A lot of girls had been knocked to pieces by Sami. She was big and tough.

Finally, Jeri went to her mom about it. She explained what had happened. Her mom said, "If you were Sami, how you would want to be approached about this?"

Jeri thought about it. "I think I'd just want me to come to her and speak the truth. To be nice and gentle, but firm."

"Then why don't you do that?"

"Because she'll lie to me."

"How do you know? Maybe she won't."

Jeri decided to try it, even though she didn't think it would work. To her surprise, Sami said, "Oh, I meant only to borrow it. Sorry." She gave it back to Jeri immediately.

Today's verse is sometimes called the Golden Rule. Whenever you're in a tough situation, think how you'd like to be treated. Then treat others that way. God will bless you for it.

**PRAYER:** Lord, help me to remember to follow the Golden Rule always. Amen.

# Come to Me!

**Come to me, all of you who are weary and carry heavy burdens, and I will give you rest.** Matthew 11:28

**Main Reading:** Matthew 11 • **Optional Reading:** Matthew 10

Do you ever get tired of trying to keep the rules?

"Read your Bible every day."

"Never miss church."

"If you ever tell a lie, you're finished!"

"Pray more. You're not praying enough."

Sometimes it seems like Christianity is nothing but rules. The people of Jesus' day had the same problem—except their rules were even stickier. They couldn't walk on grass on the Sabbath. They were forbidden from walking more than a mile from home on the Sabbath. They couldn't even spit on the Sabbath.

All these rules made some people weary. But Jesus had a completely new message: "Follow me and I'll give you rules you can keep. Follow me, and I'll take the burdens of all the rules off you."

It wasn't that Jesus meant to take away all rules. Instead, he meant that having a relationship with him would take care of most of the rules. When you know him, love him, and walk with him, the rules aren't tough anymore. Soon, you're keeping them without worrying about making a mistake. Why? Because you know Jesus. He's with you in everything.

**Prayer:** Let me not worry so much about the rules as about loving you, Lord.

Week 34: Saturday

# Different Responses to the Gospel

**He told many stories such as this one: "A farmer went out to plant some seed. As he scattered it across his field, some seeds fell on a footpath, and the birds came and ate them."** Matthew 13:3, 4

**MAIN READING:** Matthew 13 • **OPTIONAL READING:** Matthew 12, 14

Jesus told this parable to help his followers understand what happens when God's Word is preached. Not everyone has the same response.

In the parable, some seed fell on the hard ground. Birds swoop down, find that seed, and scarf it up. Jesus said that's what happens to some people. They hear God's Word, but Satan grabs it away from them. They never become Christians.

Some seed fell on the shallow soil. It started well, but when the sun became too hot, it withered away. Likewise, some people stop believing when they have problems.

Still other seed fell on the weedy ground, where it was choked by the weeds. Similarly, things like money, popularity, and pleasure can destroy God's Word in our lives.

The only seed that really ended up well was the seed that fell on the good ground. It grew up and even sent out more seed to others.

What kind of ground are you? The hard soil? The shallow? The weedy? Or the good? Guess what? You're one of them. How have you treated the gospel? Have you believed and followed it? Or are you just playing games?

**PRAYER:** Teach me to follow you always, Lord. I love you.

Week 34: Sunday

# Wanting a Miracle

**One day the Pharisees and Sadducees came to test Jesus' claims by asking him to show them a miraculous sign from heaven.**
Matthew 16:1

**MAIN READING:** Matthew 16 • **OPTIONAL READING:** Matthew 15, 17

Many people say, "If God would just prove it to me, I'd believe in him."

Have you ever caught yourself saying that? Why doesn't God do it? Why doesn't he simply do a miracle for each of us? Wouldn't we all believe, if he did that?

The answer is what we find in today's reading. The Pharisees and Sadducees were the leaders in Israel. Many of them were present when Jesus did various miracles. Healings. Feedings. Raising people from the dead. Turning water into wine. Jesus did not do his miracles only for his disciples, or for believers. He did them in front of everyone.

Then why did the Pharisees and Sadducees ask for a personal miracle? Would they have believed if he did one?

The fact is, they didn't believe when they saw the other miracles. The Pharisees and Sadducees were enemies of Jesus. They had no intention of believing in him. They simply wanted to taunt him, to put him down. Doing a miracle would only have invited their inspection and scorn.

Jesus knows our hearts. If we need proofs, we have the whole Bible full of proofs. We have the witness of friends and neighbors. We have people in our family who have believed in Jesus and been changed by him. If we won't believe all those proofs, we won't believe at all.

**PRAYER:** Jesus, you have given me plenty of proof, and I believe in you. Amen.

# Go in Private

**If another believer sins against you, go privately and point out the fault. If the other person listens and confesses it, you have won that person back.** Matthew 18:15

**MAIN READING:** Matthew 18 • **OPTIONAL READING:** Matthew 19

"He lied to me," Alex said to his friend Josh. "I'm going to pay him back."

"Wait," Josh said. "Didn't we hear about this in Sunday school?"

"What?"

"About when someone sins against you."

"I think so."

"Let's find the verse first."

Alex and Josh found their Bibles and looked up the verse we are reading today. Matthew 18:15-17 is sometimes called the passage about church discipline. What it talks about is what you are to do when someone sins against you. Do you go gossip about it to others? No. Do you go to the minister and tell him? No. What it says is that you go in private to the person who hurt you. Tell him what he did. Then see if he repents and asks your forgiveness. If he does, it's over. You forgive him and the hurt is made right. Other steps follow if he doesn't apologize, though.

The important thing is that when you are hurt by someone, when they sin against you, you don't go talking about it to everyone like most people do. Instead, you go to the person alone, in private. This way, they're protected and so are you—from sinning against them by gossiping .

**PRAYER:** Lord, praise you for giving us a way to solve problems. I'll follow it. Amen.

# Jesus Predicts His Death

**Then they will hand him over to the Romans to be mocked, whipped, and crucified. But on the third day he will be raised from the dead.**
Matthew 20:19

**Main Reading:** Matthew 20 • **Optional Reading:** Matthew 21

Few people can predict when they will die. Unless you're a murderer on death row with an exact date, most people never know. Not even up to the last minute.

This is what makes Jesus' prediction in this verse that much more amazing. Over and over Jesus told his disciples this would happen. He would be mocked, beaten, and crucified. Three days later, he'd rise from the dead.

At first, the disciples didn't like what Jesus said. Peter even argued with Jesus about it. But Jesus was firm. It would happen and for a good reason: so he could die for the sins of the world.

After Jesus rose again and the Holy Spirit reminded the disciples of Jesus' words, they remembered everything. Jesus had predicted his death. It happened just as he said.

How did Jesus know this? Because he is God. He knew the end from the beginning. He had seen everything that would happen in his life and in yours too. This was just one more proof of Jesus' divinity. When the disciples remembered it, they realized all the more that Jesus was who he said he was: the Son of God.

Do you trust him? Are you following him? If not, get with it. You don't want to be late on this one.

**Prayer:** Father, I know Jesus is the Son of God, and I trust him forever. Amen.

# Love God with All Your . . .

**You must love the Lord your God with all your heart, all your soul, and all your mind.** Matthew 22:37

**MAIN READING:** Matthew 22 • **OPTIONAL READING:** Matthew 23

"What's the greatest commandment?" the Sunday-school teacher asked.

Students responded with various commands from the Bible: "Don't steal." "Love your enemies." "Give a tithe of all you earn."

Jesus answered the question, though, for all time in today's verse. We are to love God with all our heart, soul, and mind. Some places Jesus says, "And with all your might, too."

What does this mean? To love God with your heart is to love him from the core of your being. Deep inside where no one else can see, in your greatest thoughts and feelings, you love God.

Loving him with your soul means to love him with your personality and self. That might mean letting out a shout now and then, and expressing your strongest feelings.

To love him with your mind means learning from him, studying his Word, understanding the truth about God.

And loving him with all your might means to love him from your will—obeying him no matter what he asks of you.

Are you loving God like that?

**PRAYER:** Father, I want to love you with everything I've got, ever and always. Amen.

# Signs of the End

**There will be famines and earthquakes in many parts of the world. But all this will be only the beginning of the horrors to come.**
Matthew 24:7, 8

**Main Reading:** Matthew 24 • **Optional Reading:** Matthew 25

How do we know when Jesus will come back?

The disciples asked Jesus this very question shortly before he died and rose again. "What will be the signs of the end?" they asked.

Jesus answered in Matthew 24, 25 with many things we can look for. Among them are the issues of today's verse. There will be famines and earthquakes in various places. Did you know that there are more famines on the face of the earth than ever before? And earthquakes have increased in recent times. Are these signs Jesus' coming is near? Possibly.

Jesus also told his disciples that false Christs would come saying they're Jesus. "Don't believe them," Jesus said. Angels told the disciples that Jesus would come down from the heavens, just as he went up. That's what we're to look for.

The important thing is that Jesus could come at any time. When we're awake or sleeping. When we're doing right, or doing wrong. When we're looking for him, or when we're not.

Be ready. Jesus is coming. Keep your life clean and open before him. When he comes, he will be proud of you for that.

**Prayer:** Lord, I want you to come quickly, because I want to be with you forever. Amen.

Week 35: Friday

# Peter's Denials

**But Peter denied it in front of everyone. "I don't know what you are talking about," he said.** Matthew 26:70

**MAIN READING:** Matthew 26:47-75

**OPTIONAL READING:** Matthew 26:1-46

Jesus warned Peter something terrible would happen. What was it? That Peter, the most outspoken of the disciples, would deny even knowing Jesus.

Peter, of course, was incensed. He would never deny Jesus, he told everyone. He even went out and found a sword to defend himself if anyone should attack.

But Peter wasn't ready for what happened. Jesus was at the trial of his life. Peter stood out in the courtyard, surrounded by hostile people. He didn't realize how afraid he was. Then someone asked him, "Aren't you one of them?" Peter looked around at the soldiers with their hands on their swords and shivered all the way to his toes. He didn't want to die. He couldn't face being flogged. So he said it. "I don't know him." He did this three times. After the third time, a rooster crowed as Jesus had predicted, and Peter ran out of the courtyard, weeping about his cowardice and betrayal.

Did Jesus hold this against Peter? No. In John 21, we see Jesus talking to Peter about the event. He seemed to want Peter to forget the past and to go on and preach the truth to people.

Peter did that and never turned back again. God never holds it against us when we mess up. If we ask, he forgives us as he did Peter.

**PRAYER:** Jesus, may I never deny I know you. May I always stand up for truth. Amen.

# The Son of God

**The Roman officer and the other soldiers at the crucifixion were terrified by the earthquake and all that had happened. They said, "Truly, this was the Son of God!"** Matthew 27:54

**Main Reading:** Matthew 27:32-66

**Optional Reading:** Matthew 27:1-31

The Romans took Jesus and whipped him. They beat him bloody, then stuck a crown of thorns on his head. They pressed it down till his scalp ran with blood. Then they put a stick in his hand and threw a purple cape over Jesus. Mocking him, soldiers bowed down and cried, "Hail, king of the Jews."

What did Jesus do? He could have summoned a million angels to come and kill every one of those soldiers. But he didn't. He just took it.

Later the Romans forced Jesus to march to Calvary where he would be crucified. One of them took foot-long nails and drove them through his hands and feet. They pushed Jesus up on the wood of the cross and left him hanging there. While they waited for him to die, the Romans gambled away his clothing and possessions. They always did this with a prisoner.

But suddenly, things went crazy. The sun darkened. Jesus cried out several times, and in the end he gave up his spirit. The soldiers were terrified, but they came to believe one thing: this was no ordinary man. The centurion and perhaps others cried out, "Truly, this was the Son of God!"

What was happening here? Jesus gave each of those men a chance to believe. Even as he was dying, he cared about them. If Jesus cares that much about lost people, shouldn't we too?

**Prayer:** Lord, thank you for giving us all the opportunity to believe in you. Amen.

# Go!

**Therefore, go and make disciples of all the nations, baptizing them in the name of the Father and the Son and the Holy Spirit.**
Matthew 28:19

**Main Reading:** Matthew 28:11-20

**Optional Reading:** Matthew 28:1-11

Today's verse is sometimes called the Great Commission. It's the mission that Jesus gave his disciples after he rose from the dead. These were some of his last words on Earth. If anyone wondered what Jesus wanted them to do, they could stop wondering now. Jesus spoke what has become the mission of the church ever since.

"Go, and make disciples of all the nations," he told his disciples. "Baptize them . . . and teach them . . . and I am with you always, even to the end of the age."

What is your mission in life? Why are you alive now? Why do you live where you do, go to the school you do, and attend the church you do? For one basic reason: so you can make disciples of anyone you talk to.

Of course, not everyone you talk to about Jesus will believe. Maybe it'll only be one in 10 or 20 or 30 who actually listen to you. But that doesn't mean you should stop talking about him.

The mission is GO. Make disciples. Get them baptized. Teach them everything Jesus taught you. And don't worry about anything. Jesus will be with you all the way.

Can it be any plainer?

**Prayer:** Lord, help me to get out there and share the gospel wherever I am. Amen.

Week 36: Monday

# Fishing for People

**Come, be my disciples, and I will show you how to fish for people!**
Mark 1:17

**MAIN READING:** Mark 1 • **OPTIONAL READING:** Mark 2

Have you ever been fishing?

You grab your rod and reel. You trek down to the creek or river or lake. You bait the hook with a worm, a lure, a fly, or just a small chunk of bologna. You throw in the line. And wait. And wait. And wait.

A lot of fishing is about waiting. For that first strike. For the big one. For that catfish you've seen lurking down in the depths.

Fishing is a fairly simple sport. It's not real complicated. But it's an apt illustration for what Jesus meant when he told his first disciples he would make them fishers of men.

God wants you to fish for people. He wants you to snag them, pull them out of the world, and bring them to Jesus. How do you do it? It's a lot like fishing. You have your equipment—the Bible, various opening questions, a gospel presentation. You go to your friends, throw out your line, and wait for a strike. You ask them questions that grow out of your friendship with them: What do you think life is all about? Have you ever thought about eternity? Do you know where you'll go when you die?

Some friends will ignore you. Some give you a little nibble, then walk away. But a few will take the bait and get hooked. Soon, they're walking with Jesus too.

God wants you to fish. For people. With all your heart. Don't give up when you don't get a strike. God will bless you if you wait.

**PRAYER:** Lord, grant me success as I fish for people who want to come to you. Amen.

Week 36: Tuesday

# Jesus' Anger

**He looked around at them angrily, because he was deeply disturbed by their hard hearts. Then he said to the man, "Reach out your hand."**
Mark 3:5

**MAIN READING:** Mark 3 • **OPTIONAL READING:** Mark 4

Is it ever OK to get angry?

Some Christians would have us believe that we should never get angry about anything. Anger is a sin, they say. Anger makes you lose control.

Some say, "No, righteous indignation is all right." That's when you rightly feel angry about someone doing wrong things.

Jesus became angry at the Pharisees and scribes for their hardness of heart. A man sat in the temple, probably begging. He couldn't work, because his hand (and arm?) were withered, just skin and bone. He couldn't move or manipulate things with that hand.

Jesus saw him and decided to heal him. But some in the crowd that day believed to work on the Sabbath—church day—was wrong. They didn't care about this poor man. They felt no compassion for this person who had suffered so long. All they cared about was their little man-made rules.

Jesus felt anger because these people had hard hearts. They put their little rules and laws (not God's, but theirs) ahead of everything else that God had commanded.

Jesus healed the man anyway. It's OK to get angry at sin. It's OK to be upset when you see people hurting others. That's the right kind of anger, the kind Jesus felt.

**PRAYER:** Father, may I never stop being angry about sin that hurts others. Amen.

Week 36: Wednesday

# Go Home and Tell

**Go home to your friends, and tell them what wonderful things the Lord has done for you and how merciful he has been.** Mark 5:19

**MAIN READING:** Mark 5 • **OPTIONAL READING:** Mark 6

Cal was excited. That Sunday, the minister planned to baptize him in front of the whole church. Cal had never been baptized. He felt a little nervous about it. But he wanted to obey God. He knew baptism was one of the first steps toward being a committed Christian.

The day came. Cal dressed in a special robe. He walked down in front of the whole church. The minister said some words, then asked Cal if he believed in Jesus with all his heart. Cal piped up, "I do."

Then the minister baptized him. Nothing amazing happened, but Cal felt a little different. He felt as if he'd made a real and final commitment.

The minister said then, "Go, tell all your friends what has happened to you. Never stop telling them." Cal took it seriously and began telling everyone he knew about trusting Jesus. Soon, several became Christians.

Today's verse tells us about a man who had many demons inside him. Jesus cast them out. The man became calm and normal. Before this, he had been violent and hateful. He wanted to follow Jesus. But Jesus told him to go tell his family and friends what God had done. That's what sharing your faith is all about. Telling them what Jesus has done for you.

**PRAYER:** Lord, help me to tell everyone I know about you so they'll believe, too. Amen.

# Thought-Life

**It is the thought-life that defiles you. For from within, out of a person's heart, come evil thoughts, sexual immorality, theft, murder . . .** Mark 7:20

**Main Reading:** Mark 7:1-20 • **Optional Reading:** Mark 7:21-36

Ever hear thoughts like these come into your mind:

"I hate her. She's so ugly."

"I'd like to punch his lights out. He messes with me, I'll mess with him."

"She thinks she is so hot. I'll show her."

"That guy is the biggest jerk in the class."

We have so many nasty thoughts go through our heads at times. Jesus knew what happens in our minds. In today's verse, he spoke to his disciples about what makes a person disgusting in God's eyes. They had the idea that not washing their hands, or wearing the wrong clothing was what mattered. But Jesus told them those outside-your-body things didn't really hurt you. It was what went on inside you that God didn't like.

What thoughts do you hear in your head? Are they mean, nasty thoughts? The way to stop them is simply to refuse to let them run on. When a bad thought comes into your mind, choose to say no to listening to it. Then let your mind think about something good and beautiful, a verse of Scripture, a nice thing you can say to someone else.

God will clean up your mind if you ask him. So why not ask today?

**Prayer:** Lord, help me to clear out all the junk in my head, and to replace it with good, positive thoughts. Amen.

# You Are the Messiah!

**Then Jesus asked, "Who do you say I am?" Peter replied, "You are the Messiah."** Mark 8:29

**Main Reading:** Mark 8 • **Optional Reading:** Mark 9

Who is Jesus?

Some people say he was a great teacher. He taught wonderful lessons about life and God. The only problem is, Jesus himself didn't say he was just a great teacher. He said he was the Son of God. How could he be a great teacher if he claimed to be the Son of God when he really wasn't?

Other people tell us Jesus was a prophet. Again, that's true. Jesus did predict the future and he preached some tremendous sermons. But how could he be a prophet if he was wrong about who he really was? Would a prophet have been wrong about something so important?

There are those who say Jesus was a liar. And a lunatic. And other bad things. But could a liar or lunatic have done the miracles he performed? Could a liar or lunatic have spoken the wondrous words he gave us? Would a liar or lunatic have died on the cross for the sins of the world?

Today's Scripture points out the most important question for any of us to answer: Who is Jesus?

How you answer that question is a matter of life and death.

**Prayer:** Jesus, may I always remember that you are God's Son, my Savior and Lord. Amen.

# Bring the Children to Me

**Then [Jesus] took the children into his arms and placed his hands on their heads and blessed them.** Mark 10:16

**Main Reading:** Mark 10 • **Optional Reading:** Mark 11

Does Jesus like kids?

Some adults are not nice to children. They don't want to be bothered by their questions or needs. They want the children to just disappear or go out and play.

There are other adults who think children don't have anything good to say. They're just too dumb. Or, they don't know enough yet to say something that means anything.

Jesus' disciples were a little like that. They thought children were a nuisance. They didn't want them crowding around. They told the children not to bother Jesus. After all, he had important work to do.

Jesus never felt that way about kids. Today's verse shows us the truth: Jesus loves kids and wants them to feel free to come to him anytime, anywhere. Jesus will listen to a child as attentively as he would the president of the United States. Jesus wants to nurture and comfort and build up children as much as anyone.

Do you ever wonder if you're too young to really get Jesus' attention? Stop! Jesus wants you. Come to him. Tell him your thoughts. He will always listen. And he will soon answer any needs you have too.

**Prayer:** Lord, thank you for inviting me to come to you anywhere, anytime. Amen.

Week 36: Sunday

# Give to God What Is God's

**"Well, then," Jesus said, "give to Caesar what belongs to him. But everything that belongs to God must be given to God." This reply completely amazed them.** Mark 12:17

**MAIN READING:** Mark 12:1-27 • **OPTIONAL READING:** Mark 12:28-44

The Jews laid a trap for Jesus. One of the biggest issues Jews talked about everywhere was the problem of taxes. Should they have to pay them to Rome? Weren't they free? Wasn't their money their own?

Two groups approached Jesus about the problem. One group, the Pharisees, hated taxes. They considered Roman coins a kind of idolatry because the Roman emperor's face adorned the front of the silver and gold pieces. The other group, the Herodians, liked Rome. They believed strongly that paying taxes made their lives secure and worthwhile.

Now notice: these two bitterly divided groups came to Jesus to ask about taxes. How can Jesus answer and satisfy both? If he says, "Yes, pay taxes to Caesar," the Pharisees will write him off as a heretic. If he says, "No, you don't have to," the Herodians will haul him off and have him thrown into prison as a rebel.

Jesus, though, never one to be pinned to the wall, gives the perfect answer: "Give to Caesar what is Caesar's, and to God what is God's."

That's the issue, isn't it? We need to give God the things that belong to him—our hearts, our friendship, our love. When we do that, everything else falls into place.

**PRAYER:** Jesus, may I always remember to give you what really matters first. Amen.

# The Lord's Supper

**As they were eating, Jesus took a loaf of bread and asked God's blessing on it. Then he broke it in pieces and gave it to the disciples, saying, "Take it, for this is my body."** Mark 14:22

**Main Reading:** Mark 14 • **Optional Reading:** Mark 13

What does the Lord's Supper represent in our lives?

Jesus instituted what we call the Lord's Supper the night before he was crucified as he celebrated one last Passover with his disciples. The disciples gathered around the table, eating. At one point, Jesus took the loaf of Passover bread. It was unleavened, which means it had no yeast. The bread didn't rise or have bubbles in it. Yeast represented sin to God, and in this special feast he wanted flat, unleavened bread. God wanted the people of Israel to remember they had exited from Egypt in a hurry. They didn't have time to make regular bread.

But the bread had even greater significance. It represented Jesus' body, which would be nailed to the cross and bear the sins of the world.

The cup or wine represented Jesus' blood which would be spilled.

In both cases, the Lord's Supper becomes a remembrance. We remember what Jesus did for us on the cross. It's meant to be a time of worship and reverence.

Next time your church celebrates the Lord's Supper, remember these things. It will make it more meaningful to you and everyone present.

**Prayer:** Lord, thank you that you gave your body and blood for us. Amen.

Week 37: Tuesday

# Forsaken

**Then, at that time Jesus called out with a loud voice, "Eloi, Eloi, lema sabachthani?" which means, "My God, my God, why have you forsaken me?"** Mark 15:34

**MAIN READING:** Mark 15 • **OPTIONAL READING:** Mark 16

Have you ever been lost as a child?

Maybe you were at the mall. You got separated from your family. Suddenly, strangers stood all around you. No one familiar appeared in sight. It can be very scary.

Or worse, in the woods. Perhaps you walked down to a wooded area or went on a trip to a forest. You thought you were on the trail. But you looked up and saw nothing but trees. Your dad and mom were gone.

Being lost is scary. The feeling of being lost is even worse.

Perhaps that is a little of what Jesus felt on the cross, when he cried out the words of today's verse. "My God, my God, why have you forsaken me?" In that moment, the sins of the world were laid on Jesus' body. He felt infinite and dark separation from his Father in heaven. All the anger of God was poured out on him. He felt lost, broken, forsaken—something he'd never experienced before.

Jesus was in hell.

That is what hell will be: forsaken, separated, lost from God forever. Jesus took that on himself for you and me.

**PRAYER:** Jesus, thank you for taking the punishment in my place. Amen.

# I Am Your Servant!

**Mary responded, "I am the Lord's servant, and I am willing to accept whatever he wants. May everything you have said come true." And then the angel left.** Luke 1:38

**Main Reading:** Luke 1:1-45 • **Optional Reading:** Luke 1:46-80

Picture this. You're lying in bed asleep. Suddenly, a noise awakens you. You look up. By your bed stands an angel, unlike anyone you've ever seen before. He holds up his hand and says, "Don't be afraid." Then he tells you about a mission God wants you to fulfill.

Maybe it's to go to a foreign country and tell people about Jesus.

Perhaps it's to travel to Washington, D.C., and protest against some new anti-Christian law.

It could be something as simple as playing the piano for your church.

But it's a mission from God, one he has personally selected for you to take on.

Would you do it? Would you agree to obey God?

That's what happened to Mary in today's reading. Gabriel, one of God's angels, came to her to tell her she would become pregnant and give birth to Jesus, the Savior of the world. Mary had some questions. She didn't fully understand how this could work. But in the end, she bowed her head and said, "I will do as you wish."

What great courage. What perfect obedience. That's the way God hopes all of us will respond when he gives us a mission too.

**Prayer:** Lord, whatever you want me to do, I will do it, and gladly. Amen.

Week 37: Thursday

# Born in a Stable

**She gave birth to her first child, a son. She wrapped him snugly in strips of cloth and laid him in a manger, because there was no room for them in the village inn.** Luke 2:7

**MAIN READING:** Luke 2:1-24 • **OPTIONAL READING:** Luke 2:25-52

Why was Jesus born in a stable? Why did he have such a strange and difficult way of coming into the world?

Jesus is the king of the universe. He might have come to us in purple robes, with a huge army of angels and a sword on his hip. He could have forced every one of us to bow down and worship him. He could easily have required that no one commit one more sin, on penalty of death.

But Jesus came into the world as a baby. Born of a virgin. Placed in a feed trough. Wrapped with rags. Why did he come like this?

Some say it's a stunner. It gets the world's attention. But did it back then?

Perhaps the best reason is because God wants us to know that Jesus doesn't demand the best of everything. He won't force us to bow in worship. Jesus is humble.

That's a good thing to know as a Christian. Jesus isn't proud. He has every right to be, but he isn't. He wants us to feel comfortable with him. He's a brother, a friend, as well as Lord and master. No names in lights. No top billing. He's a loving friend who wants to have an eternal relationship with each of us.

**PRAYER:** Lord, may I never forget that although you are God, you're also a friend and the leader of my family. Amen.

Week 37: Friday

# John the Baptist

**Then John went from place to place on both sides of the Jordan River, preaching that people should be baptized to show that they had turned from their sins and turned to God to be forgiven.** Luke 3:3

**MAIN READING:** Luke 3 • **OPTIONAL READING:** Luke 4

Can you see this guy? Brawny arms. Booming voice. A coat of camel's hair. Thick belt. Standing there in the middle of the Jordan River, beckoning people to come and be baptized.

Would you have gone to him? Would you have listened?

John had a simple message: "I come to prepare the way for the Messiah. I'm here just to announce that he's coming next."

John didn't try to conform to the ways of the world. He didn't make himself out to be someone special. Many people probably wondered where this strange guy had come from. What rock did he crawl out from under?

John had one mission: to get people ready to meet Jesus. He wasn't the main act. He wasn't the big show. He didn't even do miracles. He just trumpeted out his message and told everyone to get ready, the Son of God is coming. How did he feel, just playing the role of a messenger?

And yet, that's what we are too. We're just messengers telling people where to look to find life. We're just beggars who've found bread. The bread is Jesus. The one we've come to talk about is the Lord of creation.

It's a big job. Are you up to it?

**PRAYER:** Jesus, help me to be the best messenger possible. Amen.

Week 37: Saturday

# Jesus Calls a Tax Collector

**Later, as Jesus left the town, he saw a tax collector named Levi sitting at his tax-collection booth. "Come, be my disciple!" Jesus said to him.** Luke 5:27

**MAIN READING:** Luke 5 • **OPTIONAL READING:** Luke 6

Tax collectors were the worst people in all of Israel. Jews considered them traitors. They worked for Rome, the hated enemy of all the Jews. Sometimes they cheated people. Sometimes they required a lot more than what was right. But they had the power to do it. You didn't pay up, they could call out an armed guard. They were feared, hated, and rejected.

So why did Jesus step up to Matthew's (sometimes named Levi) tax table and call him? Didn't Jesus know what losers tax collectors were? Didn't he understand that many people would be angry that this was one of Jesus' disciples?

The truth is, Matthew wasn't different from any of us. Maybe he worked his job well. Perhaps he was nice to people. He might even have given some of his victims a break here and there.

But he was a sinner. He was hated, rejected. Have you ever felt like that?

It doesn't really matter, does it? Because if Jesus calls you to be one of his children, everything in your past flies out the window. It doesn't matter who you are or what you've done. You could be far worse than a tax collector—a bigot? a murderer? a traitor? But Jesus wants you anyway.

**PRAYER:** Lord, praise you that you leave no one out, not even the worst among us. Amen.

# What Amazes God

**When Jesus heard this, he was amazed. Turning to the crowd, he said, "I tell you, I haven't seen faith like this in all the land of Israel!"** Luke 7:9

**MAIN READING:** Luke 7 • **OPTIONAL READING:** Luke 8

Can God be amazed? Can you stun God with something sometime?

After all, God knows everything. He knows about everyone down to the smallest details. Nothing we could do would ever astonish him. We couldn't say any line, speak any creative piece of writing, or tell a joke he hasn't already heard.

But it's possible to amaze God. Did you know that? Yes, one thing really blows God away. What? Faith. When we show that we believe in him wholeheartedly . . . when we say or do something that demonstrates incredible faith and trust in him . . . that knocks God off his feet.

In today's verse, we see a soldier who really gave Jesus a reason to be amazed. When Jesus said he was willing to come and heal this man's slave, the man told him he didn't need to travel all that distance. "Just say the word right here, right now," he said. "My servant will be healed without your taking one more step."

Why is this such a great act of faith? Because it had never been done before. Every time Jesus healed someone before, the person was present. Jesus touched them, or put mud on their eyes, or said something directly to them. Jesus had never healed from a distance.

But this man knew. He understood things about Jesus that no one else did. He knew Jesus could do anything. Is that the kind of faith you have?

**PRAYER:** Lord, give me the same kind of faith this soldier had. Amen.

# Transfigured

**And as he was praying, the appearance of his face changed, and his clothing became dazzling white.** Luke 9:29

**Main Reading:** Luke 9:1-36 • **Optional Reading:** Luke 9:37-62

God provided many ways for the disciples to believe Jesus was the Son of God.

When John baptized Jesus in the Jordan River, the Holy Spirit came upon him like a dove and a voice called out of heaven, "This is my beloved Son, in whom I am well pleased."

Jesus proceeded to do miracle after miracle. He turned water into wine at Cana. He healed the blind, lame, withered, deaf, and dumb. He cast out demons. He did other spectacular miracles—walking on water, stilling the storm, and feeding 5,000 people with five pieces of bread and two pieces of fish.

What more did they need?

Perhaps the thing they needed most was for Jesus to look like God. Radiant. Powerful. Beautiful. Magnificent. Maybe that's why Jesus took the three disciples, James, John, and Peter, up on the mountain. There, Jesus was transfigured. That means "changed in appearance," but really he was transformed. He looked totally different. His face radiated like the sun, and his garments brightened so the disciples could hardly look at them.

God did this to convince the disciples one more time: Jesus really is the Son of God.

Do you believe it too?

**Prayer:** Lord, praise you that Jesus is the Son, whom I can believe in always. Amen.

# Keep on Asking

**And so I tell you, keep on asking, and you will be given what you ask for. Keep on looking, and you will find. Keep on knocking, and the door will be opened.** Luke 11:9, 10

**MAIN READING:** Luke 11 • **OPTIONAL READING:** Luke 10

How do you get your prayers answered? Do you ever see God answering one of your prayers? How can you be a part of the answer?

Today's verse provides some insight.

First, ask. "Keep on asking." Don't give up. Mention your request to God today, tomorrow, and the next day. Keep asking till he either says no or wait or answers yes. The main thing is that you don't stop praying about the need. If you're convinced God will answer, don't give up.

Second, look. "Keep on looking." Sometimes you have to do more than ask. You have to get out there and look around. Perhaps you'll need to go to several places. Don't just ask, but get involved. Let God lead you.

Third, knock. "Keep on knocking." Sometimes you have to go much further than asking or looking. Sometimes you have to get out there and find a friend or others (knock on their lives) who can help you.

God often expects us to be part of the answer. Today my daughter needed a baseball glove. I had several old ones and told her to look around the house. She soon found one in a closet.

God wants to answer your prayers. But don't sit on your behind. Get out there, ask, look, and go to others, if necessary. God will answer you soon.

**PRAYER:** Father, let me not give up in prayer, but help me to get out there and really beat the bushes, looking for your answer. Amen.

# Your Primary Concern

**He will give you all you need from day to day if you make the Kingdom of God your primary concern.** Luke 12:31

**MAIN READING:** Luke 12 • **OPTIONAL READING:** Luke 13

Jade had a tremendous need. Her older sister planned to get married in two months and Jade was a bridesmaid. She needed a dress. Lavender was the color her sister said to get.

Her mom took Jade to the store and they looked all around. They went to the mall and checked out every store along the walkway. But no lavender dress in their price range appeared. Jade was pretty discouraged. Then her mother said, "Why don't we pray about it? Maybe we'll have a chance to glorify God too."

"What do you mean?" Jade asked.

"Maybe we can tell the salesperson that your sister is getting married, and we want God to be the center of it. We want a dress that will be part of that."

"That sounds cool," Jade said.

That was what they did. In a little while, they found a rack of dresses by accident. One of them was the perfect lavender dress. When they paid for it, Jade said to the attendant, "We prayed about this one and God answered. He really did."

"That's great," the attendant said. "I believe that's important!"

On the way home Jade commented, "That was so cool."

"God will always provide for your needs if your focus is right," her mom replied.

**PRAYER:** Lord, let me make building your kingdom the most important thing. Amen.

# Found!

**"We must celebrate with a feast, for this son of mine was dead and has now returned to life. He was lost, but now he is found." So the party began.** Luke 15:23, 24

**MAIN READING:** Luke 15 • **OPTIONAL READING:** Luke 14

You've probably heard the story many times. We call it the Parable of the Prodigal Son. Prodigal means a person who went to bad extremes. He messed up everything.

But a better title for this story would be "The Forgiving Father." Look at the father in this parable. He gave his younger son all the money the boy would inherit one day. The boy left town and soon squandered all that money on pleasure. He drank. He gambled. He took out beautiful women. He threw parties.

One day, though, the money ran out. His day in the sun was over. He ended up working for a farmer feeding the pigs. He didn't have a thing to eat. At that point, he woke up. He knew his father's hired hands had nice beds and plenty of food. He decided to go to his father and ask if he could be a hired hand.

That father had looked for the boy every day. He sat on the porch in the evening, studying the horizon. He awoke every morning, hoping the boy had come home. One day the boy did. It was a miracle. The boy stood there, apologizing, but the father was so happy, he threw a party, and gave the boy a ring and a new coat.

That's what God says he wants to do for people who have sinned. Do you ever worry that God might not accept or forgive you? Stop! He will. And he'll even throw a party in heaven when you come back to him.

**PRAYER:** Lord, thank you for forgiving me. I'll never forget it. Amen.

Week 38: Friday

# If They Won't Listen

**But Abraham said, "If they won't listen to Moses and the prophets, they won't listen even if someone rises from the dead."** Luke 16:31

**Main Reading:** Luke 16 • **Optional Reading:** Luke 17

Some people just won't listen.

Seth told his friend Joel about how he was baptized in church and forgiven. Joel just laughed.

Seth mentioned his new faith to his Uncle Gabe. But his uncle told him, "Oh, it's all just stories. I can't believe that stuff."

One day, Seth talked to a new kid on the bus. The kid just shook his head. "I have my own religion," he said.

Sharing your faith can be like that. Sometimes, you think, "If God would just do a special miracle for them! If God would just do something spectacular that would wake them up and make them see."

Do you know what God says to that? The same thing Jesus says in today's verse. Here, he told a parable about a poor man, Lazarus, who went to heaven, and a rich man who went to hell. The rich man pleaded with Abraham to raise Lazarus from the dead and send him to the rich man's brothers and warn them about hell. But Abraham said that if his brothers wouldn't believe Moses and the prophets, they wouldn't believe even if someone went to them from the dead.

Miracles don't change hard hearts. What changes them is the work of the Spirit. Pray for God's Spirit to work in people, and maybe then they will believe.

**Prayer:** Jesus, I pray that your Spirit would work in my friends today. Amen.

Week 38: Saturday

# Never Give Up

**One day Jesus told his disciples a story to illustrate their need for constant prayer and to show them that they must never give up.**
Luke 18:1

**Main Reading:** Luke 18 • **Optional Reading:** Luke 19

What's the most important truth about prayer?

We find it in today's verse. Jesus told his disciples to keep on praying and not give up. He then gave them a parable about a nasty judge who wouldn't listen to anyone. A poor widow came to him day after day, knocking on his door and crying out to him to give her justice. The judge just told her to go away.

One day, though, he realized this widow would wear him out. So he finally granted her request. It was a selfish reason, but because the widow wouldn't give up, she got what she needed.

Jesus told his disciples then, "If this judge, who didn't care about anyone, granted the widow her request, how much more will God, who loves you, give you what you need?"

God isn't like that judge at all. God wants to answer our prayers. But sometimes he delays. Sometimes he doesn't answer immediately. Sometimes he says no. But until then, we need to keep coming to him. Keep telling God what you desire. One day he may say no by changing your heart about it. But until then, keep on praying.

**Prayer:** Father, may I not give up in prayer, but keep praying until you answer. Amen.

Week 38: Sunday

# The Gift

**"I assure you," he said, "this poor widow has given more than all the rest of them. For they have given a tiny part of their surplus, but she, poor as she is, has given everything she has."** Luke 21:3, 4

**Main Reading:** Luke 21 • **Optional Reading:** Luke 20

Jerry took his $2 to church that day with high hopes. He wanted to donate to the building fund, but he had little money. It was his last two bucks.

In the meeting, the pastor asked the people how much they would donate. One man called out, "I'll give $200."

A second lady, who was known to have a great house, said, "I'll give $1,000."

And the richest man in the church answered, "I'll give $10,000 for the new building."

Jerry sat there with his $2 and felt like an idiot. What was $2 next to all these amounts?

But then the pastor talked to the church about the poor widow who gave her two little coins (mites). As Jesus watched everyone give their vast sums, he noted the widow and said she'd actually given more. Why? Because everyone else gave out of their surplus—money they had left over and didn't need that much. But this widow gave all she had.

God wants you to give to the work of his kingdom. If you give sacrificially, an amount that really costs you something, he is mightily pleased. For then he knows you truly love him.

**Prayer:** Father, help me to learn to give from the heart, so I may please you. Amen.

Week 39: Monday

# Sift You Like Wheat

**Simon, Simon, Satan has asked to have all of you, to sift you like wheat. But I have pleaded in prayer for you, Simon, that your faith should not fail.** Luke 22:31, 32

**MAIN READING:** Luke 22:1-38 • **OPTIONAL READING:** Luke 22:39-71

Jesus had some startling news for his top disciple, Peter. Satan, Jesus' archenemy and the accuser of God's people, asked God if he could attack Peter. Satan planned to "sift [Peter] like wheat." What did he mean?

You sift wheat by putting it into a sieve. A sieve is a plate with lots of little holes in the bottom. When you sift wheat, the heavy grain slips through the holes. The chaff, the wheat's paperlike covering, is too big and light to go through the holes. It is left behind.

To sift someone meant to find out where Peter was weak. Satan wanted to show God what a poor disciple Peter was. He planned to prove to Jesus that Peter had too many flaws to be relied upon.

When Jesus told Peter about this, Peter wasn't fazed at all. He responded that even if his life was threatened, he wouldn't desert Jesus.

We know what happened. Peter ended up denying that he knew Jesus at all. Satan showed Peter up.

Now look at this. Jesus warned Peter of this doom. But he also promised Peter that after he failed, he was to go back and strengthen his brothers. In other words, Jesus knows when we'll fail, but that doesn't mean he still can't use us in his kingdom.

**PRAYER:** Lord, praise you that Peter failed, showing us all that Jesus' love is greater. Amen.

Week 39: Tuesday

# Strangely Warm

**They said to each other, "Didn't our hearts feel strangely warm as he talked with us on the road and explained the Scriptures to us?"**
Luke 24:32

**MAIN READING:** Luke 24 • **OPTIONAL READING:** Luke 23

Jesus rose from the dead on a Sunday. The city of Jerusalem soared into an uproar about it. The disciples were flung every which way. Many ran. Others hid themselves.

But two walked on the road to Emmaus, perhaps going home. On the way, the risen Jesus walked with them. As they talked, they grieved over Jesus' death and seemed to have no knowledge of his resurrection.

Jesus set them straight. He shared with them what the Old Testament said. He assured them Jesus was still alive. At one point, they finally recognized him, and at that moment, he disappeared.

They talked excitedly and remembered how their hearts were "strangely warmed" as Jesus explained the Scriptures to them. Do you ever feel such a sensation when you hear the Bible preached? Do you ever feel moved, or amazed, or "warmed" inside?

God wants the Scriptures to be a powerful resource for us. He longs that we find in them the answers we need about life, death, and hope. As you learn to drink the words of the Bible, you'll find your heart moved and warmed. God gives hope and life through the Word to each of us, if we're listening.

**PRAYER:** Father, may your Word touch me deeply as I read it and hear it preached. Amen.

# The Word

**In the beginning the Word already existed. He was with God, and he was God. He was in the beginning with God.** John 1:1, 2

**MAIN READING:** John 1 • **OPTIONAL READING:** John 2

John begins his Gospel with a sentence about the "Word." What is the "Word?"

As you read, you'll find that in John 1:14, the Word refers to Jesus. Jesus himself was the Word.

Why did God call him the Word? Just about everything has a word that names it. One word can refer to an animal we know as a cow. House is the word we use for someone's place of residence.

Jesus is called the Word of God because he is God's final message to the world. He is the ultimate picture of God in the world. When we see Jesus, we have seen God.

This "Word" was "with God" and "was God." He "already existed" at the beginning. What does this tell us? Jesus is equal to God the Father and also is God's Son, the second person of the Trinity.

It's a difficult concept, but just think of Jesus as God's word picture of himself. Jesus is God's object lesson of what God is like.

**PRAYER:** Father, thank you for sending us the Word, Jesus, so we might know you. Amen.

# Born Again

**Jesus replied, "I assure you, unless you are born again, you can never see the Kingdom of God."** John 3:3

**MAIN READING:** John 3:1-21 • **OPTIONAL READING:** John 3:22-36

You've probably heard it in church many times. "You must be born again." What does this mean? How is someone born again?

You know what it means to be born. You come out of your mother's body. You start out as a baby, then grow up and become mature.

To be born again, you experience another kind of birth. You are born into a new family and have a new home, a new destination. You start off like a little baby, no matter how old you are in human years. You need the nurture and help of older Christians to learn to walk, eat, and grow.

How do you become born again?

By repenting of your sins and giving your life to Jesus. By trusting him with your life and being obedient to him. By agreeing with God that Jesus is your Lord, master, king, and friend.

Have you taken this step? Have you believed in Jesus? Do you sense that he is now in your life, leading you, helping you? If not, why not make it sure today by asking him to come into your life and begin leading you?

**PRAYER:** Jesus, I praise you that you have made the way for us to go to heaven plain and simple—we just need to obey you. Amen.

Week 39: Friday

# In Spirit and Truth

**For God is Spirit, so those who worship him must worship in spirit and in truth.** John 4:24

**Main Reading:** John 4 • **Optional Reading:** John 5

How does God want us to worship him? What should we be doing when we go to church?

When Jesus encountered the woman at the well in today's story, he talked to her about many things. At one point, he told her that those who worship God must worship "in spirit and in truth." What does that mean?

God is Spirit, according to today's verse. He does not have a body. He is everywhere. He knows everything. He possesses total and complete power over the whole universe. And he fills the whole universe.

In the same way, our bodies are simply clothing for our spirits. Inside each of us lives a spirit that is eternal. It can never die. That's the part of us that talks to, learns from, and experiences God. When we worship in spirit, we worship God with the most basic and real part of us, the thing that really is us.

In truth means nothing is hidden. We tell no lies, hold back nothing. We admit our wrongs. We come to God openly and without pretense. We worship him in reality, in real time, in a real place, and with our real spirit—our real self.

Do you want to worship God in spirit and in truth? Then come to him. Speak to him, spirit to Spirit. Hide nothing. Be open. You will find God an amazing friend and Lord, one who loves you infinitely.

**Prayer:** Lord, teach me to worship you in spirit and in truth. Amen.

Week 39: Saturday

# The Bread of Life

**I am the bread of life. No one who comes to me will ever be hungry again. Those who believe in me will never thirst.** John 6:35

**Main Reading:** John 6:1-40 • **Optional Reading:** John 6:41-71

For centuries, the main ingredient of a good meal was bread. Ancient people made bread out of wheat, barley, or other types of grain. They baked it in ovens and slathered butter on it when it was hot. There was nothing like a meal of hot bread, butter, and maybe some meat or gravy.

One day, Jesus fed 5,000 people with five loaves of bread and two small fish. You can be sure the bread Jesus gave them was the best bread they ever tasted.

Later, Jesus told the people that he was "the bread of life." What did he mean?

Bread, the most basic part of any meal, is an essential. Today, we eat white bread, whole wheat, bologna sandwiches, hamburgers on rolls, hot dogs on buns, and subs on foot-long Italian rolls. The ingredients of bread are in the crusts of our pies and the slices of our cake. There's bread in pizza and in a sandwich. Just about everywhere you look at things that we eat, you'll find some bread.

When Jesus said he was the bread of life, he meant he is the most important staple and ingredient of life. Without him, life would be dull, dreary, and without real joy and love. Without him, nothing in life would really taste good.

When we partake of him as our bread, though, we come alive. He makes it all worth living.

**Prayer:** Father, let me eat the bread of life always. Amen.

Week 39: Sunday

# Living Water

**If you are thirsty, come to me! If you believe in me, come and drink! For the Scriptures declare that rivers of living water will flow out from within.** John 7:37, 38

**Main Reading:** John 7 • **Optional Reading:** John 8

As Holly read the Bible that morning, it seemed her heart filled with joy. The promises about God loving us and being with us cheered her. The words about following and obeying him told her what to do. And the assurances that the Bible gave her about God's protection and care comforted her. It seemed like she saw God everywhere she went.

That morning, she skipped down to breakfast in a good mood.

"What are you so happy about?" her mother asked.

"Oh, today's reading in the Bible was really great," Holly answered. "I got excited about it."

"Feel like a little river flowing through your heart?" her mother commented.

"Yes, that was it," Holly said. "Like refreshing water on my face, except on the inside, where I really am."

"That's the living water of Jesus, darling. He's giving you a taste of real living water, which is from the Holy Spirit."

Her mom showed Holly today's verses and Holly knew it was true. She was thirsty and now she'd discovered where she could get a good, refreshing drink. From Jesus. From learning about him and walking with him. He was the living water she needed every day.

**Prayer:** Lord, I am thirsty. Fill me with your living water. Amen.

Week 40: Monday

# Why He Was Born Blind

**"It was not because of his sins or his parents' sins," Jesus answered. "He was born blind so the power of God could be seen in him."** John 9:3

**MAIN READING:** John 9 • **OPTIONAL READING:** John 10

Many people believe God repays us for our sins. We reap disease, or problems, or even great disasters, because of our sin. One major religion, Hinduism, believes in the Law of Karma. This states that you get in your life (they believe in reincarnation) payment for what you did in your previous life. If you were good in your previous life, you receive good in this life. If bad, then you receive bad in your present life.

Can you see the horrible edge to this belief? It means whatever happens to you in this life—blindness, lameness, handicaps, whatever—happens because of what you did previously. No one needs to help you because you're just reaping what you've sown. You're getting what you deserved.

Jesus tells us the truth about this belief in today's verse. It's wrong. There's only one reason a person might be born with or have handicaps: so the glory of God might be displayed in the person. That person may glorify God by being healed. If not healed, he may show God's greatness by living a joyous, fulfilled Christian life despite his handicap.

People who have handicaps are meant to show off God in their lives, even if they aren't healed. That's the true path to hope and God's glory.

**PRAYER:** Jesus, I praise you for being gracious to all of us. Amen.

# Why God Delays

**Lazarus's sickness will not end in death. No, it is for the glory of God. I, the Son of God, will receive glory from this.** John 11:4

**Main Reading:** John 11:1-37 • **Optional Reading:** John 11:38-57

Sometimes God doesn't answer prayer right away. Sometimes God delays answering. Why?

Many Christians pray for months, even years, for something to happen in their lives. Healing. Job success. A spouse. Children. People pray for all kinds of things. Sometimes God answers right away. Sometimes he doesn't. Sometimes he delays for a long time because of his greater plan.

In today's verse, we see Jesus telling his disciples why he isn't going to travel to Bethany to heal Lazarus. He planned to do something greater than a healing; he wanted to raise Lazarus from the dead. Why? To show off his power and to convince more people to believe in him.

God always does what he does for a reason. When he doesn't answer prayer right away, it may be because he has another plan. He wants to do something else in your life. When answers to your prayers are delayed, talk to God about it. Ask him why. Go to him and discuss whether he has some other plan.

It will help you grow and become stronger as a Christian.

**Prayer:** Lord, I praise you for the prayers you haven't answered for me. I know you have other plans and I trust you about them. Amen.

# Remembering

**His disciples didn't realize at the time that this was a fulfillment of prophecy. But after Jesus entered into his glory, they remembered that these Scriptures had come true before their eyes.** John 12:16

**Main Reading:** John 12 • **Optional Reading:** John 13

How did the disciples write the New Testament? How did they remember all the things Jesus said and did? Matthew and John were disciples of Jesus and saw many of the works Jesus performed. But Mark, Luke, and Paul weren't part of that inner circle. How did they know what to write?

Today's verse offers us some insight. The disciples and writers "remembered" what happened after Jesus rose from the dead. When the Holy Spirit came into their hearts, he helped them remember what they had seen. In many cases, the Spirit revealed things to them that they never knew before.

This is how we got our Bible. The Holy Spirit led the writers of the Old and New Testaments to remember and see things they may have forgotten. The Spirit strengthened their minds. He spoke to their hearts. And so they knew the truth.

Do you know that God will speak to you through the Bible? Are you ever convicted by something you read or heard from the Bible? Do you ever feel great joy over some promise? Has a truth ever touched you deeply?

That's the Spirit of God speaking. He spoke to the disciples then so they could write his words, and he speaks to us now.

**Prayer:** Father, thank you for the Spirit. Let him speak to me every day. Amen.

# Live in Them

**Jesus replied, "All those who love me will do what I say. My Father will love them, and we will come to them and live with them."**
John 14:23

**Main Reading:** John 14 • **Optional Reading:** John 15

Did you know that God lives in your heart?

Today's verse reveals that great truth. When we accept Jesus, he comes to dwell in us in the person of the Holy Spirit. God lives in that little nook of our hearts that is the most private and personal part of us. There, he speaks to us, not out loud, but in the deep parts of our heart. There, faith burns.

What are some signs of Christ's presence inside you? Ask yourself these questions:

1. Does God ever speak to you through the "still small voice" in your heart? Have you been convicted or built up by something you heard in church or from your friends? He will speak at times, leading you, strengthening you, helping you.

2. Does the Spirit ever comfort you? When things go wrong, when you lose a friend or relative, does the Spirit talk to you quietly, assuring you in your heart? That's God giving you his comfort.

3. Does God ever tell you in your heart that you are his child? One of the things the Spirit does is assure us we belong to God.

These are just a few of the ways that Jesus makes his presence known in our lives. He wants to be real to you, not just someone who is distant.

**Prayer:** Lord, praise you that the Spirit is in my life. Speak to me every day. Amen.

Week 40: Friday

# Overcome the World

**I have told you all this so that you may have peace in me. Here on earth you will have many trials and sorrows. But take heart, because I have overcome the world.** John 16:33

**MAIN READING:** John 16 • **OPTIONAL READING:** John 17

James was having a bad day.

He flunked an important test in school. He knew his father would be angry about that one.

He got into a tiff on the playground, and some kids laughed at him when he backed down.

He lost his favorite hat. He thought he must have left it at a store he'd visited. But when he went back to find it, they knew nothing about it.

Have you ever had a bad day like that? Like that character Alexander who had the "terrible, horrible, no good, very bad day?"

What does a Christian do in the midst of such problems?

God promises one thing he will give us when things go wrong: peace. How can we have peace when everything in our lives has gone crazy? Because of Jesus. The world will throw all kinds of bad stuff at us, but we can still be at peace. Why? Because Jesus has overcome the world. What does that mean? It means he is greater than the world and its problems. He is the supernatural source of power and strength. He can give us peace even when everyone around is afraid and worried.

**PRAYER:** Lord, grant to me your peace at all times so I may glorify you, even when things go wrong. Amen.

# Do You Recognize the Truth?

**"You say that I am a king, and you are right," Jesus said. "I was born for that purpose. And I came to bring truth to the world. All who love the truth recognize that what I say is true."** John 18:37

**MAIN READING:** John 18 • **OPTIONAL READING:** John 19

Jesus said something startling in today's reading. "All who love the truth recognize that what I say is true." When he said this while standing before Pontius Pilate, the governor commented, "What is truth?"

Many people today believe there is no such thing as absolute truth. They say things like, "It's true to me." Meaning: "For me this is true, but it may not be for you." Or they say, "All truth is relative." Meaning: "Everything depends on the person who thinks it. If someone thinks something is true, it is for him. But it may not be true for others."

Is this correct? Can the earth be round and flat at the same time? Can gravity work sometimes but not others? Is murder always wrong, or are there situations in which it might be justified?

People argue these points all the time. But it's really as plain as day. There are many things in the universe which simply are true all the time. No matter how much we might wish we could fly like a bird, we can't. Gravity will pull us down.

Moral truth—truth about how we live our lives—is just as important as scientific truth. The truth is what Jesus said: people who love the truth will believe in him. All others will go their own way, to their own peril.

**PRAYER:** Jesus, thank you for showing me the truth. Amen.

Week 40: Sunday

# Those Who Believe Anyway

**Then Jesus told him, "You believe because you have seen me. Blessed are those who haven't seen me and believe anyway."** John 20:29

**MAIN READING:** John 20 • **OPTIONAL READING:** John 21

Thomas, Jesus' disciple, had a problem. He was so distraught over Jesus' death on the cross that he disappeared for a while. Where he went, no one knows. Maybe it was to weep by himself. Or more likely, to think about what he would do next with his life. He thought it was over. He'd thrown everything he had into Jesus' pot. Now Jesus was dead, and Thomas had nothing to live for.

The other disciples, though, informed him of the resurrection. Thomas told them he wouldn't believe it unless he could touch Jesus' nail-scarred hands as proof. Jesus appeared to Thomas and told him to touch away. Thomas fell at Jesus' feet and cried, "My Lord and my God!"

Then Jesus made the pronouncement which is today's verse. Thomas saw Jesus and believed. But Jesus said those people who didn't see and yet believed would be most blessed.

Who is that? Us. None of us ever saw Jesus resurrected. But we have believed. Why? Because the Bible or someone using the Bible has spoken to us.

Do you ever think you need a proof to believe in Jesus? Go to the Bible. Search its pages. Study the texts. God will speak to you. Faith will come to you as you accept the truth and facts about Jesus.

**PRAYER:** Lord, praise you that you give us all we need to believe. Amen.

Week 41: Monday

# Power to Tell the Story

**But when the Holy Spirit has come upon you, you will receive power and will tell people about me everywhere—in Jerusalem, throughout Judea, in Samaria, and to the ends of the earth.** Acts 1:8

**Main Reading:** Acts 1 • **Optional Reading:** Acts 2

Do you ever feel afraid when a chance to share your faith comes up?

Most Christians face the same problem. We can be talking about everyday things. Suddenly, a thought pops into your head: "Why don't you tell this person about Jesus?" Instantly, your hands get clammy. Your mouth dries up. You may even start to shake.

Most likely, in such situations you will just push the thought away. You might feel better after that. But if you're really walking closely with Jesus, you might think, "Hey, that's a good idea."

Fear in witnessing is normal and natural. Satan will attack you the moment an opportunity arises. He never wants you to share the gospel. But today's verse tells us something important. "You will receive power." God supplies us with the power at the right moment. All we have to do is expect it to come and receive it.

In your fear, you might stop, or even refuse to talk about Jesus. But take the first step. "Hey, have I ever told you about what Jesus did in my life?" If you ask a question or say a quick word like, "Can I tell you about Jesus?" you will find God will give you the power. Expect it. You will calm down. Your words will become smooth. And you will share. It's an exciting thing to happen in your life.

**Prayer:** Lord, teach me always to be ready to share the truth with my friends. Amen.

Week 41: Tuesday

# No Other Name

**There is salvation in no one else! There is no other name in all of heaven for people to call on to save them.** Acts 4:12

**Main Reading:** Acts 4 • **Optional Reading:** Acts 3

Can a Muslim be saved? Will God come into the heart of a Buddhist? Or a Mormon? Is salvation through Hinduism just another way?

Today's verse tells us the truth about other religions: none of them are the way to heaven. Only in Jesus will God save the person. Many times, Jesus speaks to such people and they become believers, even on their deathbeds. We cannot possibly know everything about a person until we meet them again in heaven.

But for those who have heard of Jesus, there is only one way to heaven: through believing in him. No matter how much they believe their own religion is right, it's not.

Why is it this way?

Jesus paid the price of his life for us. He died on the cross for our sins. If we hear about that and reject it, saying, "I'll stick with believing in reincarnation," why should God help us? We have rejected the one who paid everything for us.

Make no mistake. There is only one way to salvation, eternal life, and heaven: through Jesus. God will not listen to us if we come by another way.

**Prayer:** Lord, I have come to you through Jesus. I know he is the only way. Amen.

# Rejoicing About Suffering for Jesus

**The apostles left the high council rejoicing that God had counted them worthy to suffer dishonor for the name of Jesus.** Acts 5:41

**MAIN READING:** Acts 5 • **OPTIONAL READING:** Acts 6

Peter and John hung from the whipping post by their hands. They were tied there with a leather thong.

A burly Roman whipped them 39 times with a whip that would hurt far worse than any instrument we know today.

How did they survive? Undoubtedly, God gave them special grace for that moment. God gave them the power to withstand the punishment. That doesn't mean it didn't hurt, or they felt no pain. But supernatural power flooded them as that Roman beat them. Nothing the Romans did to them would make them give up their mission.

When they left that place, beaten and bloody, they "rejoiced." They had "suffered for Jesus," and it gave them great feelings of happiness. Why? It's a grace God gives us when we're persecuted. We find joy in knowing God has used us to do great things for his kingdom.

Have you ever been persecuted for your faith? Put down? Gossiped about? Rejected? Hated? Maybe even hit by a particularly nasty person?

That's suffering for the name of Jesus. It's a high honor for any Christian to stand up under such pressure. God will see you through it, even if it does hurt.

**PRAYER:** Jesus, if I must face persecution, help me to face it like these men. Amen.

# A Glorious Death

**But Stephen, full of the Holy Spirit, gazed steadily upward into heaven and saw the glory of God, and he saw Jesus standing in the place of honor at God's right hand.** Acts 7:55

**Main Reading:** Acts 7:37-60 • **Optional Reading:** Acts 7:1-36

Are you ever afraid of dying?

Researchers have told us that young people think about death many times a day. They wonder about it, ask themselves questions about it, and hope it doesn't happen to them for a long time. What most people fear about death is what will happen after they die. Where will they go? What will it be like? Do they live on? Is there really a heaven and a hell?

Sometimes God gives people a glimpse of life after death. People have died and been resuscitated, claiming they went to heaven or hell while they were dead. In today's verse, we meet a person who saw the afterlife. Stephen, while he was being stoned for his faith in Christ, at the last moment saw something. The Scripture says he saw "heaven opened" and saw "the glory of God." What did he see? We don't know. We only know that Stephen was not afraid. He looked forward to the moment he would go there.

If you are ever afraid about death, turn to God. Tell him about your fear. God will give you his peace. He will assure you that you will go to be with him, and that nothing from the world can ever hurt you again.

**Prayer:** Father, let me not be afraid about death. I look forward to being with you. Amen.

Week 41: Friday

# Jesus Appears to Saul

**I am Jesus, the one you are persecuting! Now get up and go into the city, and you will be told what you are to do.** Acts 9:5, 6

**MAIN READING:** Acts 9 • **OPTIONAL READING:** Acts 8

Will God stop evil people from doing their evil? Does God ever get through to murderers, bigots, and others?

Several years ago, two notorious murderers were caught. The first one was a brutal killer who murdered close to a hundred people. But before he was executed, this man was visited in prison by several Christians. Many believe this man repented of his sins and became a real Christian.

The second murderer also went to prison for his numerous crimes. He was eventually killed by another prison inmate, but not before he also repented of his sins and became a Christian.

Were these people for real? Did they truly convert?

Today's verse shows us a similar blasphemer and murderer who was turned around by God. His name: the apostle Paul, then known as Saul. One day, on the road to Damascus, Jesus confronted Saul. He soon became a Christian and one of the church's greatest apostles and writers of the New Testament.

When God chooses to move on someone, no matter how much sin they have committed, he can bring them to repentance. No one, absolutely NO ONE can be turned away from faith in Christ if he wants to believe. Even if he has committed horrible crimes, the gospel is for him too.

**PRAYER:** Jesus, thank you that your gospel goes out to all people everywhere. Amen.

Week 41: Saturday

# God Loves Us, Too

**Peter told them, "You know it is against the Jewish laws for me to come into a Gentile home like this. But God has shown me that I should never think of anyone as impure."** Acts 10:28

**Main Reading:** Acts 10 • **Optional Reading:** Acts 11

At one time, Jews had nothing to do with non-Jews, called Gentiles. They didn't eat with them. They didn't talk to them, if they could avoid it. The only time they worked with Gentiles was in necessary business matters. Otherwise, they considered Gentiles unclean, dirty, and rejected in the sight of God.

The new church, started by Jesus after his resurrection, could have had similar prejudices against Gentiles. Jesus' gospel could easily have been a new Jewish religion and for no one outside their faith.

But God didn't want that to happen. His gospel was for all the world. Anyone, anywhere could believe in Jesus and be saved. God communicated this truth to Peter one day through a vision. Today's Scripture tells us what Peter learned—that the gospel was for Gentiles too.

If you are not Jewish today, you could easily have died and gone to hell with no help from anyone. But God made sure the gospel came to you. He made sure you heard the truth. And he made sure you listened until you believed.

**Prayer:** Thank you for making me yours. Amen.

# The First Missionaries

**The Holy Spirit said, "Dedicate Barnabas and Saul for the special work I have for them."** Acts 13:2

**MAIN READING:** Acts 13 • **OPTIONAL READING:** Acts 12

You'll find their pictures on refrigerators. We pray for them in church. Sometimes they come to visit us when they come home for a period of time. They go to the ends of the earth—Africa, Australia, the Philippines, India, China, Russia—to tell those people of Jesus. Who are they?

Missionaries. A missionary is a person sent on a mission. He receives support from people in his church or denomination. He goes to another country, or to a university campus, or somewhere else where people haven't heard the gospel. Sometimes missionaries go to provide medical help. Sometimes they work as electricians or carpenters or teachers. But their mission is always the same: share Jesus. Tell the world the good news of salvation in Christ.

In today's verse, we meet the first two missionaries: Paul and Barnabas. Never before had this been done (although Jonah might have been the first real Jewish missionary). No one had thought of it. But Jesus told the disciples in Matthew 28:18-20 and Acts 1:8 to go into all the world. He gave them the Great Commission.

Paul and Barnabas actually took several missionary journeys. They planted churches all over the world. We believe today because of their work 2,000 years ago.

**PRAYER:** Father, please help me to be open to being a missionary. Amen.

Week 42: Monday

# God Spoke to Them

**But [God] never left himself without a witness. There were always his reminders, such as sending you rain and good crops and giving you food and joyful hearts.** Acts 14:17

**Main Reading:** Acts 14 • **Optional Reading:** Acts 15

Jesse wondered if there was a God.

His friend Stephen had a strong faith. He believed Jesus worked in his life and in others', doing good things for us that often we don't notice. Jesse just wasn't sure.

So he decided to do a test. He thought he would simply pray, "God, if you're really there, show me. Show me the good things in life."

On Monday, while taking a test, Jesse found that he knew the answers well. His mind never seemed to click so perfectly. He remembered his prayer too.

On Tuesday, he noticed that his mother's plants were growing nicely. They sat all over the house and looked beautiful. Was this God doing good too?

On Wednesday, he found himself laughing merrily when he spotted two squirrels fighting in his backyard. The laughing felt good, and something inside him reminded him of his prayer.

On Thursday, his heart kept telling him to apologize to a friend he called a "jerk." He wondered if this was God doing something else that was good.

And on Friday, his headache went away without his taking aspirin.

At the end of the week, Jesse decided he believed good things happened to people because God cared about them. Eventually, he took it a step further by giving his life to Jesus.

**Prayer:** Lord, thank you that you don't leave us without evidence of your love. Amen.

# God Opened Her Heart

**As she listened to us, the Lord opened her heart, and she accepted what Paul was saying.** Acts 16:14

**MAIN READING:** Acts 16:1-15 • **OPTIONAL READING:** Acts 16:16-40

You could be sitting in church. The pastor says something about helping people in need. You suddenly remember you should visit your grandmother in a nursing home.

You might be walking along the street. You spot a dog running around without a leash. Your heart suddenly says, "Hey, why don't you grab that dog and see who he belongs to?"

It may happen as you're eating dinner. "Shouldn't you thank Mom for such a great meal, really do it up?" your mind suggests.

What is happening here? God is opening your heart. It's what happened to Lydia in today's verse. God works in our hearts to make us more willing to accept him, or obey him, or listen to him. God doesn't expect us just to do everything right on our own. Instead, he works behind the scenes. He touches us, speaks to us, motivates us in the quiet of our hearts. That way we want to do what he asks us to do.

Have you found God speaking to you lately? What is he saying? What do you need to do, or say, or think?

**PRAYER:** Father, praise you that you lead me every moment. Otherwise, I know I'd lose my way. Amen.

# God Is Not Far from Any

**His purpose in all of this was that the nations should seek after God and perhaps feel their way toward him and find him—though he is not far from any one of us.** Acts 17:27

**Main Reading:** Acts 17 • **Optional Reading:** Acts 18

God is not far from anyone. Did you know that?

God is there when you sleep, watching over you. Perhaps tonight, he stopped a robber from coming into your room. You'll never know about it until you meet God in person. But he did it just the same.

God is there when you get up in the morning. He gives you that little jolt of pleasure as you brush your teeth. The toothpaste just makes your mouth feel cleaner.

God is there as you sit on the bus. He's there, encouraging you to talk to other kids. He's there, giving your friend Bill a joke that makes you laugh. He is there, making sure that drunk driver doesn't veer his car into the bus accidentally.

God is always there, everywhere. Wherever you are, he is. You cannot flee from him. You can't hide from him. He wants to be friends with you. He wants to speak to you as you lie in bed at night waiting for sleep. He wants you to get to know him so well that he'll become your greatest leader and helper.

God is there. You just have to be looking to see him.

**Prayer:** Lord, I want to see you in everything. Open my eyes. Amen.

Week 42: Thursday

# Miracles

**God gave Paul the power to do unusual miracles, so that even when handkerchiefs or cloths that had touched his skin were placed on sick people, they were healed of their diseases, and any evil spirits within them came out.** Acts 19:11, 12

**Main Reading:** Acts 19 • **Optional Reading:** Acts 20

Have you ever wished you could see a miracle? Or do one?

In the days of Jesus and the apostles, God performed many miracles in the land. Deaf people had their ears opened. The blind gained their sight. Disabled people walked and leaped and pirouetted. Mutes spoke and demon-possessed men became clean and new inside. At one time, Jesus stilled a storm. It stopped, as fast as snapping your fingers.

Don't you wish you could have seen those things?

Why did God do miracles then, but doesn't seem to today?

Actually, God probably does miracles today too. Many times very sick people will get well after the doctors have given up. Isn't that a miracle? When someone almost hits your car on a trip but at the last second misses, isn't that God's miraculous protection? When God speaks to a friend's heart and he accepts Jesus, isn't that a miracle too?

God did miracles back then, to prove Jesus really is the Son of God. He did miracles through the apostles to show they were the real thing. We don't need that proof today like they did then.

God does good things today, too, if you're looking. The question is, are you looking?

**Prayer:** Jesus, open my eyes that I might see what you're doing all around me. Amen.

Week 42: Friday

# God Chose You

**The God of our ancestors has chosen you to know his will and to see the Righteous One and hear him speak. You are to take this message everywhere, telling the whole world what you have seen and heard.**
Acts 22:14, 15

**MAIN READING:** Acts 22 • **OPTIONAL READING:** Acts 21

Have you ever been in gym class when a couple of kids chose up teams? When were you picked—first, second, fifth, last? How did it feel to be chosen early? Did you feel embarrassed if you were chosen late? Or last? Choosing teams like that can hurt deeply. Many young people have felt insulted and rejected because of the way team-picking worked out.

Did you know, though, that God also chose you? According to today's verse, God chose Paul so he could know him. The same application is true for you. He chose you so you would believe in and follow Jesus. God wanted you on his team. And he didn't pick you second, or eighth, or last. No, he chose you first thing. All of us were his number one pick.

How can that be? God's love—not when we were picked—makes us number one. And God's love is perfect, powerful, infinite. He loved you so much that he picked you to be on his team from the very beginning. You weren't an afterthought. God didn't say, "Oh, yeah, him. I almost forgot." No, God started off wanting you. He never hesitated or had second thoughts. He wanted you all along, and he made sure he got you.

He loves you that much.

**PRAYER:** Father, thanks for choosing me. I won't let you down. Amen.

Week 42: Saturday

# Terrified

**As he reasoned with them about righteousness and self-control and the judgment to come, Felix was terrified.** Acts 24:25

**MAIN READING:** Acts 24 • **OPTIONAL READING:** Acts 23

Sometimes hearing the gospel can be terrifying. After all, part of it deals with things like blood and death and judgment. People don't want to hear about that. They don't want to think that if they die without Jesus they could go to hell. Many people don't want to talk about it, or think about it. They'd rather be ignorant, pretending they just didn't know, rather than face the truth.

Perhaps that was what Felix the governor was thinking when Paul appeared before him. Paul talked about "righteousness and self-control and judgment." What are these things? Righteousness is obeying the truth and the law. Paul probably told him anytime he broke any of God's rules he was in danger.

Self-control related to keeping the rules too. The rules about sex and loyalty and not overeating and not living for pleasure. That might have scared Felix too. As a Roman governor he must have had a lot of opportunity to get involved with pleasures that were forbidden.

Finally, there was judgment. The very idea that each of us will stand before God and explain why we did what we did for our whole lives terrifies many people. If you have to do that without Jesus in your life, you're done for.

No wonder Felix was terrified. He realized without Jesus he was doomed. And yet, he didn't want to accept Jesus, because that would change his life. Sad, isn't it?

**PRAYER:** Lord, I'm glad you don't terrify me. I'm glad you're my best friend. Amen.

Week 42: Sunday

# Quickly a Christian?

**Agrippa interrupted him. "Do you think you can make me a Christian so quickly?"** Acts 26:28

**MAIN READING:** Acts 26 • **OPTIONAL READING:** Acts 25

How quickly can a person become a Christian?

In today's story, we see King Agrippa, the ruler of the Jews, sitting and listening to the apostle Paul. Undoubtedly, Paul spelled out the gospel. He told Agrippa everything he needed to know about Jesus in order to believe. Agrippa seemed to be interested. That is, until Paul encouraged him to become a Christian. Agrippa didn't think that could happen that fast.

After all, shouldn't you think about such a decision for a long time?

Shouldn't you be concerned about what changes will come into your life?

Shouldn't you consider how your family might be affected?

All these things make some people think they should delay becoming Christians. They want to wait for a better time. Some want to commit a few more sins before they take that step. Others honestly want to study more about Jesus. After all, this is a life-changing decision.

But really, becoming a Christian can happen very quickly. Do you admit you're a sinner? Do you believe in Jesus? Will you confess that you trust him? Will you be baptized?

That's all a person needs do. After all, how many facts do you need?

**PRAYER:** Jesus, I believe in you and I want to walk with you. Amen.

Week 43: Monday

# Even Paul Used the Bible

**[Paul] told them about the Kingdom of God and taught them about Jesus from the Scriptures—from the five books of Moses and the books of the prophets.** Acts 28:23

**Main Reading:** Acts 28 • **Optional Reading:** Acts 27

Esther argued with her mother about her new faith in Jesus.

"But it's so real, Mom," she said. "And I think I'm changing."

"I don't want you to change," her mom answered.

"But I want to be a better person. I need to be more patient. And I want to be more loving to people I don't love right away."

"It's all hokey," Mom replied. "I can't believe you accept this stuff."

Esther felt frustrated. Her friend, Joylie, had invited her to church. The service was moving, and Esther accepted Jesus at the invitation. It seemed everything in her life had changed. And now her mother was against her.

"The Bible says something about me and you, Mom," Esther finally said.

"What?"

"The pastor told us last Sunday. That we should obey our parents and honor them."

Her mother was suddenly silent. "It really says that?"

Esther showed her the passage in Ephesians 6:1, 2. For a second, her mother was stunned. Speechless. Then she said, "I never knew that," and went back to work.

The Bible has power. That's why it says that Paul used it when people came to him in prison. That's why you should use it when you talk to others.

**Prayer:** Lord, let me learn your Word well enough to use it all the time. Amen.

Week 43: Tuesday

# Where the Power Is

**For I am not ashamed of this Good News about Christ. It is the power of God to work, saving everyone who believes—Jews first and also Gentiles.** Romans 1:16

**MAIN READING:** Romans 1 • **OPTIONAL READING:** Romans 2

Jason said to his friend, Robert, "It's in John 1:12. 'But to all who believed him and accepted him, he gave the right to become children of God.' You can be a child of God."

"It really says that?" Robert asked.

"Look." Jason opened his Bible and found the verse. Robert stared at it.

"It's kind of like being part of a royal family," Robert mused.

"Yeah, and God becomes your friend. He protects you and guides you and helps you in problems in life."

"Helps you?"

"Yeah, look at this." Jason found 2 Timothy 2:1. "Be strong with the special favor God gives you in Christ Jesus."

"Special favor, huh?"

"Yeah. Like special help. Like when the teacher keeps you after school to help you figure something out."

"Cool," Robert commented.

In today's verse we see that Paul said the gospel has power. In the above story, you see that kind of power. Jason helped Robert see that the Bible isn't just a book. It's full of great truth to help us and change us.

**PRAYER:** Father, let me learn to use the Bible for every situation of life. Amen.

# All Fall Short

**For all have sinned; all fall short of God's glorious standard.**
Romans 3:23

**MAIN READING:** Romans 3 • **OPTIONAL READING:** Romans 4

Kenna held up the bow and aimed the arrow at the target. Her first shot went over the target completely. The second one nicked the side, but went askew. The third one was better. It stuck in the biggest outside circle, the black one.

"I'm not a very good shot," she said to her instructor, Mrs. Morris.

Mrs. Morris smiled. "It's kind of like what it says in Romans 3:23." Kenna was a new Christian and Mrs. Morris had been nurturing her along for several months.

"What's that?" Kenna asked.

"We all fall short of God's glorious standard," she said. "In the Bible, to fall short or to 'sin' meant to miss God's bull's-eye. That's what happens when we try to live up to God's laws on our own. We 'miss the mark.'"

Kenna picked up another arrow. "This time I'm going to hit it."

She drew back, aimed carefully, then shot. The arrow struck the target, but only in the yellow, not the red bull's-eye. "I'll never do it," she said.

"In the Bible, though, you hit the bull's-eye when you let the Spirit guide you. When you let God fill your life. That's when he's pleased."

"So I may not hit the bull's-eye with my arrow, but I can with my life?"

"Absolutely."

Have you missed the mark? Confess it, and thank God for forgiving you. And then go on, in his power. That's when we really please him.

**PRAYER:** Lord, teach me to hit your standard with everything I do. Amen.

# Rejoicing About Problems

**We can rejoice, too, when we run into problems and trials, for we know that they are good for us—they help us learn to endure.** Romans 5:3

**MAIN READING:** Romans 5 • **OPTIONAL READING:** Romans 6

Gabe ran hard. It was his first mile race, and he started off in second place. But now he'd slipped back to fifth.

His legs felt wobbly. His breath came in chuffs. His chest burned. His thighs began to ache.

Still, he pressed on. He didn't expect to win. That wasn't the point. He just wanted to finish, to run his own race, a good race.

In the end he finished fourth, not a bad showing.

The Christian life is like running a long-distance race. It's hard work. Sometimes you feel like giving up. Your body grows weary. You're tired and just want to lie down and forget you're in a race.

At times, you get a second wind and you feel stronger. But soon that passes and you're back to slogging along. Everywhere you look, you see a problem. Your legs hurt. Your lungs burn. You hands feel like lead.

But when you keep running, when you endure, you're doing the main thing that pleases God. He wants you to learn to endure, like today's verse says. It's not always easy. It's rarely pretty. But in the end, you get where you're going.

That makes it worth the struggle.

**PRAYER:** Jesus, help me to run my race without giving up. Ever. Amen.

# God Causes Good to Come

**And we know that God causes everything to work together for the good of those who love God and are called according to his purpose for them.** Romans 8:28

**Main Reading:** Romans 8 • **Optional Reading:** Romans 7

Jennie knew she couldn't stop her parents' divorce. She'd prayed for them. She'd pleaded with her father not to leave. She'd cried herself to sleep many nights. Alone. Tired. Fearful. Broken.

In the end, her dad left her mother for good. He got remarried to someone he met at work, a woman he said he "really loved." Hadn't he ever loved Jennie's mom?

Jennie tried to understand it, but it just seemed everything in life went wrong from that point onward. She was depressed, and her grades slipped. She felt lonely at dinnertime when it was just her mom and her brother. When she did see her father, he was distant and didn't say much. She felt as if he didn't love her anymore.

One day, her youth minister reminded her of today's verse. "God causes everything to work together for good." She didn't see how God could do anything good in her situation. But she prayed about it.

Gradually, she realized there were some good things. Peace at home. No more arguing. Spending time with each of her parents when there wasn't a fight going on. Being able to help and encourage friends who also had divorced parents. In many ways, Jennie could see God had done some great things in her family. It was still hard, but she decided all she could do was trust that God would do more in the days ahead.

**Prayer:** Lord, help me to see the good behind some of my problems. Amen.

Week 43: Saturday

# Believe and Confess

**For if you confess with your mouth that Jesus is Lord and believe in your heart that God raised him from the dead, you will be saved. For it is by believing in your heart that you are made right with God, and it is by confessing with your mouth that you are saved.**
Romans 10:9, 10

**MAIN READING:** Romans 10 • **OPTIONAL READING:** Romans 9

How do you make sure Jesus is in your life?

A little acrostic I learned years ago helps. A-B-C. A—Admit your sin and Agree with God that you have done things wrong in your life. B—Believe in Jesus. Trust that he really was God. Accept the fact that he came to die for your sins. Look to him to be your Savior and Lord. And third, C—Confess Jesus to others. Tell them you believe in Jesus. Get baptized at church. Don't be afraid to let anyone know that you belong to him.

Today's verse tells us what happens when we B-Believe and C-Confess. When we believe, our heart is "made right with God," like the verse says. And when we confess him before others, we "are saved."

Why are believing and confessing so important? They are the first steps toward walking and obeying God. Believing is simply accepting the facts about Jesus and making an act of trust in him through prayer. Confessing lets the world know what you've done.

You can't be a Christian without doing A, B, and C. But when you do—watch out! God's going to do big things in your life.

**PRAYER:** Lord, I believe and I have confessed you. Be near, let me feel you in my life. Amen.

Week 43: Sunday

# Be Devoted!

**Love each other with genuine affection, and take delight in honoring each other.** Romans 12:10

**MAIN READING:** Romans 12 • **OPTIONAL READING:** Romans 11

At one time I had a dog named Jacques. He was a big poodle, not one of those little dinky ones with jeweled collars. He was as big as a Lab or a German shepherd.

You know what I liked most about Jacques? Every day when I came home from school, he ran to greet me at the door. He barked with joy. He jumped up and down, fetched his ball, rolled over, and made a regular fool of himself.

It seemed I didn't have a bigger fan out there than Jacques. He just made it real clear that I was number one in his book.

Have you ever thought that's how we're to treat others in the church? We're to be so glad to see them, to smile, to speak uplifting words. Paul said it that way in today's verse. "Love each other!"

Couldn't you use some people in your life like that—people who are devoted to you?

It's really great to have people who are glad to see you, isn't it?

But let's turn it around. Are you glad to see others when they show up at church or at your house? Do your eyes light up? Do you say something friendly in greeting?

If you're friendly, you'll have friends. If you're kind to others, most will be kind to you. How can you show love today to the people who are important to you?

**PRAYER:** Help me to show love to everyone, Lord. Everyone! Amen.

# Accept Them

**Accept Christians who are weak in faith, and don't argue with them about what they think is right or wrong.** Romans 14:1

**MAIN READING:** Romans 14 • **OPTIONAL READING:** Romans 13

The new kid had purple hair, a nose ring, and a tattoo. He was the weirdest kid David had ever seen. Still, David decided to be nice to him and sat down with him at lunch.

"What's your name?"

"Lennie," the kid mumbled.

"Where you from?"

"Chicago."

That was about as far as they got the first day. The next day, David took a seat by Lennie again. "What you want?" Lennie asked between bites.

"Just bein' friendly," David said.

"Hmmm . . . OK," the boy said.

It was hard going, but over the next few months, Lennie began to talk a little more. David listened and prayed repeatedly about inviting Lennie to church. That was when he found out Lennie was already a Christian. "I go to church," Lennie said. "I accepted Jesus about a year ago, so I'm still pretty new to the whole thing."

David was amazed, but then he realized that was all the more reason to accept Lennie for who he was. Just because he dressed differently and liked a different type of music didn't mean Lennie couldn't also be a Christian. Besides, he could probably use a strong Christian friend to help him grow in his new faith.

**PRAYER:** Lord, may I always accept other Christians, even when they seem weird to me. Amen.

# Encouragement

**Such things were written in the Scriptures long ago to teach us. They give us hope and encouragement as we wait patiently for God's promises.** Romans 15:4

**Main Reading:** Romans 15 • **Optional Reading:** Romans 16

Kinzie needed some encouragement. It had been a bad day at school, and she was tired and wanted to quit. Her mom suggested she read a story in the Bible about Moses and some of his trials.

Kinzie began in Exodus and followed Moses' story along for a few pages. She saw how Moses didn't want to do what God called him to do in Exodus 3 and 4. She noticed how discouraged Moses was in Exodus 5 and 6. She saw him battling Pharaoh and trying to free the Jews. She read how the Jews fought Moses too.

"He had a hard time," Kinzie said to her mother after reading.

"What did you learn?"

"That Moses didn't give up even when things went wrong."

"Then don't you give up, either."

Kinzie began reading the Bible specifically to be encouraged. She found that many stories had the power to make her feel better.

The Bible was written to encourage you, not beat you down. Read it with that in mind, and you'll find it an amazing book.

**Prayer:** Jesus, help me to find the great stories that will encourage me and help me to learn them well. Amen.

# God Will Keep You

**He will keep you strong right up to the end, and he will keep you free from all blame on the great day when our Lord Jesus Christ returns.**
1 Corinthians 1:8

**Main Reading:** 1 Corinthians 1 • **Optional Reading:** 1 Corinthians 2

Do you ever feel like you won't make it to heaven? Do you ever worry that you'll give up the faith? Or just drift away?

God wants you to know that it's not all up to you. You're not the only one in this battle. God is in it with you. He keeps you going and sticking with the faith, as today's verse says. He keeps encouraging you, strengthening you, leading you. He will never give up on you.

How does God keep us going? Here are three thoughts.

1. God keeps you going by speaking to your heart. He will talk to you when things are tough. He will lead you when you don't know what to do. He will always speak to you, if you ask him.

2. God keeps you going by speaking to you through the Bible. The Bible gives you great stories, great promises, and great encouragements. Look for verses you like. Write them down and memorize them. They will "keep" you through many hard times.

3. God keeps you going through the words of others. Other Christians should be building you up and helping you along the way. Build good Christian relationships and they will give you strength when you're weak.

God will use these ways to keep you going. He will never stop, either. He wants to get you through to his new heaven and earth.

**Prayer:** Lord, keep speaking to me and leading me. I need it today. Amen.

# Put Through the Fire

**But there is going to come a time of testing at the judgment day to see what kind of work each builder has done. Everyone's work will be put through the fire to see whether or not it keeps its value.**
1 Corinthians 3:13

**MAIN READING:** 1 Corinthians 3 • **OPTIONAL READING:** 1 Corinthians 4

Have you ever looked at some of the great people who have lived—Mother Teresa, the apostle Paul, Martin Luther King, Jr.—and felt like you can never live up to what they did?

Many great people have helped the world. In our time, you can't pass a day without hearing of some amazing thing done by someone. Even celebrities sometimes do heroic acts. The world reports it, and everyone is astonished.

Sometimes when you look at these great deeds, you can feel like a spiritual midget. "How can I ever do something like that?" you ask. Or, "I have never even led one person to Christ, let alone millions."

But you see, God doesn't worry about publicity or great deeds. Every one of us is different and has a special job to do. Your job may be simply to lead a quiet life and build up others. When you stand before Christ, he'll reward you for living up to what he gave you.

Today's Scripture is scary, but God doesn't want that fire to burn up your work. Listen to him, walk with him, and one day when you get to heaven, you'll be amazed at all the great things God will reward you for.

**PRAYER:** Lord, help me to do little things in little places, a little bit at a time. Amen.

Week 44: Friday

# Temple of the Holy Spirit

**Don't you know that you body is the temple of the Holy Spirit, who lives in you and was given to you by God?** 1 Corinthians 6:19

**Main Reading:** 1 Corinthians 6 • **Optional Reading:** 1 Corinthians 5

"Your body is a temple," said the young woman giving her testimony to the youth group. "It's a temple that God lives in. So we shouldn't mess it up by putting bad things into it."

"You mean drugs?" one of the boys asked.

"Drugs, alcohol, smoking—I did them all before I became a Christian, and they're all ways to mess up God's temple."

"What about sex?" one of the girls asked, to a few giggles from the group.

"Before I gave my life to Christ, I made some mistakes in that area as well, and I can tell you that it only leads to pain and heartache. On top of that, it can also be dangerous! Do yourself a favor and don't get involved in sex till you're married. God knows what he's talking about!"

God wants us to treat our bodies with respect. Like today's verse says, the Holy Spirit lives inside each and every Christian. God doesn't tell us to avoid things like drugs, alcohol, and premarital sex in order to deprive us of fun. He does it because he wants what's best for us, and he knows these things can be destructive.

**Prayer:** Lord, help me always to treat my body like a temple. Amen.

# Knowing All the Answers

**While knowledge may make us feel important, it is love that really builds up the church. Anyone who claims to know all the answers doesn't really know very much.** 1 Corinthians 8:1, 2

**MAIN READING:** 1 Corinthians 8 • **OPTIONAL READING:** 1 Corinthians 7

You think you just know everything, don't you?" Sami said to Laurie. "Well, you don't."

Laurie had been talking to Sami for months about Jesus. Every time Sami asked a new question, Laurie went to her Bible, or to her Mom, or to her youth pastor, and found an answer. Sami had asked, "What about people who have never heard about Jesus?" "How do we know the Bible is true?" And, "Wasn't Jesus just a great teacher?" Each time, Laurie had given strong, convincing answers. Now Sami was mad.

"I'm just trying to give you decent answers," Laurie said. "I'm not trying to prove anything."

"Well, I'm tired of it," Sami cried. She started to walk away, but Laurie caught up to her.

"Hey, come over my house and we'll have pizza and a sleep-over," Laurie said.

Sami turned around. "Really?"

"Sure," Laurie answered.

Sometimes knowing all the answers isn't the answer. Sometimes unbelievers just want to be loved. It's good to have answers and know the reasons you believe what you believe. But sometimes just loving a lost person is where real change happens.

**PRAYER:** Lord, may I always choose love over trying to overload people with facts. Amen.

Week 44: Sunday

# Fitting In

**When I am with the Jews, I become one of them so that I can bring them to Christ. . . . When I am with the Gentiles who do not have the Jewish law, I fit in with them as much as I can.** 1 Corinthians 9:20, 21

**MAIN READING:** 1 Corinthians 9 • **OPTIONAL READING:** 1 Corinthians 10

How do you communicate the gospel with people who are different from you?

Muslims believe very different things from Christians. They wear different clothing. They follow different rituals. How does a Christian speak to them?

Hindus and Buddhists also have practices strange to us. What could a Christian do to convince them we care?

Paul had an answer in today's reading. He became like a Jew to Jews, like a Gentile to Gentiles. Whoever he met, he tried to fit in with them. He worked at using their practices to break down barriers. How did he do that? If the people had a custom of wearing some specific clothing, Paul may have worn it too. If they stopped work at a special time to pray, Paul did that too. However, he prayed to God, not their god.

There are many ways to show others that Christianity is worth looking at. People who want to witness to bikers wear biker clothing and ride motorcycles. Kids who want to reach fans of rock music might start up a Christian rock band. It's not complicated.

What can you do today to break down a barrier with someone you know?

**PRAYER:** Jesus, let me learn to major on important things and not worry about minor issues such as clothing. Amen.

Week 45: Monday

# If One Suffers

**If one part suffers, all the parts suffer with it, and if one part is honored, all the parts are glad.** 1 Corinthians 12:26

**MAIN READING:** 1 Corinthians 12:12-30

**OPTIONAL READING:** 1 Corinthians 12:1-12

Jason came to church with a heavy heart. His father had been laid off from his position at work, and they might have to move. Jason's friends all lived in that area. His buddies at church were the best friends he'd ever had.

He didn't say much that morning at church, but a couple of his friends noticed he was quiet and looked a little depressed. Finally, they began asking questions. For a moment, everyone sat there stunned and quiet, but no one knew what to say until Jennifer said, "I feel really bad about this. What can we do about it—anything?"

Jason didn't know. "I don't think we're going to be able to give my dad a job."

Everyone agreed about that, though Jennifer suggested they ask their parents if any of them knew about any company that was hiring.

In the end, Jason did have to move. It was a sad time for everyone, but his friends from church came to his house and helped him and his family pack. One day, Jennifer gave Jason a "book of remembrance" with words of encouragement written down by everyone in the youth group.

When our Christian friends are hurting, sometimes a pep talk isn't what they need. What they need is for us to sympathize, hang in there with them, and do what they can through it. Do you know anyone in need like that today?

**PRAYER:** Help me, Lord, to offer comfort to those who hurt. Amen.

# Meaningless Noise

**If I could speak in any language in heaven or on earth but didn't love others, I would only be making meaningless noise like a loud gong or a clanging cymbal.** 1 Corinthians 13:1

**MAIN READING:** 1 Corinthians 13 • **OPTIONAL READING:** 1 Corinthians 14

"Turn or burn," Kenny yelled. "Go to heaven or go to hell!"

Alonzo watched his friend "talk" to the group of boys about Jesus. Kenny seemed a bit nasty about it, and Alonzo wasn't sure how he liked it.

"Go to hell, I don't care," Kenny said finally. He started walking away.

Alonzo caught up to him.

"Why didn't you say anything?" Kenny asked immediately.

"I wasn't sure what to say," Alonzo answered honestly.

"Just tell them if they don't believe, they'll go to hell. That's what my dad says."

"Yeah, but shouldn't we be nice about it?"

Kenny and Alonzo talked more, but Alonzo couldn't convince Kenny his approach was wrong. Today's verse shows us the problem. When we have all the truth, but use it like a club, we rarely get anywhere. Love, though, can break through the barriers.

Love your friends, then give them the truth. It's the only way to an open door.

**PRAYER:** Lord, may I always love people and not bash them with the gospel. Amen.

Week 45: Wednesday

# Seen By Many

**He was seen by Peter and then by the twelve apostles. After that, he was seen by more than five hundred of his followers at one time, most of whom are still alive, though some have died by now.**
1 Corinthians 15:5, 6

**MAIN READING:** 1 Corinthians 15

"What proof is there?" Bran asked Josie. "It happened 2,000 years ago."

"People saw him alive," Josie answered, trying to help Bran understand the facts about the resurrection of Jesus.

"Where?"

"In the mountains, in rooms, at dinners," Josie replied.

"No, I mean where did you find this out?"

"In the Bible."

"Let me see."

Josie had just been reading the verses in today's reading at church. She turned to 1 Corinthians 15 and read.

Bran pursed his lips. "That doesn't convince me, but I didn't know that was in there. I thought it was all made up."

"There are some good reasons to believe the Bible is factual."

Bran wasn't convinced, but as Josie showed him other verses and material from other books, he began to listen.

When you talk to outsiders, show them what the Bible says. Use books that refer to it. It has the real power.

**PRAYER:** Jesus, thank you for giving us great proofs of your power in the Bible. Amen.

# God Comforts Us

**All praise to the God and Father of our Lord Jesus Christ. He is the source of every mercy and the God who comforts us. He comforts us in all our troubles so that we can comfort others.** 2 Corinthians 1:3, 4

**MAIN READING:** 2 Corinthians 1 • **OPTIONAL READING:** 2 Corinthians 2

Marshall came home from school and began making a sandwich in the kitchen. In the next room, he heard someone. Zeroing in, he soon realized it was his grandmother. She was crying again.

Marshall's grandfather had died just a week before. Grandma came to stay with Marshall's family after the funeral.

At first, Marshall didn't know what to do, but he made a second sandwich, then walked into the family room and sat down by his grandmother. "I'm sorry, Grandma," he said. "I wish Grandpa hadn't died." He put his arm over her back and offered her a sandwich. She began eating quietly.

"If only we had another year together. That's all I wanted."

Marshall nodded. He pulled a slip of paper out of his pocket. "I wrote this down today," he said, and handed it to her.

"Trust in the Lord with all your heart," the paper said. "Do not lean on your own understanding."

Marshall said, "I guess that's all we can do."

Grandma stared at it, then clutched it. "I'm going to keep this," she said.

"I wish I could comfort you better," Marshall said.

"God comforted me, through you," Grandma said, and ate the sandwich.

**PRAYER:** Lord, help me to be a comforter wherever I go. Amen.

# Renewed Every Day

**That is why we never give up. Though our bodies are dying, our spirits are being renewed every day.** 2 Corinthians 4:16

**Main Reading:** 2 Corinthians 4

**Optional Reading:** 2 Corinthians 3

Jake's dad hefted the ax. He swung and split the log in half. Jake grabbed another piece of wood and set it on the block. "Go ahead, Dad."

His father swung again and another log was cleaved in half. They worked for a long time, creating a pile of split logs laying on the ground. The twosome gathered up the wood and stacked it.

"Aren't you tired?" Jake asked after a while.

"Of course," his dad said. "My body's tired. But God renews the spirit when you're doing his work. It makes me happy to help someone in need."

He looked toward the minister's house. They had cut the wood for their minister. "God gives you power, a recharge when you ask," Jake's dad said.

"What do you mean, a recharge?"

"I mean God gives you the strength and you are like new inside. That's what I think."

It's true. When we walk as Christians, God continually builds up and strengthens our inner spirit. Even though our outer bodies may be weak, tired, and drained, our inner spirit is refreshed.

**Prayer:** Jesus, renew me each day so that I have vigor for your work. Amen.

Week 45: Saturday

# Like New Clothing

**We grow weary in our present bodies, and we long for the day when we will put on our heavenly bodies like new clothing.** 2 Corinthians 5:2

**Main Reading:** 2 Corinthians 5 • **Optional Reading:** 2 Corinthians 6

Do you ever long for a new, heavenly body?

Paul did. He knew one day, his old, tired, used up body would disappear and he would have a new, powerful, spiritual body. That body will never wear out. It'll never get old. It's perfect.

If we look at what Jesus could do after he was raised from the dead, we get the idea. He could walk through doors. He could appear in a room seemingly out of nowhere. He could eat things (he ate some fish, according to Luke 24:41-43). He could be touched and seemed as real as any of the others. Yet, he possessed incredible power. His wounds on the cross didn't slow him down at all.

For a person who suffers from physical problems, this verse is a great promise. One day we won't any longer have pain, or fear, or physical difficulties. We'll have new, spiritual, powerful, immortal bodies.

Do you long for that day? Do you wish it would come soon?

That's part of what it means to be a Christian. We aren't part of this world anymore. We belong to a new heaven and a new earth that God will make. We're citizens of a great world that will make this one look cheap and fake.

**Prayer:** Lord, I look forward to the day you come and make me all new. Amen.

Week 45: Sunday

# Give What You Have

**If you are really eager to give, it isn't important how much you are able to give. God wants you to give what you have, not what you don't have.** 2 Corinthians 8:12

**MAIN READING:** 2 Corinthians 8

**OPTIONAL READING:** 2 Corinthians 7

Katie heard about a woman who gave over a million dollars to a church. She read in the paper where it said that a television businessman had given over a billion dollars to the United Nations. And she had heard of others, like Bill Gates, who gave billions to various charities.

Staring down at the $5 bill she planned to give that Sunday, she realized it didn't look like much. Five dollars? What was that next to all these huge sums?

Her grandmother had sent her $50 for her birthday. Katie wanted to give a tithe of that to the Lord. That's how she ended up with $5. It looked so little and insignificant. Even when the offering plate was passed, Katie noticed checks in it. There were several $20 bills too.

What was her $5?

Today's verse can be a great encouragement to us when we can't give that much to God's work. It tells us God is pleased when we give what we have. Don't worry that you can't give millions, or even hundreds, like other people. God accepts your gift when you give out of love. He is pleased when we give from the heart.

Even if it's only a couple of cents!

**PRAYER:** Lord, let me be cheerful in what I'm giving, knowing you'll use it for your kingdom. Amen.

Week 46: Monday

# Plant Generously

**Remember this—a farmer who plants only a few seeds will get a small crop. But the one who plants generously will get a generous crop.**
2 Corinthians 9:6

**MAIN READING:** 2 Corinthians 9 • **OPTIONAL READING:** 2 Corinthians 10

Are you a generous person?

Generosity is helping people who have needs when they need it. Like offering a hand after a meeting to put away the chairs. Or giving the new kid some extra time to help him understand his homework.

Generosity is giving just a little more for the work of God's kingdom. When you give to God's work, you decide to give even more than a tithe. When you donate something to a charity, you offer them a few dollars more than you originally intended.

Generosity is a spirit always ready to pitch in. Helping the sound man get ready for the big service. Listening to your aunt for the tenth time as she tells you about her operation.

God tells us in today's verse that generosity pleases him. When we give, help, and encourage with a generous spirit, God says we'll reap rewards here and in heaven.

What are you holding back? Decide today not to hold back any word of encouragement, any way to help out, any opportunity to build up. Give all you have, and you will receive all God has.

**PRAYER:** Give me a generous spirit, Lord, so I may share with everyone. Amen.

Week 46: Tuesday

# False Apostles

**These people are false apostles. They have fooled you by disguising themselves as apostles of Christ.** 2 Corinthians 11:13

**Main Reading:** 2 Corinthians 11:1-15

**Optional Reading:** 2 Corinthians 11:16-33

False apostles hide everywhere.

You can find them in the church, teaching a class on the Bible. They say mostly the right things, but then they add or subtract a few other things that make their teaching false.

You can find them on the street. Many people go door-to-door, spreading the news about their religion. Be careful. Some of these people teach wrong things. They don't care about Christian faith and they want to steal you away from it. The Bible warns us repeatedly to stay clear of these people. They will even lie about what they truly believe to suck you in. Then when you're caught, they reveal the real truth.

Look at what it says in today's verse: "They fool you by disguising themselves." In another passage (Matthew 7:15) they are referred to as wolves in sheep's clothing. What was this all about? True shepherds often used the wool of the sheep they guarded to make coats and other articles of clothing. A sheep got used to seeing its shepherd look like this, and felt comfortable with him or her.

However, spiritual wolves can put on the same kind of clothing. They look just like the real thing. But they're not.

Be on guard. Wolves out there want to devour you. The best defense is to know your beliefs inside and out. That way you won't be tricked.

**Prayer:** Jesus, protect me from these false teachers who try to suck us in. Amen.

# Power in Weakness

**Each time he said, "My gracious favor is all you need. My power works best in your weakness." So now I am glad to boast about my weaknesses, so that the power of Christ may work through me.**
2 Corinthians 12:9

**Main Reading:** 2 Corinthians 12 • **Optional Reading:** 2 Corinthians 13

A Japanese sport called judo specializes in pitting smaller opponents against larger ones. It often looks like a wrong match. Surely the bigger guy will win.

Inevitably, though, the smaller, more versatile and tricky opponent takes down the big guy. Why? Because a judo expert knows how to use his weaknesses as strengths. He also knows how to exploit the big guy's strengths so that they turn into weaknesses. The smaller person uses weight differences to trick the larger person. He specializes in making himself look weak until he strikes.

There are many times that our weaknesses are a source of strength, as with judo. How? Because when we know we're weak in an area, we rely more on God and others. We're more apt to ask for help when we're weak. In that sense, our weakness is a strength, because it drives us to God.

Paul knew about this and wrote in today's verses how he found out that his weakness was actually a source of spiritual power. He wasn't a great speaker, so he relied more on God. That enabled God to work more through him and have a greater effect on his listeners.

Where are you weak? Rely on God and he will make you strong.

**Prayer:** Lord, use my weaknesses and help me to rely on you always. Amen.

# Crucified with Christ

**I have been crucified with Christ. I myself no longer live, but Christ lives in me.** Galatians 2:19

**Main Reading:** Galatians 2 • **Optional Reading:** Galatians 1

You are there the day Jesus was crucified. You stand in the crowd, weeping. The greatest man you ever knew is about to die.

You look down and pray a bit. But you're too depressed to think about anything else. Then you look up and suddenly everything has changed. Another person hangs from that cross. It's no longer Jesus.

You look closer. You realize you recognize the person now on the cross. It's you!

What has happened? Where did Jesus go? How did you get up there?

This is a spiritual reality Paul talks about in today's verses. When Jesus was crucified, a spiritual transaction happened. It was as though you were crucified there too. Jesus was crucified for your sins. He took your punishment. But in another sense, you were crucified with Jesus. That is, your old nature—the one that always wants to do the wrong thing—hung up there with him. After Jesus died, you died with him spiritually. Now your old nature has no right to rule you. It died with Jesus.

Do you see what happened? When you give Jesus full power in your life, you no longer have to listen to the taunts and temptations of your "flesh," the old you. That person died. It can still talk to you, but it has no power to make you do what it says.

**Prayer:** Lord, praise you for dying for my sins on the cross so I no longer have to live according to my old nature. Amen.

Week 46: Friday

# Calling God Father

**Because you Gentiles have become his children, God has sent the Spirit of his Son into your hearts, and now you can call God your dear Father.** Galatians 4:6

**Main Reading:** Galatians 4 • **Optional Reading:** Galatians 3

What do you call your father?

Daddy? Papa? Dad? Pop?

Kids have all kinds of names for their fathers. When my mother became a grandmother, she told us to call her Mimi. My father was known as Bapa. The grandkids called my father Bapa all his days.

What kind of name is Bapa, or Pop, or Daddy? It's a special name we give to someone special in our lives. It's an intimate name, one we use only for our dad. Nobody else can call him that.

In the same way, when we become Christians, we begin to call God our father or "Abba" or Daddy. Why do we do this? Because now we're intimate with him. He is our heavenly daddy and we know him personally. We can go to him anywhere, anytime. He's like a real daddy. He's special to us, and we're special to him.

**Prayer:** Father, thank you for being my heavenly daddy. Amen.

# Life in the Holy Spirit

**So I advise you to live according to your new life in the Holy Spirit. Then you won't be doing what your sinful nature craves.**
Galatians 5:16

**Main Reading:** Galatians 5 • **Optional Reading:** Galatians 6

Imagine if you could be patient when your little brother pesters you. Or, when you go to church, you could be full of joy. Or, when bad things happen in your life, you calmly face them with peace in your heart.

That's what today's verse is talking about. If you live "according to your new life in the Holy Spirit," you will produce the fruit of the Spirit. What is that fruit? Love, joy, peace, patience, kindness, goodness, faithfulness, gentleness, self-control. Imagine if all the time you let these qualities shine in your life! What a life it would be!

The Spirit wants to help you become all these things. When your little sister socks you in the chest, you remain patient and gentle. You don't sock her back. When other kids give up, you hang in there. You're faithful to the end. When some kids react with anger, you have self-control. Kids look to you for leadership.

As the Spirit produces these qualities in your life, you will become a person others want to be with. People will want to know, "How could you be like that in that situation when everyone else just lost it?" They will trust you and love you for your character.

Let the Spirit work in your life every day. Soon, you will be producing the qualities that make the world stand up and cheer.

**Prayer:** Father, produce in me the qualities I need to live well. Amen.

# Blessed with Every Blessing

**How we praise God, the Father of our Lord Jesus Christ, who has blessed us with every spiritual blessing in the heavenly realms because we belong to Christ.** Ephesians 1:3

**MAIN READING:** Ephesians 1 • **OPTIONAL READING:** Ephesians 2

What blessings would you like to have in your life?

Eternal life? If you're a Christian, you already have it.

A place in heaven? Ditto!

A God who loves you infinitely? Yup!

A Lord who will be with you through every hard time? Definitely!

A Spirit who will give you power and strength when you need it? Of course.

Today's verse says that God has given us "every spiritual blessing." Does that mean we have all the money we want? No, these are spiritual blessings. Does it mean we'll get a car when we're 17? Not necessarily. These blessings are for you on the inside, not the outside.

Some people might say, "Big deal. Spiritual blessings? I have plenty of them. What I need is a new bike."

The truth is, spiritual blessings often lead to physical blessings. Maybe you're blessed spiritually with a good head for numbers. Maybe you can get a paper route or a job mowing lawns. That way you can earn the money you need to get the bike.

Never discount God's spiritual blessings. They're really what life is all about.

**PRAYER:** Father, thank you for giving me all the blessings you have. And if you want to send more, that's OK too. Amen.

Week 47: Monday

# Infinitely More

**Now glory be to God! By his mighty power at work within us, he is able to accomplish infinitely more than we would ever dare to ask or hope.** Ephesians 3:20

**Main Reading:** Ephesians 3 • **Optional Reading:** Ephesians 4

John knelt down by his bed and began to pray. "Please help me get a bike for Christmas," he said.

Within his heart, he suddenly heard voice. "More," it said. He looked around, saw nothing, and continued. "Um, help me make enough money to get a bike for the school year."

For a second he waited, then his heart spoke again, "More."

He stared about him, but saw nothing. "Uh, let's see. Help me to get six lawns to cut this summer so I can make the money to buy a new bike very soon."

He smiled. Now that was good. But this time the still, small voice in his heart said, "More! Make it hard!"

He didn't know what to think, but said, "OK, here goes. Help me get eight lawns to cut and make enough money to buy a bike and donate $200 to the church building fund too."

He waited. Then the internal voice said, "Good!"

John was amazed, but he decided maybe he wasn't praying enough and for big enough things. Maybe he was expecting too little of God. You don't need to hear a voice in your heart, or even out loud. Today's verse tells us God can do more than we ever think or ask. So start asking! Ask for things that require faith, not just work!

**Prayer:** Lord, teach me to expect big things from you. Amen.

Week 47: Tuesday

# The Real Battle

**For we are not fighting against people made of flesh and blood, but against the evil rulers and authorities of the unseen world, against those mighty powers of darkness who rule this world, and against wicked spirits in the heavenly realms.** Ephesians 6:12

**MAIN READING:** Ephesians 6 • **OPTIONAL READING:** Ephesians 5

Are you in the real battle?

You may think that kid at school who's always razzing you is the enemy.

But he's not.

You may think your teacher in sixth period can't wait to flunk you. She's an enemy for sure.

But she's not.

You may think that the kids down the street who threatened to wreck your tree fort are against you. Surely they're real enemies.

But they're not.

The real enemies you fight are spiritual enemies. Demons who are invisible. The cohorts of the Devil attacking others so they'll attack you. The Devil himself trying to mess up your life.

The world is full of bad people. But ultimately, the Bible teaches, they're not your real opponents. Behind them are spiritual forces who goad them into doing their foul deeds. When you meet them, remember who your real enemies are. And pray that God will defeat them.

**PRAYER:** Protect me, Lord, from the real enemies of my soul. Amen.

# What We Can Be Sure Of

**And I am sure that God, who began the good work within you, will continue his work until it is finally finished on that day when Christ Jesus comes back again.** Philippians 1:6

**MAIN READING:** Philippians 1 • **OPTIONAL READING:** Philippians 2

God will never let you go. He will never stop working in your life. You might give up. You might say, "This is too hard." But God won't give up on you. He'll keep giving you the strength and resources to win.

You might feel like the Christian life is too hard. There are just too many rules and you can't keep them all. But God says to you, "Draw on my power. Rely on me and I will give you what you need."

Perhaps some day things will get so bad that you think God has forgotten about you. Or given up on you. Or deserted you. But God promises, "I will never desert you or forsake you. I'm with you to the end."

When God began his work in you after you became a Christian, he meant to see it through. He took you on for the whole journey. He won't quit in the middle. He won't drop you and say, "You're just too dumb." Or, "You've lost your temper for the last time."

No, God will stick with you to the very end. And there, he will bring you into heaven where you'll be with him forever.

**PRAYER:** Jesus, I know you began a good work in me and I'm confident you'll take me through to the end. Amen.

# Thought Life

**And now, dear brothers and sisters, let me say one more thing as I close this letter. Fix your thoughts on what is true and honorable and right. Think about things that are pure and lovely and admirable.**
Philippians 4:8

**Main Reading:** Philippians 4 • **Optional Reading:** Philippians 3

Many thoughts flit through your brain all day.

"My mom is so old-fashioned. She just doesn't get it."

"Why do we have to take this test now? Can't the teacher see we're all tired and we still don't get it?"

"Ah, a nice little breeze. Now that feels good."

"Hey, get that bee. It'll sting somebody."

We have all kinds of thoughts, don't we? And about every little thing that happens. But God wants you to learn to channel your mind, to make it flow into the good things he has prepared for you. Today's verse tells us what to think about. What are those things? Things that are . . .

True—the truth, the Bible, the things that don't change.

Honorable—what honors God and pleases him.

Right—the right thing to do in a situation.

Pure—things that are clean and holy.

Lovely—those things that are beautiful to look at, and loving.

Admirable—what everyone admires and says is good.

Think on these things and your mind won't be filled with junk.

**Prayer:** Jesus, let my mind be full of good things, not bad or stupid things. Amen.

Week 47: Friday

# The Visible Image of God

**Christ is the visible image of the invisible God. He existed before God made anything at all and is supreme over all creation.** Colossians 1:15

**MAIN READING:** Colossians 1 • **OPTIONAL READING:** Colossians 2

What does God look like?

Does he look like Santa Claus, big and fat and roly-poly?

I don't think so.

Does he look like a movie star, with perfect hair, teeth, nose, and smile?

Probably not.

Does he look like a big cloud in the sky? A billowing blip of white that can shape itself into anything?

Nah.

How about a policeman, or a king, or a president, or a great sports personality?

Perhaps not.

History says one person showed us what the invisible God was like. Who was that? Jesus. But it wasn't his looks that pictured what God was like. It was his personality, his perfect character, his loving actions, and his amazing miracles.

That is what God looks like.

**PRAYER:** Father, help me to remember always that Jesus shows us exactly what you are like. Amen.

Week 47: Saturday

# Let the Word Live in Your Heart

**Let the words of Christ, in all their richness, live in your hearts and make you wise. Use his words to teach and counsel each other. Sing psalms and hymns and spiritual songs to God with thankful hearts.**
Colossians 3:16

**MAIN READING:** Colossians 3:16-25

**OPTIONAL READING:** Colossians 3:1-15

Gabe worked hard at memorizing the new verse of Scripture for that week. His Sunday-school teacher had explained. Now Gabe knew it backwards and forwards. He had it imbedded in his brain.

But was that verse really living in his heart?

A truth of Scripture lives in your heart when it changes you. It lives when it has an effect on your life. It lives when you use it to help others. It lives when you encourage and build up your friends with its truth.

How can you make the truth of Scripture live in your heart?

1. Memorize it and meditate on it. Think about it. Ask it questions. Try to find out about its depth of meaning.

2. Think of ways it can apply to your life. What change can you make because of what this verse teaches? Should you pray more? Should you be more patient? What does it say to you?

3. Strive for opportunities to share the verse with others. Ask God to give you a chance to tell a friend about it.

When God's Word lives in your heart, you will begin to live like he wants!

**PRAYER:** Father, make your Word to live in me even as I live in you. Amen.

Week 47: Sunday

# Devoted to Prayer

**Devote yourselves to prayer with an alert mind and a thankful heart.**
Colossians 4:2

**Main Reading:** Colossians 4:1-6
**Optional Reading:** Colossians 4:7-18

How does a person become devoted to prayer?

Allison was devoted. She prayed every night before bed. She prayed for her family, for her friends, for her country, and for the world. She kept a list of needs she knew people had and prayed about them.

Jenna was also a devoted pray-er. She often prayed during the day, stopping in her classes to pray in her mind about something that was happening or had happened. She also tried to pray each night as she lay in bed waiting for sleep.

Alden prayed a lot too. As he sat in church, he prayed about each part of the service, asking God to encourage the people who were there. In school, he prayed for his teacher as she taught. At home, when others were watching TV, he sometimes prayed for the people on TV, that they would hear about Jesus.

Being devoted to prayer simply means making prayer a high priority. It's important to you. You want to pray as much as possible, so you pray at all times during the day. You never stop praying.

When you pray like that, God will answer. You will see amazing things happen in your life and in the lives of others. God changes the world through prayer, and he will change your world when you pray to him about it.

**Prayer:** Lord, remind me to pray about everything. Amen.

# Faithful Work, Loving Deeds

**As we talk to our God and Father about you, we think of your faithful work, your loving deeds, and your continual anticipation of the return of our Lord Jesus Christ.** 1 Thessalonians 1:3

**Main Reading:** 1 Thessalonians 1

**Optional Reading:** 1 Thessalonians 2

What does God most look for in his people? What does he most want us to be doing with our lives?

Today's verse is a good indication. Here, the apostle Paul refers to three things that impressed him about the Thessalonians.

1. Their faithful work. They served God and the people of God faithfully. They didn't give up, or get mad and stomp off. They didn't slack off when things got tough. No, they were faithful. They stuck with the job till it was done.

2. Their loving deeds. The Thessalonians did much good for their church and friends. They helped where help was needed. They gave their money to good causes. They pitched in when someone needed a hand. And they did it all with love.

3. Their continual anticipation of Jesus' coming. They looked forward to Jesus' coming back. Every morning they arose, thinking, "Today could be the day." Every night before bed, they prayed, "Lord, please come soon." It wasn't that they were depressed or hurt or dying. They just wanted to see Jesus.

Such actions win the pleasure and blessing of God every time.

**Prayer:** Lord, may I be as faithful and loving as the Thessalonians. Amen.

Week 48: Tuesday

# May Your Love Overflow

**May the Lord make your love grow and overflow to each other and to everyone else, just as our love overflows toward you.**
1 Thessalonians 3:12

**Main Reading:** 1 Thessalonians 3

**Optional Reading:** 1 Thessalonians 4, 5

Lydia helped serve dinner with her mom. She set the table and brought out the food. When she was done, her mom was pleased. But the still, small voice in Lydia's heart said, "Make it overflow."

She made sure each place setting was just right. Then she folded napkins and put them under the fork by the side of each plate. She knew she had done a good job, but that little voice said, "Make it overflow."

Lydia was feeling a little frustrated, but when everyone came to the table, she greeted them happily. She told everyone she loved them. She offered to pray a prayer and asked if anyone had something on their mind. Then she prayed for them.

The little voice in her heart said, "You did it!"

Making your love overflow is all about going the extra distance, helping just a little better. Sometimes God will speak to you about it in your heart; most of the time he won't. It's a matter of excellence, kindness, and faithfulness. When we make our love overflow, God sees what we do with pleasure in his heart. He knows we're learning to be the kind of people he wants for his kingdom.

**Prayer:** Jesus, make my love overflow toward everyone. Amen.

# Endurance and Faithfulness

**We proudly tell God's other churches about your endurance and faithfulness in all the persecutions and hardships you are suffering.**
2 Thessalonians 1:4

**MAIN READING:** 2 Thessalonians 1

**OPTIONAL READING:** 2 Thessalonians 2:1-10

Jeff didn't budge. One of the kids at school told him to stop talking to everyone about Jesus. Jeff said he had to "do what God told him to do."

One afternoon, several kids cornered him on the way home from school. "Let's see if Jesus protects you now," one of the bigger boys said.

He was about to slug Jeff in the face, when a teacher came around the corner. Everyone stepped back and pretended nothing was wrong. The teacher said, "Oh, Jeff, would you come back in? I have that test for you."

"Sure," Jeff said, giving the boys a dark look. He went back inside and the teacher gave him his test. When he came back outside, the boys were still there.

"This time your little teacher isn't going to protect you," the leader of the group yelled.

Jeff stood his ground. He didn't want to get hit. He knew what it was like to have people turn against him. But he also wanted to please his Lord.

Then an idea came into his head. "Look, it's OK if you beat me up," Jeff said. "But first, can I pray for you?"

The boys roared, but Jeff bowed his head and began to pray. When he finished, he looked up. All the boys were gone.

Sometimes it's hard to be a Christian. Stand firm, and God will be with you.

**PRAYER:** Lord, let me not be afraid of being persecuted. Amen.

# May It Spread Rapidly

**Pray first that the Lord's message will spread rapidly and be honored wherever it goes, just as when it came to you.** 2 Thessalonians 3:1

**Main Reading:** 2 Thessalonians 3

**Optional Reading:** 2 Thessalonians 2:11-17

The gospel is the most important message you can tell anyone. It can change a person's life. It offers them eternal life and a relationship with God that everyone would want. God will lead a person, through the gospel, to help many others. You plant one seed, someone else plants two seeds, and on and on it goes. God brings many through one witness.

In some places in the world, the gospel is not welcome. Muslim countries often restrict missionaries from ever telling anyone there the gospel. In other places, such as Communist countries like China, the gospel is forbidden. Many secret churches meet there and many people become believers. But they can't do it openly.

Today's verse is telling us to pray that the gospel will gain a hearing everywhere we take it. Paul is telling us to pray that God will break down walls put up against hearing the gospel. He wants it to be honored and listened to everywhere.

Are you praying for that? You need to be. Pray for specific places and countries. Pray for missionaries. And pray that you yourself will have opportunities to tell your friends and neighbors the gospel.

That's the only way it will be heard.

**Prayer:** Jesus, help the people who are spreading your gospel around the world. Amen.

Week 48: Friday

# Pray for Your Leaders

**I urge you, first of all, to pray for all people. As you make your requests, plead for God's mercy upon them, and give thanks.**
1 Timothy 2:1

**Main Reading:** 1 Timothy 2 • **Optional Reading:** 1 Timothy 1

Allie sat down with the group of girls. She had been asked to lead the prayer circle that afternoon. "Well, what should we pray about?" she asked the six girls.

Chandra raised her hand. "I think we should pray for the president."

"What should we pray for him?" Allie asked, following the guidelines she'd learned from her teacher.

"That he has wisdom," one of the girls said.

"And that he will feel God's strength as he leads the country," said another.

"Let's pray that his family life be good," a third girl said. "I think he should have a happy family."

"Good idea," Allie answered. She asked more questions and soon the group began to pray. It was exciting to pray for so many things for one person. It was also exciting to realize that they had a hand in making a better life for the President.

Prayer should be specific. When you pray for others, don't just mention their name. Pray for specific things—wisdom, strength, happiness, guidance. Pray that God will work in their lives. When we pray specifically, God answers specifically.

**Prayer:** Father, help me always to pray about as many people as I can. Amen.

Week 48: Saturday

# The Last Days

**Now the Holy Spirit tells us clearly that in the last times some will turn away from what we believe; they will follow lying spirits and teachings that come from demons.** 1 Timothy 4:1

**Main Reading:** 1 Timothy 4 • **Optional Reading:** 1 Timothy 3

Some Christians believe we're in the last days. Because of so many wars in the world, because of famines and earthquakes and things like that, they think we're near the time when Jesus will come back.

Do you ever worry that you could be living in the last days? It's nothing to be afraid about. It's rather something to rejoice in. Jesus may come in our lifetime. We will meet him "in the air," it says in 1 Thessalonians 4, and we will always be with the Lord from then on. What do you think that new world will be like? The Bible tells us many things about it. In Revelation 21 and 22 we learn that there is no pain in heaven, not like on Earth. God will wipe every tear from our eyes. There will no longer be any death. None of our friends or relatives will ever die again. And the world will be a good, righteous, kind, and loving place. Everyone will be good, without sin.

Do you look forward to it? We could be in the last days. Jesus could be coming any day now. Keep your heart strong. No matter how hard it is now, think of what it will be like then, and you will be able to stand strong.

**Prayer:** Lord, I hope you come soon. Amen.

Week 48: Sunday

# Wanting to Get Rich

**But people who long to be rich fall into temptation and are trapped by many foolish and harmful desires that plunge them into ruin and destruction.** 1 Timothy 6:9

**Main Reading:** 1 Timothy 6 • **Optional Reading:** 1 Timothy 5

Laura watched the news that night with great hope. Her mom had bought a lottery ticket and she wanted to see if the numbers matched.

Laura and her mom watched the news program. At the end, they always did the lottery numbers. Her mom pulled out the ticket and watched as the numbers unfolded.

"Seven," the announcer said.

"I have a seven," Mom cried.

"Twenty-two!"

"That's what I selected."

The excitement was building. But then the next three numbers were all wrong. Laura's mom had lost. She hadn't won a thing.

"It's a waste," she finally said. "Next time I'm listening to the Bible."

Wanting to get rich is a dangerous thing, today's verse says. When you want riches, you are apt to do things that are wrong. You might even violate the laws of God. People all over the world want to get rich today. Some ways are honest. But many are not.

It's better, though, to be honest and poor, than rich and evil. Don't you think?

**Prayer:** Jesus, let me not worry about riches. You'll meet my needs, I know. Amen.

Week 49: Monday

# An Apostle's Love

**Timothy, I thank God for you. . . . Night and day I constantly remember you in my prayers. I long to see you again, for I remember your tears as we parted. And I will be filled with joy when we are together again.** 2 Timothy 1:3, 4

**Main Reading:** 2 Timothy 1 • **Optional Reading:** 2 Timothy 2

Paul loved Timothy like a son. He loved him by praying for him. Paul said that he "constantly" remembered Timothy in his prayers "night and day." Imagine what those prayers were doing in Timothy's life.

Paul also remembered how Timothy wept when they parted. It takes deep emotion to weep like that, deep love. Paul had been through many trials with Timothy. They also experienced many great victories. With Timothy at his side, Paul taught, led, and planted churches all over the world.

Another way Paul loved Timothy was by encouraging the young man. As you look in the verses of today's Bible passage, you see many things Paul said to his disciple. He believed Timothy was a man of "sincere trust" in God. Paul was also the one God used to give Timothy spiritual gifts. Paul encouraged Timothy to "fan into flames the spiritual gift God gave you."

Finally, in verse seven, Paul reminded Timothy of the great power of the Holy Spirit. He said, "God has not given us a spirit of fear and timidity, but of power, love, and self-discipline."

Would you like to have had Paul as a friend? Guess what? You can. Just by reading his mail to Timothy. Paul meant it for everyone.

**Prayer:** Jesus, thank you for giving us encouragement through Paul. Amen.

Week 49: Tuesday

# The Power of the Bible

**All Scripture is inspired by God and is useful to teach us what is true and to make us realize what is wrong in our lives. It straightens us out and teaches us to do what is right.** 2 Timothy 3:16

**Main Reading:** 2 Timothy 3 • **Optional Reading:** 2 Timothy 4

But what can the Bible really do for you?" Terri asked her mother. "It just seems like an old book to me."

Terri's mom opened up to today's verse and read it to her daughter. She said, "First, it's 'useful to teach us what is true.' Truth is a valuable thing. Many people wonder all their lives what the truth is about our world, about us, about life, and heaven. We have that truth all in one book, and if we study it, we will learn it.

"And look at this: The Bible can 'make us realize what is wrong in our lives.' It can point out any bad things we're doing."

"Lots of people do bad things and they don't think they're bad," Terri said.

"That's right," her mom answered. "But with the Bible we can know what is right."

"I guess it's not so bad," Terri said. "It's just that it's so hard."

"It gets easier, honey," her mom said. "Just study it day by day, memorize important verses, and gradually it will become the number one book to you."

The Bible has power. According to today's verse, it can and will change your life. Let it fill you up with its wisdom, and you will become a wise person too.

**Prayer:** Father, lead me to grow in my study and understanding of the Bible. Amen.

# Live Wisely

**In the same way, encourage the young men to live wisely in all they do.** Titus 2:6

**MAIN READING:** Titus 2 • **OPTIONAL READING:** Titus 1

What is wise living?

Is it doing something wrong, and then having to pay for it when you're caught?

Probably not.

Is it thinking bad thoughts and then wondering why your mind is always filled up with junk?

Don't think so.

Is it saying something that hurts others, and then having everyone mad at you?

Nope.

Wise living means we live with skill. We're good at the program of life. We know how to solve problems quickly and completely. We learn what to say in various situations. We begin to encourage others and help them on their way.

Wise living is hard for a lot of people. They just don't know what to do, and they make all kinds of mistakes along the way. But if you want to learn to do what's right the first time every time, study the Bible. It will give you the wisdom you need for wise living.

Then people will come to you with their problems and ask you what you would do in their place. That's a fun place to be in.

**PRAYER:** Lord, may I always live wisely before you, before my family, before the world. Amen.

# Why God Saved Us

**[God] saved us, not because of the good things we did, but because of his mercy. He washed away our sins and gave us a new life through the Holy Spirit.** Titus 3:5

**MAIN READING:** Titus 3:1-8 • **OPTIONAL READING:** Titus 3:9-15

Why did God save you?

Was it because of that home run you hit last year in Little League?

Lots of kids hit home runs. And some of those kids are downright nasty to be around. Hitting a home run certainly doesn't make any big points with God.

Were you saved because of that lady whose grass you mowed last year with the church team?

Doing good is always appreciated. But how many good things would you have to do to get God's attention? How many would you have to do to get into heaven? Surely it would take much more than one.

Doing great things, even doing good things, doesn't get you into heaven. God says only one thing does: faith in Jesus. When you put your faith in Jesus, he comes into your life and makes you new inside. He gives you a new heart, and he puts the Spirit inside you. He gives you all his good deeds, and he takes all your sins onto himself.

That's how you're saved. By trusting Jesus every day forever.

**PRAYER:** Jesus, I want to trust you always. Help me to do that starting today. Amen.

Week 49: Friday

# Because You Wanted To

**I didn't want to do anything without your consent. And I didn't want you to help because you were forced to do it but because you wanted to.** Philemon 14

**MAIN READING:** Philemon 8-25 • **OPTIONAL READING:** Philemon 1-7

How does God want you to serve him? Because someone—your pastor, your mom or dad, your brother or sister—forced you do something? Or because you really want to, out of a desire to please God?

Paul wrote today's letter to Philemon, a good friend of his. Philemon had a slave, Onesimus, who ran away and may have stolen some things before he left. Onesimus ended up visiting Paul in Rome. They became friends. Soon, Paul led Onesimus into a relationship with Jesus, just like his master Philemon had been.

It was then Paul had to make a tough decision. Should he keep Onesimus with him as a helper? Or should he send him back to Philemon? Paul chose to send the young man back. Undoubtedly, Onesimus was afraid. But with Paul's letter in hand, he hoped for the best. It's in that letter that Paul talked about "wanting to" and "being forced to" do something good for Onesimus.

We don't know what Philemon did. But the teaching is a great one.

Do you feel like you're forced to serve God? Or do you really want to?

Whichever way you answer will reveal much about what kind of relationship you have with Jesus.

**PRAYER:** Father, make me a person who wants to serve you with all my heart. Amen.

# God's Exact Representative

**The Son reflects God's own glory, and everything about him represents God exactly. He sustains the universe by the mighty power of his command.** Hebrews 1:3

**Main Reading:** Hebrews 1 • **Optional Reading:** Hebrews 2, 3

Imagine you're studying a story about Jesus. You come to the passage about how Jesus helped Thomas with his doubts. Remember that one? Jesus had risen from the dead, but Thomas didn't see him with the other disciples. Thomas refused to believe until he actually saw Jesus, and then everything was OK.

Suppose you're a little like Thomas. You have doubts. You wonder whether all the stuff you've heard about Jesus is really true. Do you think God likes it when we doubt him? After all, isn't the Bible about trust? Isn't the whole point of faith about trusting that God is there, he loves us, and wants to be with us? Wouldn't doubt make him mad?

If you want to know how God would feel about that, just look at Jesus. In today's verse from Hebrews 1, we learn that Jesus "represents" everything about God. If you want to know what God is like, look at Jesus.

What did Jesus do with Thomas? He didn't put the man down. He didn't yell at him or send him packing. No, he offered his hands to Thomas and said, "Feel the scars and see if it's really me." Thomas fell at Jesus' feet and said, "You are my Lord and my God."

No matter what it is that you need to know about God, look to Jesus. He's the perfect example of everything God is and does.

**Prayer:** Lord, thanks for giving me Jesus so I can know what you're like. Amen.

Week 49: Sunday

# Come Boldly

**Let us come boldly to the throne of our gracious God. There we will receive his mercy, and we will find grace to help us when we need it.**
Hebrews 4:16

**Main Reading:** Hebrews 4 • **Optional Reading:** Hebrews 5, 6

Josh had a lot of questions about prayer. He said to his teacher, Mr. Sampson, "But why should God hear my prayers? Aren't a lot of people praying all over the world? How does God sift out just mine?"

Mr. Sampson was about to answer, when Josh added, "Will God get mad if I ask him for something for just me? Like a minibike? Or a go-cart? Can I ask him for stuff that only I want?"

Mr. Sampson cleared his throat and was just about to say something, when Josh said, "And what if someone's praying the exact opposite prayer as me? Like when our Little League team prays. What if we pray to win and they pray to win? What happens then?"

Finally, Josh gave Mr. Sampson enough silence to let the man answer. "You'll find the answers in the Bible, Josh," he said. "God can hear everyone's prayers at once because he's eternal and not bound by time like we are. When two groups of people are praying opposite things at the same time, maybe God finds a middle way to answer, or he does something else. Sometimes he just says no. He knows what's best for us, even better than we do. But the most important thing is what Hebrews 4:16 says. God wants us to come to him "boldly." That means no fear, no hesitation, no worrying. God wants to answer our prayers even before we make them."

"Cool," Josh said, and went back to his seat.

**Prayer:** Lord, let me always remember that you want me to come to you. Amen.

Week 50: Monday

# Drinking Only Milk

**And a person who is living on milk isn't very far along in the Christian life and doesn't know much about doing what is right.** Hebrews 5:13

**MAIN READING:** Hebrews 5 • **OPTIONAL READING:** Hebrews 6, 7

Rebekah watched as her mother fed the baby from a bottle. "How come babies only drink milk?" she finally asked. "Doesn't it get boring?"

"When you're hungry, no food is boring," her mother said. "But we feed babies milk because that's all they can take in and digest. They have an instinct to suck but not to mouth food and swallow. So if we gave them regular solid food, they would choke. Also, their stomachs aren't developed enough yet to digest anything but milk. They have to grow a little before they can take in a cheeseburger."

Rebekah laughed. "Did you know that's what the Bible says?"

"What's that?"

"That when we're new Christians—baby Christians—we can only drink milk. We have to grow to be able to eat the solid stuff."

"Yes, honey, I know about that. And it's true," Rebekah's mother said. "So what are you eating these days—spiritual milk or solid spiritual food?"

Rebekah wasn't sure how to answer, and maybe you aren't either. Today's verse points out this truth, though. It helps us understand the need to graduate from milk—issues like faith and repentance, as the author to the Hebrews says—to more solid food like the more difficult teachings of the Bible, whatever they may be for you.

What are you dining on?

**PRAYER:** Jesus, help me to learn to eat up those more difficult truths. Amen.

Week 50: Tuesday

# We Die Only Once

**And just as it is destined that each person dies only once and after that comes judgment, so also Christ died only once as a sacrifice to take away the sins of many people.** Hebrews 9:27, 28

**MAIN READING:** Hebrews 9 • **OPTIONAL READING:** Hebrews 8

Lukas gazed at the still form of his grandfather in the coffin. Grandpa had died the week before, and now Lukas's family attended the funeral. As he waited for the service to begin, he said to his dad, "My friend Tony says that Grandpa will come back to Earth, maybe as a spider or a goat or even another man or woman."

"That's Hinduism," Lukas's father said. "Hindus believe in reincarnation. But that is not what the Bible says."

"Kent told me that Grandpa would go to hell because he wasn't a Muslim," Lukas added.

"That's Islam. Again, that's the not the biblical way."

"Then what happened to Grandpa?" Lukas stared up at his father.

"The Bible teaches that all of us will die once. If we are Christians in this life, we go to be with Jesus. Then, at the end, he will give us new, spiritual bodies. We'll live forever with him."

"Grandpa was a Christian, wasn't he?"

"Definitely."

Yes, today's verse shows us the truth about death. We will go to be with Jesus in heaven and will live with him forever.

**PRAYER:** Guide me, Father, into all good truth so I may tell others. Amen.

# Impossible!

**So, you see, it is impossible to please God without faith. Anyone who wants to come to him must believe that there is a God and that he rewards those who sincerely seek him.** Hebrews 11:6

**Main Reading:** Hebrews 11 • **Optional Reading:** Hebrews 10

What is faith all about? What are we to believe in?

Faith involves many beliefs about God, Jesus, the Holy Spirit, life, death, heaven, hell, and many other subjects. But at the start, faith requires two things. Today's verse tells us what they are.

First, we must believe there is a God. I have heard people pray, "God, I want to believe in you, but please show me that you exist." God will often answer such prayers. He wants us to know that he is there, in heaven, watching us, protecting us, helping us find him. If we don't believe God exists, there's no faith. And without at least that bit of faith, we cannot possibly please God.

The second thing is we must believe God will reward us for our faith. What does it take to gain God's blessings in life? Faith. Pure and simple. If we believe God blesses those who have faith, we show that we believe God is also good, kind, loving, and gracious.

If you believe those two things about God, you have started on the journey. Now go the rest of the way and put your trust in Jesus too.

**Prayer:** Lord, I believe you exist and that you love me. Help me to believe strongly. Amen.

Week 50: Thursday

# Run Your Race

**Therefore, since we are surrounded by such a huge crowd of witnesses to the life of faith, let us strip off every weight that slows us down, especially the sin that so easily hinders our progress. And let us run with endurance the race that God has set before us.**
Hebrews 12:1

**MAIN READING:** Hebrews 12 • **OPTIONAL READING:** Hebrews 13

When I was in school, we had something called the 600-yard run. It wasn't that far, about one and one-third laps around the track. But it was hard for me.

After the first 200 yards, my breath came hard. I wheezed and my side felt as if a knife had been driven into it. By the next 200 yards, my legs began to feel like lead. I wanted to quit with every step. I usually came in as one of the last people in the race, just ahead of all the fat kids. I just didn't have a runner's stamina, or a runner's will.

Today, my 13-year-old daughter has to run a whole mile. She hates it, too, like I did. She doesn't have the stamina or the breath for it. I don't blame her for hating it.

There is a race, though, a little like a footrace. It's the race of life, the race of Christian living, that God wants us all to run in. Around us, all the great saints of the faith watch, as today's verse says. They cheer us on. Moses. Elijah. David. Paul. Hannah. Esther. Ruth. They all tell us to keep on going.

How are you doing in the race of life? Is it difficult? Do you feel like giving up? Call on God's power to stick with it. If you do, you will never be sorry.

**PRAYER:** Jesus, help me to run my race without giving up. Amen.

Week 50: Friday

# The Opportunity for Joy

**Dear brothers and sisters, whenever trouble comes your way, let it be an opportunity for joy. For when your faith is tested, your endurance has a chance to grow.** James 1:2, 3

**Main Reading:** James 1 • **Optional Reading:** James 2

There is a great painting hanging in an art gallery. It pictures a bird sitting on a nest. But this bird and nest are unusual. For she is sitting contentedly on her nest in the middle of a rock jetty. She's in a little niche. The sky above her is black. Lightning flashes and rain pelts the stones. Huge waves roll and smash into the jetty, tearing away any trees and plants.

But the bird seems undisturbed. It sits there without blinking an eye. It doesn't appear to know that a hurricane rages around her.

At the bottom of the picture is a little brass plaque. It gives the painter's name and also the title of the painting. Can you guess what that title is? It's Peace.

That's really what today's verses are talking about. When trouble strikes, when the waves get high and the heavens roar with wind and rain, what do you do? Do you run for the hills? Do you sit down and cry? Or can you stand up and say, "God is with me. He'll help me through this. And I will be a stronger person because of it"?

That's what James wants all of us to do when we experience trouble. Why? Because it shows we really believe in a good, loving, protecting God.

**Prayer:** Father, may I have peace in the midst of trouble too. Amen.

Week 50: Saturday

# The Tongue

**So also, the tongue is a small thing, but what enormous damage it can do. A tiny spark can set a great forest on fire.** James 3:5

**MAIN READING:** James 3 • **OPTIONAL READING:** James 4, 5

Isn't it amazing some of the things our tongues can say?

"I hate you."

"I hope you die!"

"I wish you would just dry up."

"I'd like to smack you!"

"Did you hear what stupid thing Sarah did the other day? Let me tell you."

Gossip, lies, curses, put-downs, slander—they all come off our tongue. Like James says, that tongue can be like a flame set in a dry forest. It starts out small and insignificant, but it can build up to something awesome in a matter of minutes.

The tongue can bless and encourage people. Or it can tear them down. It can tell the truth. Or it can lie. It can praise God. Or cuss.

Who controls your tongue? Is it your emotions? When you get angry, do you just let your tongue rip? Or do you watch what you say?

When you're feeling down, do you complain and whine?

Don't let your emotions rule your tongue. Instead, ask God to give you a heart of praise that speaks truth and love everywhere you go.

**PRAYER:** Jesus, help me to control my tongue. Amen.

Week 50: Sunday

# Boundless Mercy

**All honor to the God and Father of our Lord Jesus Christ, for it is by his boundless mercy that God has given us the privilege of being born again.** 1 Peter 1:3

**MAIN READING:** 1 Peter 1 • **OPTIONAL READING:** 1 Peter 2

Why are you a Christian?

Because you prayed a prayer? Perhaps, but who got you to pray the prayer? Who worked in your heart to make you open to praying that prayer?

Are you a Christian because you went forward at a church service? Or a Bible camp? Or got baptized? Yes, that speaker was persuasive. Yes, his words made you feel deeply about God and Jesus. But who gave him the words? Who worked in your heart to make you want to accept Jesus?

Or maybe your mom or dad talked to you one night about Jesus. They made it all so clear. You just decided then and there to become a Christian. Was that what made you a Christian? Sure, but who gave your mom and dad the words? Who opened your heart to want to listen?

The truth is that none of us ever become Christians simply because we made a decision. No, God himself works in us, draws us, speaks to our hearts, nudges us toward him. He does this in all people. Many do come to him. Some never do, or don't until much later.

Thank God for your salvation. He is the one who wanted you from the beginning.

**PRAYER:** Lord, may I always remember that you saved me from the very start. Amen.

Week 51: Monday

# Use Your Gifts

**God has given gifts to each of you from his great variety of spiritual gifts. Manage them well so that God's generosity can flow through you.** 1 Peter 4:10

**Main Reading:** 1 Peter 4 • **Optional Reading:** 1 Peter 3

Do you like gifts? Christmas gifts? Birthday gifts? Other special times of the year?

Gifts are wonderful. They come in nicely wrapped packages and are often a big surprise. God has given you gifts, too. Spiritual gifts. These gifts give you the ability to help, love, and nurture others. From your gifts you receive:

1. A special kind of ability no one else has. Although others may have a similar gift to yours, it won't be used in the same way and the same place. You will be unique. Many times God gives more than one gift. So your combination becomes unique only to you.

2. The power to serve powerfully. Your gift will give you the ability to serve in special ways that will greatly help others. Many times you won't even realize you're using your gift. You're just ministering to someone in some way. God wants you to feel loved and special, and to use you to make others feel loved and special.

3. Personal significance. You matter. Your place in the world matters. God will use you in his kingdom in great ways if you let him.

Use your gifts well. They will leave your mark on the world.

**Prayer:** Jesus, help me to discover and begin using my spiritual gifts. Amen.

Week 51: Tuesday

# The Roaring Lion

**Be careful! Watch out for the attacks from the Devil, your great enemy. He prowls around like a roaring lion, looking for some victim to devour.** 1 Peter 5:8

**MAIN READING:** 1 Peter 5:1-9 • **OPTIONAL READING:** 1 Peter 5:10-14

Have you ever seen a lion roar? Like the one that appears in the studio logo at the beginning of certain movies? That roar is deep and powerful. Some say a lion can be heard for miles, so powerful is its roar.

Why does a lion roar like that? Some say it's because when it pounces, it wants its victim to give up right away. The roar scares the victim so much that it doesn't even try to fight. An animal who doesn't fight back is easy pickings for a hungry lion.

The Devil does the same thing. He comes with powerful temptations and strong words. He overwhelms you with his presence if he can. He makes you feel small and stupid if you don't do what he says.

But remember: if you fight back, if you resist him, he will flee because God himself is with you. The Devil doesn't want a fight. He wants someone who just gives up easily.

When the Devil roars at you, fight back. Don't give up. Trust God, and stand firm and strong. That Devil may roar loudly, but he'll whimper when God roars back!

**PRAYER:** Father, may I always resist the Devil, no matter how loud his roar. Amen.

Week 51: Wednesday

# The Spirit Moved Them

**Above all, you must understand that no prophecy in Scripture ever came from the prophets themselves or because they wanted to prophesy. It was the Holy Spirit who moved the prophets to speak from God.** 2 Peter 1:20, 21

**MAIN READING:** 2 Peter 1 • **OPTIONAL READING:** 2 Peter 2, 3

Do you ever wonder how we got the Bible?

History tells us many of the details. Initially, a prophet wrote down what he learned, or heard, or had seen, from God. Today's Scripture tells us that these men were "moved" by the Holy Spirit. That is, the Spirit took hold of their hearts and gave them the information they needed, helping them put it into human words. Their words ultimately weren't their own. Rather, they were the words of the Spirit.

These men wrote down what the Spirit told them on various kinds of paper or skin— papyrus, sheepskin, and other materials. Their message was passed along from believer to believer. Many times it was copied and passed on when others wanted copies. Eventually, a whole group of scribes arose who passed the Scriptures down from person to person. Today, we have thousands of these old manuscripts in museums. When the printing press was invented, the Scriptures became available to common people.

When you read the Bible, don't be deceived. It is truly the Word of God, and you can trust it as that.

**PRAYER:** Lord, I trust my Bible and know it is from you. Amen.

# Confess Your Sins

**But if we confess our sins to him, he is faithful and just to forgive us and to cleanse us from every wrong.** 1 John 1:9

**Main Reading:** 1 John 1 • **Optional Reading:** 1 John 2, 3

During World War II, a brutal man worked in the concentration camps of Hitler. He hurt many people and even had Jews and others put to death. One of the people he persecuted was named Corrie ten Boom, a Christian Dutch woman.

Corrie survived the war and the death chambers. She went on to become a powerful speaker of the great things God did for her and her sister while she was in the concentration camp. A movie about her life was made years ago. It powerfully shows the struggle Corrie and her sister faced. But Corrie's sister died in the camps.

Some time after the war, Corrie spoke at a church. This brutal man from the camps was in the service. Afterward, he came up to her. She recognized him immediately. When he stuck out his hand, she was reluctant to take it. But he told her he'd become a Christian and saw the wrong of what he'd done. He wanted to confess to her his sin and ask for forgiveness.

Corrie gave her hand and forgiveness to him, and that man went away changed and refreshed.

Confession of sin and forgiveness are possible only when we truly repent. But when you confess your sins, God does forgive. And they are wiped away forever.

Just like they were that day when Corrie confronted her torturer.

**Prayer:** Lord, may I always be quick to confess my sin to you. Amen.

Week 51: Friday

# God Is Love

**We know how much God loves us, and we have put our trust in him. God is love, and all who live in love live in God, and God lives in them.**
1 John 4:16

**MAIN READING:** 1 John 4 • **OPTIONAL READING:** 1 John 5

You've probably heard it many times. God is love. What does that mean? Does it mean he will never punish anyone for sin?

No, because we know God is also holy and just. He can't let people get away with their sins.

Does it mean he will overlook anything bad that we do?

No, God knows all and he must stop us when we sin. Love does not mean he'll let us get away with everything.

Does it mean that God will never send anyone to hell?

Unfortunately, the Bible teaches over and over that people who refuse to believe in Jesus will go to hell when they die. God's love does not mean he will eliminate hell or let people off who have rejected him.

What then does "God is love" mean? It means everything he does, even the just and righteous things, are done in love. It means God is characterized by love in all he does. In love he protects us from bad people. In love he saved us from our sins. In love he will bring us to heaven to live forever with him. In love he blesses us every day.

Because God is love, he loves you. And that can never change.

**PRAYER:** Lord, may I always rely on your love to fill and strengthen me. Amen.

Week 51: Saturday

# The Deceivers

**Many deceivers have gone out into the world. They do not believe that Jesus Christ came to earth in a real body. Such a person is a deceiver and an antichrist.** 2 John 7

**MAIN READING:** 2 John • **OPTIONAL READING:** 3 John

"Jesus was a good man. He wasn't God," some preachers said. "He was just one of us, but very good and very loving."

"The Bible is full of errors. It's not the Word of God," another commented. "The Book of Mormon is the real word from God for this time and place."

"Sure, God exists," say others. "But you can't know him. He's too far up there to speak to us."

"I don't know if there is a God," say some. "I guess we won't know till we die."

People who say these kinds of things are often nice people. They don't hurt anyone. They may be good friends with you. But they are wrong about their beliefs. When they try and make you believe what they do, the Bible calls them deceivers. They're people who really are doing the Devil's work for him. They speak lies, even though they may not know they're lies.

Beware of them. Don't let them into your heart. Because Satan's goal is for you to follow them into their lies.

**PRAYER:** Jesus, do not let me ever be deceived by those who don't know the truth. Amen.

Week 51: Sunday

# God Keeps Us

**And now, all glory to God, who is able to keep you from stumbling, and who will bring you into his glorious presence innocent of sin and with great joy.** Jude 24

**Main Reading:** Jude 17-25 • **Optional Reading:** Jude 1-16

Do you ever worry that you could do something so bad that God would kick you out of his kingdom? That you could tell a lie, or commit a sin that would lose you your salvation?

Many Christian people worry about those things. But today's verse shows us the truth about our salvation: it's not just for us to keep.

Look at what Jude says. God is able to "keep you from stumbling." That means sinning in such a way that you leave the faith. Many people commit such bad sins that they think God will reject them. But if God is truly working in your life, he will keep you from doing that terrible thing. He will help you keep your faith strong and committed.

Notice it also says God is able to bring you into heaven "innocent of sin and with great joy." God is able to work in you, work in your heart, to keep you pure and healthy as a Christian. God will not let you go, no matter what you might think or what others say.

God wants you to be there in his heaven. He will make sure you get there, too, if you trust him.

**Prayer:** Lord, I trust you to get me all the way to heaven like Jude says. Amen.

Week 52: Monday

# He Wrote It All Down

**Write down what you have seen—both the things that are now happening and the things that will happen later.** Revelation 1:19

**Main Reading:** Revelation 1 • **Optional Reading:** Revelation 2, 3

Revelation is a hard book to understand. It's full of symbolic pictures of things that John saw but did not understand. Scholars today wonder if what he was describing were modern aircraft, tanks, and other vehicles.

It's possible. But the key to the book of Revelation is found in the first chapter, in today's verse. Here, Jesus tells John to write down what he has "seen," as well as what "is happening now" and "what will happen."

When you look at Revelation, you see three sections. What John had seen is in the first chapter. He had seen Jesus high, lifted up, almighty. He wrote all he saw down in the first chapter and it's a majestic picture.

What was happening now is found in Revelation 2, 3. Here, John tells us about individual letters to seven of the first churches of faith. Each letter is different and deals with different problems or concerns. From them you can learn what Jesus says to just about any type of church.

From Revelation 4 on is about what will happen in the future. We don't know how far in the future this was, but many think it all applies to the last days.

However you look at Revelation, one thing is true: it tells us Jesus is coming again, he is going to reign forever, and his kingdom will never end. That's encouraging.

**Prayer:** Jesus, may I learn from Revelation these next few days. Amen.

Week 52: Tuesday

# Holy, Holy, Holy

**Day after day and night after night they keep on saying, "Holy, holy, holy is the Lord God Almighty—the one who always was, who is, and who is still to come."** Revelation 4:8

**Main Reading:** Revelation 4 • **Optional Reading:** Revelation 5—7

What is the only characteristic of God that is repeated three times?

You find it in Isaiah 6 and several times in Revelation. It's the expression "holy, holy, holy." Why is this one repeated three times while others, like love or grace or justice, are not?

God's ultimate and most beautiful quality is his holiness. Why is holiness so important?

1. Holiness tells us God is utterly above and different from us. He is "high and lifted up" as some verses say. We can trust him completely because he will never change. He is all-powerful, all-knowing. and all-loving.

2. Holiness means God can never sin against us or anyone. God not only won't do anything wrong, he can't. He is incapable of ever committing a sin. He will never violate one of his characteristics—patience, kindness, goodness, or whatever. We can completely trust him, knowing he will never sin against us.

3. Holiness teaches us that God is utterly perfect and he intends to make us perfect too.

You can trust God with everything in your life, because he is holy, holy, holy.

**Prayer:** Let me learn, Lord, to trust you completely. Amen.

# Wipe Away All Their Tears

**For the Lamb who stands in front of the throne will be their Shepherd. He will lead them to the springs of life-giving water. And God will wipe away all their tears.** Revelation 7:17

**MAIN READING:** Revelation 7 • **OPTIONAL READING:** Revelation 8, 9

Shauna stood by the grave of her beloved uncle. Uncle James was killed in a recent war. He was a good soldier and a loving friend. Shauna loved him dearly. He told her stories, tickled her, and as she grew up, he taught her every good thing he knew—how to garden, how to ride a horse, how to throw a ball.

Shauna wished he had never died. And she wept.

The difference for Shauna and her uncle, compared to many other people, is that they were both Christians. Shauna knew her uncle was in heaven with Jesus because of what the Bible said. She knew she'd see him again.

But still she cried. It was hard. It hurt her deeply inside to miss him. Why did this have to happen? Why couldn't he have fought and survived, like so many others?

Those questions one day might be answered for Shauna. By Jesus himself. We don't know for sure. But today's verse assures us of one other thing: God will wipe every tear from our eyes. God will comfort us now and in heaven. He will show us the truth and reunite us with all our loved ones.

What a great promise! And a great truth!

**PRAYER:** Lord, I look forward to the day I will join you in heaven and you will wipe every tear from my eyes. Amen.

Week 52: Thursday

# The Whole World God's Kingdom

**The whole world has now become the kingdom of our Lord and of his Christ, and he will reign forever and ever.** Revelation 11:15

**MAIN READING:** Revelation 11

**OPTIONAL READING:** Revelation 10, 12

One day, Jesus will walk among us. We don't know what he will look like, but we will know him.

One day, God will reign over the whole earth, and everyone will know he is God and that he cares about us and loves us. We won't need faith in the same way, because we will see him. And everyone will know him.

One day, all the pain and misunderstanding and hatred will cease. No more terrorists. No more plagues. No more famines. Jesus will reign supreme.

Many people long for those days to come. Do you? Don't you ever get tired of this world? Yes, it's full of wonders like its animals and flowers and people. Yes, it can be a fun place at times. Yes, we can gather together great possessions.

But don't you long for something better?

That's what Revelation promises. One day Jesus will reign. The kingdom of God will be in our midst.

**PRAYER:** Jesus, may I always long for you to come. Amen.

Week 52: Friday

# Great and Marvelous

**Great and marvelous are your actions, Lord God Almighty. Just and true are your ways, O King of the nations. Who will not fear, O Lord, and glorify your name? For you alone are holy.** Revelation 15:3, 4

**MAIN READING:** Revelation 15 • **OPTIONAL READING:** Revelation 13, 14

Do you ever think of God as being great?

How about marvelous? Is God marvelous to you?

Today's verse tells us about God's works as being "great and marvelous." Have you ever seen works like that? Do you want to?

Let me offer you several ways you can begin to see God work in your life in great and marvelous ways.

1. Pray. Pray about anything and everything. Whatever need you have, whatever concern, whatever problem, pray about it. The more you pray, the more God will answer. The more you pray, the more things God can do in your life.

2. Serve. The more you serve, the more things you do for God, the more God will work through you. When you see God working like that, you will be encouraged.

3. Share. When you share your faith and share your possessions, you will see God work and bless.

Do you want to see God work in your life? Do these things, and surely God will answer powerfully.

**PRAYER:** Jesus, help me to get out there and do the things that will release your power in my life. Amen.

Week 52: Saturday

# Armageddon

**And they gathered all the rulers and their armies to a place called Armageddon in Hebrew.** Revelation 16:16

**Main Reading:** Revelation 16

**Optional Reading:** Revelation 17, 18

Many people fear the Battle of Armageddon. Many Christians believe it will be the last battle that occurs on Earth. It will involve all the nations coming together against God's people. God himself will come down and fight for God's people. Armageddon will be the most horrible battle that ever takes place in the history of the world.

Many other Christians believe other things about Armageddon. The important thing is that God doesn't want us to worry about Armageddon. He doesn't want you to be afraid that it will happen in your life. Why? Because God fights for you even now, if you're a Christian. God himself will stop all our enemies one day, regardless of what happens at the end of time. The main thing to know is that God is with us and will be with us to the very end of our lives. There is nothing to fear, no one to run from. We can be bold and courageous in every situation. Why? Because God is there. He goes before us and protects behind us. He will do all we need to succeed.

Don't worry about things like Armageddon. Whether it's an actual future event or whether it refers to something else, the important thing is that God is with you now. He will be with you forever. That's enough to quell any fear we might have.

**Prayer:** Father, let me never fear while you are with me. Amen.

Week 52: Sunday

# Jesus' Coming

**Then I saw heaven opened, and a white horse was standing there. And the one sitting on the horse was named Faithful and True. For he judges fairly and then goes to war.** Revelation 19:11

**Main Reading:** Revelation 19 • **Optional Reading:** Revelation 20

What will it be like?

Will thousands be standing there, looking up into the sky to see Jesus return to Earth? Will he be riding a white horse? Will angels or others be with him? Will the whole world see him coming back? Will it be on television?

What will he do when he comes?

In today's verse we see Jesus coming to the world at the end of the Battle of Armageddon. He will return in might and power and stop the battle. Everyone will see him. All the world will bow down to him. The whole world will know that he is God, the ruler of the universe. All people alive at that moment will realize the mistake they made if they didn't believe in him. But no one will ever make that mistake again.

Do you look forward to Jesus' coming? God says he will reward you just for waiting for him, just for looking for the moment when he comes. God will bless us because, by faith, we expected him to come.

Keep your heart on Jesus. He will come and bless you for your commitment.

**Prayer:** Lord, I wait for you. I know you will come, and I look forward to meeting you personally. Amen.

Week 53: Extra Day

# Seeing God's Face

**And they will see his face, and his name will be written on their foreheads.** Revelation 22:4

**Main Reading:** Revelation 22 • **Optional Reading:** Revelation 21

According to today's verse, we will one day see God's face.

No one in all of human history has ever seen God's face. Why? Because according to a conversation God had with Moses in Exodus 33, no one can see God's face and live.

Some say God's face will be like the sun shining right into our eyes. But without the right powers or special protection, we would never survive a face-to-face meeting with God. Our eyes and bodies could not handle such a glorious sight.

But one day we will have spiritual eyes. One day we will have spiritual bodies. We will be holy, perfect, sinless. We will be able to stand before God without being accused of wrongdoing. In that day we will have the power to see God as he is. We will be able to look upon the face of the one who has loved us all these years.

Seeing his face will be the climax of all our journeys. Because when we see him, we will be like him. We will shine forever before all creation. Angels will be amazed at us. All creatures will know we belong to God.

The day is coming. Be ready. Be happy. God will bless you mightily for your faith now.

**Prayer:** Lord, I praise you that the day will soon be here when I see you in all your perfection. Amen.

# Index


| SUBJECT | LOCATION |
|---|---|
| Acceptance of others | Week 44: Monday |
| Accusations | Week 16: Sunday |
| Admitting guilt | Week 17: Saturday |
| Advice | Week 15: Monday |
| Angels in heaven | Week 29: Wednesday |
| Angels, fallen | Week 25: Thursday |
| Anger | Week 1: Thursday |
| Anger, Jesus' | Week 36: Tuesday |
| Anger of God | Week 9: Monday |
| Armageddon | Week 52: Saturday |
| Attack of Satan | Week 12: Sunday |
| Battle for soul | Week 47: Tuesday |
| Believing in Jesus | Week 40: Sunday |
| Belonging to God | Week 24: Thursday |
| Bible, encouragement | Week 44: Tuesday |
| Bible, inspiration | Week 30: Saturday, Week 40: Wednesday |
| Bible, lives in us | Week 47: Saturday |
| Bible, power of | Week 49: Tuesday |
| Bible, Spirit inspired | Week 51: Wednesday |
| Bible, using it | Week 43: Monday |
| Bible, written down | Week 52: Monday |
| Blessing, every | Week 46: Sunday |
| Blessing, seeking | Week 13: Wednesday |
| Blessings from God | Week 18: Tuesday, Week 20: Tuesday |
| Blood | Week 4: Friday |
| Body, a temple | Week 44: Friday |
| Boldness | Week 23: Saturday |
| Born again | Week 39: Thursday |
| Caution | Week 23: Wednesday |

| | |
|---|---|
| Choices | Week 8: Friday |
| Christian, becoming | Week 42: Sunday |
| Christian life | Week 2: Wednesday |
| Come to Jesus | Week 34: Friday |
| Comfort of God | Week 45: Thursday |
| Confession of sin | Week 2: Saturday, Week 24: Saturday, Week 51: Thursday |
| Confidence | Week 3: Monday |
| Confidence in God | Week 47: Wednesday |
| Confronting others | Week 35: Monday |
| Conversion of Paul | Week 41: Friday |
| Conviction | Week 8: Wednesday |
| Courage | Week 5: Saturday |
| Covetousness | Week 12: Thursday |
| Criticism | Week 5: Friday, Week 10: Thursday |
| Crucified with Christ | Week 46: Thursday |
| Cursing | Week 3: Friday |
| Death | Week 10: Sunday, Week 17: Monday |
| Death of wicked | Week 29: Sunday |
| Deception | Week 1: Wednesday |
| Deceivers | Week 51: Saturday |
| Delay of God | Week 40: Tuesday |
| Demons | Week 10: Friday |
| Denials, Peter's | Week 35: Friday |
| Depending on God | Week 31: Sunday |
| Desiring God | Week 19: Sunday |
| Devotion | Week 43: Sunday |
| Disaster | Week 28: Friday |
| Disciples, call of | Week 37: Saturday |
| Discipline | Week 23: Monday |
| Discouraged | Week 28: Saturday |
| Dishonesty | Week 22: Sunday |

| | |
|---|---|
| Doing what is right | Week 12: Tuesday, Week 15: Sunday |
| Dreams | Week 2: Thursday |
| Encouragement | Week 8: Thursday |
| Endurance | Week 48: Wednesday |
| End times | Week 33: Wednesday |
| Enemies | Week 31: Tuesday |
| Envy | Week 18: Saturday |
| Eternal security | Week 44: Wednesday |
| Evangelism | Week 36: Monday, Week 48: Thursday |
| Excellence | Week 24: Wednesday |
| Experience | Week 16: Thursday |
| Face of God | Week 4: Tuesday |
| Faith, pleases God | Week 50: Wednesday |
| Faithfulness | Week 8: Monday |
| Faithfulness, God's | Week 29: Tuesday |
| False apostles | Week 46: Tuesday |
| Fame | Week 29: Saturday |
| Fear | Week 6: Sunday, Week 22: Monday |
| Fear, does God? | Week 25: Wednesday |
| Feelings, God's | Week 1: Friday |
| Fitting in | Week 44: Sunday |
| Forgiveness | Week 21: Monday |
| Foolishness | Week 23: Thursday |
| Friends | Week 12: Monday |
| Friendship of God | Week 17: Wednesday |
| Giving | Week 7: Monday, Week 13: Saturday, Week 14: Sunday |
| Glory of God | Week 3: Saturday |
| God, amazed | Week 37: Sunday |
| God, choosing us | Week 42: Friday |
| God, close to us | Week 42: Wednesday |
| God, doing more | Week 47: Monday |

| | |
|---|---|
| God is holy | Week 52: Tuesday |
| God is love | Week 51: Friday |
| God the Father | Week 46: Friday |
| God, jealousy | Week 29: Thursday |
| God, keeping us | Week 51: Sunday |
| God, knowing him | Week 32: Sunday |
| God, love of | Week 41: Saturday |
| God, nature of | Week 4: Monday |
| God, doesn't change | Week 34: Monday |
| God, presence | Week 30: Sunday |
| God, promises | Week 31: Wednesday |
| God, rejoicing | Week 33: Tuesday |
| God, sanctuary | Week 29: Friday |
| God, seeking us | Week 27: Wednesday |
| God, speaking to us | Week 42: Monday |
| God, what he wants | Week 32: Saturday |
| God's face | Week 53: Extra Day |
| Golden Rule | Week 34: Thursday |
| Good, working for | Week 2: Sunday, Week 16: Tuesday |
| Good works | Week 14: Friday |
| Gospel, believe | Week 43: Saturday |
| Gospel, power of | Week 42: Saturday, Week 43: Tuesday |
| Gospel, responses | Week 34: Saturday |
| Gospel, sharing | Week 36: Wednesday |
| Gratitude | Week 13: Thursday |
| Greatness of God | Week 17: Friday |
| Guilt | Week 4: Thursday, Week 18: Friday |
| Handicaps | Week 40: Monday |
| Harmony | Week 22: Tuesday |
| Hatred | Week 27: Friday |
| Healing | Week 26: Monday |
| Heart | Week 13: Sunday |

| | |
|---|---|
| Heart, clean | Week 19: Tuesday |
| Heart, hard | Week 31: Saturday |
| Heart, new one | Week 30: Friday |
| Heart, opening | Week 42: Tuesday |
| Heart, sick | Week 27: Saturday |
| Heaven | Week 27: Monday |
| Help of God | Week 15: Friday |
| Holiness of God | Week 24: Sunday |
| Holiness, personal | Week 9: Saturday |
| Holy Spirit, in us | Week 9: Sunday, Week 12: Friday |
| Holy Spirit, living water | Week 39: Sunday |
| Holy Spirit, poured out | Week 32: Monday |
| Holy Spirit, power | Week 33: Thursday |
| Honesty | Week 7: Thursday |
| Hope | Week 28: Monday |
| Human body | Week 22: Wednesday |
| Humility | Week 14: Tuesday |
| Idolatry | Week 3: Sunday |
| Israel, restored | Week 32: Wednesday |
| Jesus and children | Week 36: Saturday |
| Jesus, birth | Week 25: Monday, Week 37: Thursday |
| Jesus, bread of life | Week 39: Saturday |
| Jesus, image of God | Week 47: Friday, Week 49: Saturday |
| Jesus, live in us | Week 40: Thursday |
| Jesus, predicting death | Week 35: Tuesday |
| Jesus, prophecy | Week 33: Saturday |
| Jesus, prophet | Week 7: Tuesday |
| Jesus, Redeemer | Week 28: Sunday |
| Jesus, Son of God | Week 35: Saturday |
| Jesus, temptation | Week 34: Wednesday |
| Jesus, the branch | Week 27: Sunday |
| Jesus, the Word | Week 39: Wednesday |

| | |
|---|---|
| Jesus, took guilt | Week 26: Friday |
| Jesus, virgin birth | Week 34: Tuesday |
| John the Baptist | Week 37: Friday |
| Joy | Week 15: Tuesday, Week 50: Friday |
| Judgment, after death | Week 50: Tuesday |
| Judgment day | Week 44: Thursday |
| Justice | Week 29: Monday |
| Kindness | Week 11: Tuesday |
| Kingdom of God | Week 38: Wednesday |
| Kingdom, world | Week 52: Thursday |
| Knowledge, personal | Week 44: Saturday |
| Knowledge of God | Week 1: Sunday |
| Last days | Week 48: Saturday |
| Lawlessness | Week 9: Wednesday |
| Leaders, prayer for | Week 19: Saturday |
| Leading, God's | Week 5: Thursday |
| Leading people | Week 6: Friday, Week 11: Thursday |
| Learning, from God | Week 32: Friday |
| Life | Week 15: Saturday |
| Life in Holy Spirit | Week 46: Saturday |
| Life, not your own | Week 27: Thursday |
| Life, race of | Week 50: Thursday |
| Light of God | Week 21: Saturday |
| Listening | Week 24: Tuesday |
| Listening for God | Week 17: Thursday |
| Living wisely | Week 49: Wednesday |
| Lord's Supper | Week 37: Monday |
| Love, friend | Week 49: Monday |
| Love for others | Week 45: Tuesday |
| Love of God | Week 1: Monday, Week 20: Friday, Week 24: Friday |
| Love, overflow | Week 48: Tuesday |

| | |
|---|---|
| Loving God | Week 35: Wednesday |
| Loyalty | Week 9: Thursday |
| Lying | Week 2: Tuesday |
| Majesty of God | Week 18: Monday |
| Mary, mother of God | Week 37: Wednesday |
| Meaning of life | Week 24: Monday |
| Meditation | Week 19: Thursday, Week 22: Thursday |
| Messiah | Week 36: Friday |
| Mercy of God | Week 50: Sunday |
| Mind, renewed | Week 45: Friday |
| Miracle, doing | Week 42: Thursday |
| Missionaries | Week 41: Sunday |
| Money | Week 36: Sunday |
| Obedience to God | Week 1: Saturday, Week 5: Tuesday, Week 31: Monday |
| Obedience to parents | Week 7: Wednesday |
| One way | Week 41: Tuesday |
| Overcoming sin | Week 21: Friday |
| Passover | Week 5: Monday |
| Peace | Week 20: Wednesday, Week 25: Friday |
| Peace, for nation | Week 31: Thursday |
| Persecution | Week 28: Thursday |
| Perseverance | Week 38: Saturday |
| Persistence | Week 22: Saturday |
| Plans | Week 23: Tuesday |
| Plans for you, God's | Week 28: Tuesday |
| Planting seeds | Week 46: Monday |
| Pleasing God | Week 10: Monday, Week 30: Monday, Week 48: Monday |
| Poor people | Week 14: Wednesday, Week 23: Sunday |
| Pornography | Week 20: Sunday |
| Power of God | Week 3: Tuesday, Week 8: Tuesday |

| | |
|---|---|
| Power in weakness | Week 46: Wednesday |
| Prayer | Week 9: Tuesday, Week 13: Friday, Week 15: Thursday |
| Prayer, being bold | Week 49: Sunday |
| Prayer, devoted to | Week 47: Sunday |
| Prayer, God hears | Week 21: Thursday |
| Prayer, persistence in | Week 38: Tuesday |
| Prayer for leaders | Week 48: Friday |
| Preaching | Week 39: Tuesday |
| Presence of God | Week 2: Friday, Week 7: Sunday |
| Pretending | Week 32: Tuesday |
| Pride | Week 14: Saturday |
| Privileges | Week 23: Friday |
| Problems | Week 6: Thursday, Week 16: Friday |
| Problems, rejoicing in | Week 43: Thursday |
| Prodigal son | Week 38: Thursday |
| Proof of God | Week 12: Wednesday |
| Promises of God | Week 8: Saturday |
| Prophecy | Week 6: Tuesday, Week 11: Monday |
| Prophecy, nations | Week 30: Tuesday |
| Protection, God's | Week 12: Saturday, Week 13: Monday |
| Provision, God's | Week 6: Monday |
| Punishment | Week 25: Tuesday |
| Questions | Week 28: Wednesday |
| Refuge, God is | Week 19: Monday |
| Rejection of truth | Week 38: Friday |
| Remembering | Week 20: Monday |
| Repentance | Week 15: Wednesday, Week 30: Thursday |
| Resurrection, Jesus | Week 45: Wednesday |
| Resurrection, ours | Week 6: Wednesday, Week 45: Saturday |
| Return to God | Week 31: Friday |
| Reverence | Week 33: Monday |

| | |
|---|---|
| Riches | Week 48: Sunday |
| Sacrifice, Jesus' | Week 2: Monday, Week 3: Thursday, Week 4: Wednesday |
| Sacrifice, personal | Week 9: Friday |
| Salvation | Week 49: Thursday |
| Satan, end of | Week 30: Wednesday |
| Satan, prowls about | Week 51: Tuesday |
| Second chance | Week 32: Thursday |
| Second coming | Week 21: Wednesday, Week 25: Sunday, Week 52: Sunday |
| Secrets of God | Week 7: Friday |
| Serving God | Week 1: Tuesday |
| Shepherd | Week 18: Wednesday |
| Silence, of God | Week 16: Saturday |
| Sin | Week 5: Sunday, Week 17: Sunday |
| Sin, consequences | Week 11: Wednesday |
| Sin, all fall short | Week 43: Wednesday |
| Sin, swept away | Week 26: Wednesday |
| Sin and God | Week 26: Sunday |
| Singing | Week 8: Sunday, Week 19: Wednesday |
| Sleep | Week 21: Sunday |
| Spiritual gifts | Week 51: Monday |
| Spiritual warfare | Week 10: Tuesday |
| Strength from God | Week 11: Friday, Week 26: Tuesday |
| Suffering for Jesus | Week 41: Wednesday |
| Suffering of Jesus | Week 37: Tuesday |
| Suffering, personal | Week 45: Monday |
| Suicide | Week 10: Saturday |
| Swearing | Week 7: Saturday |
| Tears, wiped away | Week 52: Wednesday |
| Temple | Week 4: Saturday |
| Testimony | Week 19: Friday |

| | |
|---|---|
| Testing | Week 16: Wednesday, Week 17: Tuesday |
| Testing, Satan's | Week 39: Monday |
| Thankfulness | Week 20: Saturday |
| Thirst for God | Week 18: Sunday |
| Thoughts | Week 36: Thursday, Week 47: Thursday |
| Thoughts of God | Week 26: Saturday |
| Time | Week 20: Thursday |
| Tongue | Week 50: Saturday |
| Trouble | Week 3: Tuesday |
| Truth | Week 40: Saturday |
| Waiting | Week 18: Thursday |
| Walking with God | Week 6: Saturday |
| Will of God | Week 10: Wednesday, Week 14: Thursday |
| Will of man | Week 49: Friday |
| Wisdom | Week 11: Saturday, Week 22: Friday |
| Witchcraft | Week 4: Sunday |
| Witnessing | Week 21: Tuesday, Week 35: Sunday |
| Witnessing, power | Week 41: Monday |
| Word of God, power | Week 13: Tuesday |
| Work of God | Week 14: Monday, Week 16: Monday |
| World, overcome | Week 40: Friday |
| Worship | Week 5: Wednesday, Week 11: Sunday<br>Week 33: Friday, Week 39: Friday |
| Youth | Week 27: Tuesday |

# Here's What I Think . . .

# Here's What I Think . . .

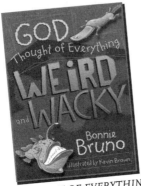